White

2

Black

Black to Move.

4

More Doubt.

CHESS

A HISTORY

CHESS
A HISTORY

Harry Golombek

G. P. PUTNAM'S SONS
New York

Library of Congress Catalog Card Number: 76-6033

SBN: 399-11575-7

Designed and produced by Walter Parrish International
Limited, London

Designer Roger Hyde

Set in 11 pt Bembo

Printed and bound in Spain by Novograph, S.A., Madrid
Dep. Legal M 20584/1976

In memory of that grandmaster of chess historians,
the learned and industrious
H. J. R. Murray

CONTENTS

Foreword   8

1 The beginnings   10
2 The game spreads to Persia and elsewhere   20
3 The game becomes shatranj   30
4 Shatranj develops its theorists
   and great masters   42
5 The game comes to Europe   49
6 Early medieval times
   the spread to Western Europe   59
7 Late medieval and early modern times
   the game becomes dynamic   81
8 The new game   95
9 The eighteenth century
   the age of the savants   113
10 The early nineteenth century
   France, England and Germany   124
11 The advent of Paul Morphy   134
12 Steinitz, the founder of modern chess   149
13 Capablanca and the hypermoderns
   from war to war   184
14 The Soviet School triumphs   208
15 The age of Fischer   219
16 The post Fischer era 1972–?   228

   Appendix   Chess notations   240
   Bibliography   242
   Further reading   245
   Acknowledgements   246
   Picture credits   247
   Index   248

FOREWORD

When, some fifteen years ago, I was invited to give a talk on chess to the apprentices in England of the Imperial Chemical Industries at the Wilton Works on Teesside, the only stipulation was that the subject matter should be of interest to chessplayer and non-chessplayer alike. I chose to speak on the history of chess and, according to the personnel officer, it was the most successful lecture they had ever had there.

It was in fact a matter of astonishment to him that no one fell asleep during the course of the talk and that everybody stayed right to the end. I was not, however, at all surprised. My audience was an intelligent one, and the fascination of the history of the game clearly enthralled them.

I thought it would for one particular reason. To me it has always seemed that the history of chess is closely interwoven with the course and history of our civilization, using this term in its broadest sense. Starting off as a war game and always indeed retaining some of that warlike quality because, alas, our civilization has been much concerned with wars, it has expanded and refined as the centuries have gone by into a remarkable and unique blend of game, sport, art and even culture. So much is this true that I think it is fair to say of the chessmasters of our time (the last hundred years or so), 'Scratch a chessmaster and you will find a philosopher'.

The intimate relationship between the game and civilization is best demonstrated by defining the layers of society in which the game has been popular and practised. In origin it was a pastime for kings and nobility, a court game encouraged among the aristocracy and discouraged among the lower levels of society. But, as civilization progressed, a new class—the middle class—made its appearance, so chess became popular in circles beyond the courts. The great merchants replaced the kings as patrons and fosterers of the game, and the professionals—doctors, lawyers, the clergy, writers, artists of every kind—all joined in.

The final popularization came with the establishment of genuine democracies during the last 200 years, when cross-sections of whole peoples played—and continue to play—chess.

It is my endeavour in this book to trace the history of the game from its inception in the sixth century AD to the present day; to show the fascinating patterns of chess affairs that arose through the wanderings and shifts of peoples and to demonstrate how the very rules changed in accordance with these shifts.

But, being a chessmaster myself, I have yet another objective: I want to give a history of the actual play of the game, to show the continual evolution of chess style and, since this too depends on people and their personalities, to describe the great players and their methods of play through the ages.

Commencing with the, alas, featureless and anonymous person or persons who invented the game in north-west India some time during the sixth century AD I will go through the various stages (Persian, Muslim and European) to the beginning of modern times, with the great Italian and Spanish schools of the sixteenth century; then I will move on to Philidor, Anderssen, Morphy, Steinitz, Lasker and Capablanca in the early twentieth century, and right down to the present Bobby Fischer era.

Since the chess world contains, and always seems to have contained, as many colourful characters as are to be found in stories by the great novelists, I hope the reader will find the book entertaining. I hope too that the non-chessplayer who happens to read this book will discover that chess is far from being a dry-as-dust pursuit and that its exponents are all essentially artists—great or small.

Harry Golombek
Chalfont St Giles, England

chapter **1**

The beginnings

Where exactly, when exactly, how exactly and by whom exactly the game of chess was invented we do not know. Its very ancientness provides a full explanation for this ignorance. Indeed, any glib exact reference to its origin must be more than suspect. No reasonably plausible explanation as to its invention exists. All sorts of picturesque and poetic legends have been constructed to fill the gap. Consider, for instance, the reference to chess in Robert Burton's *Anatomy of Melancholy* written in 1626:

> Chesse-play is a good and wittie exercise of the mind for some kinds of men, and fit for such melancholy persons as are idle and have impertinent thoughts, or troubled with cares; nothing better to distracte their minds and alter their meditations; invented (some say) by the general of an army in a famine to keepe his souldiers from mutiny.

It is possible that Burton was referring to a Chinese legend which said that a general who was besieging a city in the second century BC devised the game to distract his soldiers from the bitter winter conditions of the siege. Needless to say, this legend appeared many centuries after the time it was supposed to have occurred, and has not the slightest authenticity. However, I have seen a poem dating from the second century BC in which, according to the translator, there are two references to the playing of chess. If the game were indeed played then, it would completely upset all present-day theories; but there are two possible explanations for the references, either of which would leave modern theories untroubled. They could be to the game of 'wei-chi', or 'go', which is known to be considerably older than chess (or to another board-game, backgammon for instance). Or they could refer to the Chinese riverside game of chess, which is in fact not chess at all as we know it.

Another war-like explanation for the invention of chess is given by the great Persian poet, Firdausi, in the eleventh century. I include this beautiful and sad story in the chapter on chess in Persia (p. 26) but, briefly put, it tells how a son invented chess to console his mother, the queen, on the death in battle of his brother, her favourite son.

This, like the other fable, ascribes the invention to the influence of conditions of war. I could pile legend on legend and they would all have this martial factor in common. The other common denominator would be their incredibility.

It might be as well here to dispel as firmly as possible all the popular illusions as to the vast antiquity of chess. Possibly to attempt this is just as vain as trying to blow away the dandelion puff-balls from one's garden, since as soon as one blows them away so they are blown back by some item of news in the popular press about chess having been played by the ancient Pharoahs or by Romulus and Remus or by the Sirens in between combing their sea-wet hair upon the rocks.

Yes, the game of chess is old but, *as we know it,* it is hardly a thousand years old. In its origin perhaps 1,500 years old, it is a comparative newcomer in the history of board-games. Some, such as go and backgammon, are older, while those that are played with dice on a board of sixty-four squares (or eighty or one hundred, for that matter) are even older and do go back to ancient Egyptian times.

It is true that boards constructed of squares indicating some sort of game have been found in tombs or in ruins of all the three civilizations I have mentioned. But they are not boards for games which either anticipate or form the origin of chess. If they were, then quite clearly references would have appeared to them as such in the literatures of ancient Egypt, Rome or Greece.

That they do not seems conclusive evidence that chess was not played either in ancient Egyptian or classical times.

The first written evidence of the game appears in Sanskrit in a charming romance entitled *Vasavadatta* written by Subandhu in the late sixth or early seventh century: 'The time of the rains played its game with frogs for chessmen which, yellow and green in colour, as if mottled with lac, leapt up on the garden-bed squares.'

A more beautiful reference to chess it would be hard to find in the whole of literature since then. Rather closer to the more popular spirit of modern times (indeed this could have been written by

An ivory gaming-box with one surface marked out for senet, a board-game whose history reaches back to Ancient Egyptian times. The drawer for the pieces is fastened by an ivory bolt sliding into bronze staples. The box is of the New Kingdom type—the pieces may be of an earlier period.

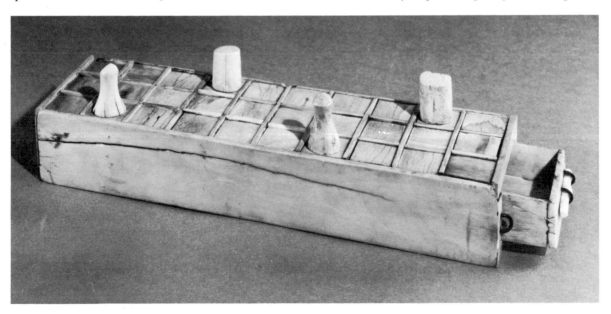

Thomas Hood in the early nineteenth century) is the next reference to the game in the early seventh century, again in Sanskrit. The writer, Bāna, in *Harshachārita,* describes the peaceful times enjoyed in northern India under the benevolent rule of King Sriharsha of Kanauj: 'Under this monarch only bees quarrel in collecting dews; the only feet cut off are those in metre; only ashtapadas teach the position of the chaturanga.'

A little explanation is required to clarify the last phrase; but inherent in these eight words is indeed a description of the origin of chess. By 'ashtapadas' the writer means boards on which games were played and the 'position of the chaturanga' means the points where the four arms of a mock army were placed on the board. In fact 'ashtapadas' refers to backgammon, which, as I have said, is older than chess, and this of course indicates a possible derivation.

So then, 'chaturanga' is what the game was called in its first mention in written form in Sanskrit about the years 590–610. It should be emphasized that no earlier written reference exists. Professor Willard Fiske, the American Icelandic scholar who did so much to show how the early form of the European game came to Iceland (and whose library is still preserved at Reykjavik, where I had the pleasure of examining it during the Fischer–Spassky match in 1972) wrote in *The Nation* (New York, 1900) that 'before the seventh century of our era, the existence of chess in any land is not demonstrable by a single shred of contemporary or trustworthy documentary evidence.'

This would discount any supposed reference to chess in China on the lines I have already mentioned; H. J. R. Murray, in his monumental *History of Chess,* agrees with him fully.

But when Professor Fiske goes on to say that 'down to that date it is all impenetrable darkness', he is perhaps a little too emphatic; recent archaeological research has shed some light in that impenetrable darkness since his day. Modern Russian archaeologists, in fact, have claimed that chess spread from India to central Asia some three centuries before the game was supposedly invented in northwest India. Excavating a site of the ancient town of Dalverzin-tepe in the Surkhan-Darya region of Uzbekistan in 1972, they found animal figures, one of an elephant and another of a zebu (a small humped ox) which, they say, are chessmen (p. 13). The town of Dalverzin-tepe was part of an empire, Mush-tik, that existed during the first to fourth centuries AD and included parts of modern Afghanistan, Pakistan, north-west India and southern Uzbekistan.

The pieces have been dated as second century AD, and Russian chess historians use this as evidence that chess came to what is now the USSR at a much earlier date than was supposed by Murray and others. The pieces are presumed to have been brought from India, but A. S. M. Dickins in the *British Chess Magazine* (July, 1973) thinks that the find is in reality a strong pointer 'towards a Chinese origin of the game'. For, he says, the place where they were found would be 'more or less on the very caravan route along which cultural exchanges took place between China and India from the earliest times before Alexander the Great until at least the time of the Mogul Emperors, if not later.'

Naturally, this is far from positive proof. For one thing, the pieces, if they were on the caravan route, might equally well have gone from India to China. And for another, they might be ornaments rather

Animal figures of the second century AD, thought to be chessmen, discovered at the ancient site of Dalverzin-tepe, Uzbekistan, in the USSR.

than chess pieces. The fact that they are tiny (the elephant is 2.4 cm high, and the zebu, 1.8 cm) and, even more important, that they are on a cylindrical base, might be a sign that they were a derivative of an ancient board-game of China in which the pieces were of cylindrical shape. This game had some resemblance to chess, but was nevertheless much further away from chess than chaturanga itself. Nor is the presence of a zebu particularly reassuring evidence.

Support for this explanation is given by passages in a commentary by Wang Po to the Emperor Wu-Ti's book on the old Chinese game written in 569 AD. The pieces were circular and flat, and the game was known as astrological or elephant chess. It could be that this was indeed the game to which the allusions were made in the poem of the second century AD already mentioned. That it was played by throwing these 'chessmen', each of which had some astrological inscription on it, haphazard over the board, shows how far away it was from chess as we know it. Dr Jack Good, who recently advocated a form of random chess, might find himself anticipated by some 2,000 years!

Nevertheless, there now exists enough evidence—obscure, unverified and conflicting though it may be—to cast more than a glimmer of light into Willard Fiske's 'impenetrable darkness'.

This evidence too would seem to militate somewhat against Murray's hypothesis that the game of chess (or perhaps chaturanga would be the better term for it at this stage) was the invention of one single individual at one single time in the sixth century in northwest India. One can accept that chaturanga was becoming popular round about that period; but the likeliest explanation as to its invention is that, basically, it was a derivation rather than an invention. It could have evolved gradually, possibly from the Chinese game or possibly from a game played in India, with the Chinese deriving the game from that country. And it could have been so devised and derived gradually by a number of people rather than springing, goddess-like, from the brain of one particular individual, 'the Philosopher', as Murray likes to term him.

That it was in origin a war game and that it was a direct product of Indian civilization in the form of chaturanga is quite certain. The reflection of the manners and mores of an Indian state of the sixth century AD is too faithful to be mere chance. Chaturanga, and its successor, chess, was and is a game that could be conceived and played only by a people of comparatively civilized and cultured character. War is the setting for the game, but it is a war waged between two advanced and highly-organized states. There is a leader, king or rāja who directs the whirlwind and controls the storm. But he is advised by a prime minister or general, and relies heavily on his judgment. It is interesting to observe that the political set-up is more like that of an oligarchy than a democracy—that idea was to come much later. It is interesting too to note that the idea that each soldier has a marshal's baton in his knapsack was anticipated by some 1,200 years with the concept of pawn promotion.

When Alexander the Great invaded north-west India in 326 BC he found himself opposed by an Indian army consisting of four divisions: 30,000 infantry, 4,000 cavalry, 300 chariots and 200 elephants. This was the normal type of well-equipped Indian army and it remained so for many hundreds of years. Chaturanga, meaning 'four-membered', was a game based on these four arms.

The inventors (or inventor—pace Murray) of the game added two vital figures, the King or Rāja and the Adviser or Minister. Since these two forces, important though they were, did not and do not take part in actual hand-to-hand fighting, they were endowed with little real force in the extent of their powers. Later on, much later on, as attempts were made to speed up the game, their powers did indeed increase, notably in the case of the Adviser, who was eventually to become the most powerful piece on the board. But no such change had been made by the sixth, seventh and eighth centuries. This argues quite a static condition in the way of life in India for almost a thousand years. It also seems to me to provide yet another argument against Murray's assertion that the game was invented by one single person sometime in the sixth century AD.

It is, however, certain that chaturanga was the conscious adaptation of the methods of Indian warfare to a board-game of a highly-stylized content. Confirmation of this is given in striking fashion by some pieces of Sanskrit poetry of a later period—sometime in the ninth century AD. Just as in England in the seventeenth century there was a school of poetry, the Metaphysicals, who used symbolism for religious and literary effects, or as in Spain you had the conceits of Gongorism, so the later Sanskrit poets made immense use of the pun for literary purposes. One can see how this brilliant transposition of ideas reproduced itself in the shaping of chaturanga which is, basically, a pun on war.

In an epic called *Haravijaya,* or the *Victory of Siva,* a Kashmir poet named Ratnākara described a highly-successful general, Attahasa, one of Siva's army, as continually defeating an opponent despite the latter's abundance of troops in the classic four-membered combination and despite his opponent's skilful diplomacy and military strategy. But all this description was done as a series of elaborate puns so that the whole passage could be read as a complete parallel with chess. In this latter form the passage, given by Jacobi in 1896 in the *Zeitschrift der Deutschen Morgenlandischen Gesellschaft* and later

The Elephant of Chaturanga, in modern chess the Bishop; a twelfth century Arab ivory in the Museo Nazionale, Florence.

by H. J. R. Murray in his 1913 *History of Chess,* runs as follows:

> . . . who turned not into a chess-board (an-ashtāpadam) the enemy who had a four-square (chaturasra) form, who abounded in foot-soldiers (patti), horses (ashwa), chariots (rat ha) and elephants (dvipa) and who had the form of combination.

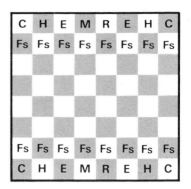

1 : *The initial placing of the men.*

The pieces mentioned in this passage have their modern equivalents as follows: Foot-soldiers = Pawns; Horses = Knights; Chariots = Rooks; Elephants = Bishops. The somewhat mysterious form of combination is explained by Jacobi as the equivalent of two halves folding together, which in turn means that the forces of each side were symmetrically disposed.

If there were any doubt as to how the game of chaturanga came to be conceived, this passage would settle it once and for all.

In the same style of simile and parallels is an equally-important poem called *Kavyalankara* by another poet, Rudrata, who wrote towards the end of the ninth century. He drew a parallel between various everyday objects and also the weapons of war (wheel, sword, bow, plough etc) and the moves of pieces on the chaturanga board. He did this by taking half the board (thirty-two squares) and demonstrating a tour of every square by three pieces, the Chariot, the Horse and the Elephant.

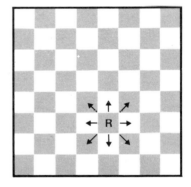

2 : *The Rāja moves to one adjacent square.*

In effect Rudrata was working out an ingenious puzzle that would have pleased the acrostic-makers of a later age. The Chariot, which became the modern Rook and had the same powers as that piece, obviously provided no difficulty as regards the actual tour of the board. The Horse (modern Knight) was more intricate but still perfectly natural and feasible; but the Elephant (modern Bishop) did not have anything like the Bishop's powers and its tour could be accomplished only by adding on powers which, according to Jacobi, were to be found in chess in the Punjab and later appear in Burmese and Siamese chess. When one realizes that all this had to be accomplished in accordance with a metrical scheme of verse, one is lost in admiration at the writer's ingenuity.

But the outstanding importance of Rudrata's writings is that they enable us to establish how the pieces moved in chaturanga. We are also greatly helped in the matter of the rules of chaturanga in that the game seemed to have persisted in India with little change for centuries (though there were differences, in accordance with which part of India one was dealing). So the Muslim writers on chess, who came some three centuries later and could well be described as the first real chess theoreticians, were in fact describing the game of chaturanga when they wrote about chess in India.

From the Sanskrit and the early Muslim writers then we get a full picture of how the pieces moved and where they were originally placed.

The Rāja (modern King) was placed originally on K1 directly opposite to the opposing Rāja (also on his K1). It moved as the modern King does, that is to say, to any adjacent square that was not attacked by an enemy piece. It could not in fact move into check. Nor could it castle, this rather more sophisticated operation not coming into being for some centuries. There was good reason for this. Chaturanga was, as will be seen, a slow game by comparison with its descendant, chess. It took a great deal of time to open up the

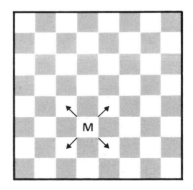

3 : *The Minister moves to one adjacent square, diagonally only.*

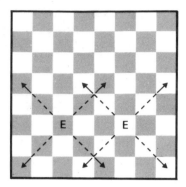

4: *The Elephant leaps over one square and moves two squares, diagonally only.*

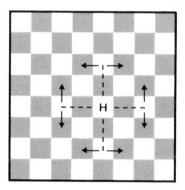

5: *The Horse moves like a modern Knight, two squares either vertically or laterally and then one square either laterally or vertically. It leaps over the intervening squares.*

centre, i.e. to strip the Rāja of its central protection. Hence the main piece could remain with equanimity in the centre for most of the game. Moreover, with some of the other pieces (notably those which were eventually to become the Queen and the Bishop) being very much less fierce and powerful than their modern equivalents, the Rāja had no reason to fear any major attack.

The Minister (modern Queen) could move to any diagonally adjacent square and was a pitifully-weak forerunner of what was to become far and away the most powerful piece on the board. It was originally placed on Q1, again vis-à-vis its opponent's Minister.

The Elephant (modern Bishop) was originally placed on QB1 and KB1. Its opposing pieces too were directly opposite. It moved diagonally, like its modern equivalent; but it was much more limited in scope as it could traverse only two squares. It was, however, rather like the modern Knight in that it leapt over one square. Presumably this quality of bridging a gap was some recognition of the usefulness of the elephant division in battle as a cavalry force. But all the same it seems a little puzzling that such a powerful beast should have been so limited in its field of action. That this also soon became recognized is illustrated by the fact that in various parts of India additional powers were given to the Elephant and that eventually its powers were indeed much increased. Nevertheless, in origin it was a piece of limited force.

The Horse (modern Knight) was initially placed on QKt1 and KKt1, again directly opposite its enemy counterparts. It moved exactly as a Knight does in modern chess: two squares vertically or laterally and then one square laterally or vertically. It could also leap over pieces just as the modern Knight does. It is significant that this move has never changed, obviously having been deemed a success for some fifteen hundred years. The millions of beginners who experience such difficulty in mastering this move should reflect that they have been preceded by still more millions, all of whom eventually have heartily approved of its somewhat complicated nature.

The Chariots (modern Rooks) were placed initially on QR1 and KR1 and the opponent's Chariots were likewise placed on his QR1 and KR1. Like the Knight, the Rook's move has not changed and it could be played right along the whole length of the board, either vertically or laterally. It was thus far and away the strongest piece, and this was exactly right having regard to the worth of the chariot in warfare of the time. In war it united speed with force to the highest degree possible in that period. It should be noted that after the game had been in existence for some time (probably about 100 years) there was confusion between the placing of the Chariot and the Elephant so that in some parts of India the Elephants were placed where Chariots should have been and vice versa. This explains why some Indian and Chinese sets have Elephants positioned where Rooks would normally be.

There were eight Foot-soldiers on either side placed initially on the second row. These were our modern Pawns and like them, they moved one square upwards and captured by taking the enemy piece on the adjacent square diagonally, again upwards. On reaching the eighth square a Foot-soldier was promoted into a Minister, but in these early stages of the game it did not have the choice of being promoted into any other piece. Nor was it able to move two squares

The Ancient Egyptians played
board games, but not chess. Here,
the scribe Ani and his wife are
shown playing draughts. From the
papyrus of Ani, Theban Book of
the Dead; XIXth dynasty,
c. 1250 B.C.

*Ancient Egyptian animals also
enjoyed playing board games!
A satirical drawing from the
period of the New Kingdom.*

at a time on its initial move. This refinement was added when the game came to Europe.

It was played by two players taking alternate turns on a board of sixty-four squares, but, unlike our modern chess-board, this was not chequered. After the game had been in existence for a couple of hundred years a variation was introduced for four-handed chaturanga with pieces being arranged on all four sides of the board. Some historians have in fact been led to believe that four-handed chess was the original game. One of the most recent books on the subject, *Historia General del Ajedrez,* published in Madrid in 1966 by Julio Ganzo, follows Duncan Forbes in this mistake. Forbes too asserts wrongly that the Chariots were originally boats. Clearly he was misled by the circumstance that this is indeed the case in the four-handed game. It is interesting to observe that Russian chess must have been derived from the four-handed type since to this very day they call the Rook (the modern form of Chariot) 'Ladia' which is indeed Russian for boat.

The object of the game was, as in modern chess, to deliver checkmate, i.e. to place the opposing Rāja in such a position that it was threatened with capture on the next move and that this threat was not to be parried. But in chaturanga one could also win by depriving the enemy Rāja of all its troops. The game was also won for the side that was stalemated, i.e. when a player had no legal move he could make with any of his pieces. In modern chess stalemate is a draw, but clearly the devisers of the game thought the paradox was worth the full point, as one might have expected from the subtle minds that played with such fancies as those in Sanskrit literature. Stalemate in fact has had an up-and-down career and has counted as a win, draw or loss at different times and in various places.

So the initial placing of the men was as in Diagram 1. The initial letter (or, in the case of the Foot-soldier, letters) of the pieces is used to indicate them.

Diagrams 2–7 show how the pieces moved.

This was a slow and subtle game as befits the slowness and subtlety of Indian warfare of the sixth century AD. Without the speed of modern transport or the destructive quality of modern armaments, warfare was inevitably a matter of slow positioning. In Indian warfare too a campaign could only be won when the Rāja was either captured, destroyed or so placed that his army had been wiped out. But so much concession was made to the inviolability of a monarch that, in the game, he was never actually captured and removed from the board.

To modern western eyes chaturanga was a tedious game, devoid of dynamism, but it should not be thought that because it lacked speed it also lacked artistry. It owed its continuous and lengthy popularity to the fact that its nature was thoroughly in accord with the spirit of the times. Luck or gambling was absent from the two-sided game though dice were used with the four-handed type.

Unfortunately it is not possible to give examples of actual games since none was preserved from this period. Indeed one had to wait till chaturanga received a fresh impetus from the Arabs and became the Muslim game of Shatranj. Then the theoreticians took charge and game scores were recorded.

But before the game went to the Arabs it spread to Persia, a westernization which will be described in our next chapter.

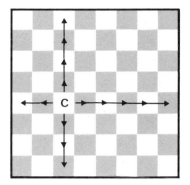

6: *The Chariot moves like a modern Rook, either vertically or laterally as far as it likes.*

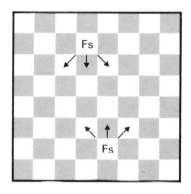

7: *The Foot-soldier moves upwards one square like the modern pawn, and, again like the modern pawn, it captures one square, diagonally and upwards.*

chapter **2**

The game spreads to Persia and elsewhere

In the name of God! It is related that in the reign of Khusraw-i-Anushakruban, Dewasarm, the great ruler of India, devised the chatrang with 16 emerald and 16 ruby red men in order to test the wisdom of the men of Iran, and also from motives of personal interest. With the game of chess he sent 1,200 camels laden with gold, silver, jewels, pearls and raiment, and 90 elephants.

This colourful story, though it possesses some uncanny overtones as a sort of modern parable about attempts to persuade Bobby Fischer to play chess, is in fact taken from the *Chatrang-namak* (written about the seventh or eighth century AD) and describes, in legendary fashion. how the game came from India to Persia.

Persia was far from being the only country to which chatrang spread. It reached all of Asia by the two great methods through which knowledge and culture, sciences and the arts, inventions and the general embellishments of everyday life have all been diffused—by trade routes and by conquest or by a mixture of the two. This blend does indeed have much bearing on the history of chess. One has only to think of the Vikings who spread the light (including chess) by travelling throughout the known (and sometimes even the unknown) world, trading, as it were, with their friendly left hand and enforcing the relationship with a sword in their right. As we shall see later, they were great pioneers in the cause of chess.

Wherever great empires were created or existed, there chatrang blossomed and flourished. The game and civilization went hand in hand, partly because its subtlety appealed to the cultivated intellect and partly because its warlike connotations coincided with even more fundamental human feelings. Chess inherited these attributes which made and make the game so enduring and pervasive; thus, it could be said that chess will come to an end when mankind ceases to make war and when he no longer delights in using his mind at play.

The first and most important expansion of chatrang was to Persia some time in the sixth century, probably towards the end of that century, if the *Chatrang-nāmak* is to be believed.

But there were other expansions, almost as important and just as enduring. One was via Afghanistan, Pakistan and Outer Uzbekistan to what would nowadays be called the Soviet republics of

Central Asia. The importance of this expansion is that it was eventually to prove, again by trade routes and conquest, a way into Europe for chess. Recent archaeological finds all tend to confirm this. Murray says that Savenkov, who published a monograph on the *Evolution of the Game of Chess* in Moscow in 1905, was claiming too great an antiquity for Russian chess in stating that the introduction took place in the fifth or sixth century AD, and that it came from Sassanian Persia. However, the speed with which the game has always travelled is quite remarkable, and it may well be that Savenkov was not so far out in his time scheme after all.

Another most enduring expansion was southwards, via southern India to the lands occupied by the Malayans, to Borneo, Java and Sumatra and so to what is now known as Indonesia. The game took root here so lastingly that even today there are many places in Indonesia where something like chatrang is still played. Its very name, 'main chator', shows the derivation, 'main' being Malay for 'game' and 'chator' obviously deriving from chaturanga. Malayan chess pieces are much more elementary than the normal pieces to which one is accustomed and, by an amusing turn of the wheel, they strongly resemble some modern artistic sets from which all frills and furbelows have been banished and strictly geometric patterns are used.

This is no doubt an exceedingly practical way of making and using chess pieces. In Sumatra, for example, a new chess set is used for each game by the instant method of carving new pieces out of bamboo or the centre of a palm leaf.

Trade routes were again responsible for the expansion of the game via Kashmir to China. This was, however, much later, round about

The chess hall of the Moscow 'Palace of the Young Pioneers', with wall panels illustrating legends about the origins of chess.

the eighth century AD, and from China it eventually made its way to Korea and Japan. But it made little headway in these eastern countries. It came up against a figurative Chinese wall in the shape of the game of Go which was and is far more popular.

Go, a much older game than chaturanga, bears no resemblance to chess. Known as wei-chi, there are many references to it in ancient Chinese literature. I have seen translations of these which, wrongly in my opinion, render them as chess. An example is the *Golden Palace,* an anonymous poem of the first century BC which runs charmingly as follows:

> In the Eastern Kitchen the meat is sliced and ready—
> Roast beef and boiled pork and mutton
> The Master of the Feast hands round the wine
> The harp-players sound their clear chords.
> The cups are pushed aside and we face each other at chess;
> The rival pawns are marshalled rank against rank.
> The fire glows and the smoke puffs and curls;
> From the incense-burner rises a delicate fragrance
> The clear wine has made our cheeks red;
> Round the table joy and peace prevail.
> May those who shared in this day's delight
> Through countless centuries enjoy like felicity.

What game is this which the translator so lightly terms chess? Modern chess it certainly is not. Many kindred souls may no doubt enjoy it for countless centuries in the future, but the number of centuries in which chess as we know it has been enjoyed can almost be counted on the fingers of one hand.

Was it then chaturanga, or chatrang as the Persians called it? Hardly, if the game originated in north-west India and spread from there to Persia and then on to China. Could it have been go? The line, 'The rival pawns are marshalled rank against rank', hardly tallies with wei-chi, nor with chatrang for that matter, even allowing for poetic licence.

Presumably the word that the translator has taken to mean chess is 'siang-chi' which seems to have been used for any kind of board-game. 'Siang' originally meant elephant, and then, by an obvious extension, it came to mean ivory or figure. The most important chess historian before Murray, Antonius van der Linde, maintains in his *Geschichte und Litteratur des Schachspiels* published in Berlin in 1874, that it means figure game, and he may well be right.

This figure game, which was played along the lines of the board rather than on the squares, bore very little resemblance to chatrang. But it is possible that the Chinese river game, which is still played in China, may have been a sort of blended derivative from the figure game and chatrang. The figure game survives but the pieces no longer look like figures and are merely draughtsmen on which are inscribed their names.

So the modern form of chess in China is played on a board consisting of eight times nine squares. Each side sets out his pieces on the first four rows and these are divided by one row of squares known as the river, hence its name. As in chess each side has sixteen pieces, one opponent's being red and the other's black, traditionally, at any rate, for there are many variations of colour. The pieces are circular discs and their names are written on top. They are not placed on the squares of the board but on the corners, edges and intersections, as in the diagram (Diagram 8).

The River Game has resemblances to chaturanga and chess which are quite remarkable. But so too are the differences—so much so that it is still unproven whether it is a variant or a derivative from chaturanga, or whether it stems from some more ancient game (perhaps that described in *The Golden Palace*) and was then blended with or strongly influenced by chaturanga as it made its way to China from India.

The fact that Black moved first and not Red is neither here nor there. In the history of the game, many variations of this nature can be noted, and it was only in comparatively modern times that White (which corresponds to Red) always had the first move.

The names of the pieces and their moves are of supreme significance in this connection. Each side has a General which moves one square vertically or laterally. This is clearly the King. The General has two Counsellors which move one square diagonally. These correspond to the modern Queen, but are closer to the chaturanga Minister. I use the term 'squares' but since the pieces move from line to line and from intersection to intersection 'square' is not perhaps quite accurate; in any case, the difference from chaturanga and chess is here quite startling.

There are two Elephants (our modern Bishops) and these very nearly approximate to the chaturanga pieces since they move two squares diagonally; but they cannot leap over any piece as their chaturanga equivalents were wont to do. In the case of the Red side, the Elephants are called Assistants who move as they do. Then there is the Horse, which is our modern Knight, although it differs quite considerably from the Knight in its moves. It cannot leap over any piece and its power is modified to moving one square vertically or laterally and then one square diagonally. Two Chariots have exactly the same powers as those of chaturanga or as those of our modern Rook.

Each side has two Cannons, pieces that are not to be found in either chaturanga or chess, presumably because the Chinese came to this invention earlier than the rest of what we would call the civilized world and they would term the barbarian. Inasmuch as their methods of warfare were more advanced, they would, no doubt, have the right in the matter. The Cannon moves like a Rook, but with one odd difference: it can capture only when there is a piece between itself and its target. Presumably the Chinese had already invented their own version of the howitzer, and, as one who received his early training in the artillery in the last war, I can testify to its being a most subtle and civilized arm of warfare.

Then come the Infantry. Each side has five Foot-soldiers. These are our modern Pawns and like them they advance one square. Once past the river, however, they can move forwards or sideways. But there is no promotion, an idea which would have been repugnant to ancient Chinese civilization.

The object of the game is to deliver checkmate, but stalemate also counts as a win. Here again there is no great difference from chess, since stalemate has varied in value from time to time in its history. One important difference, however, from both chaturanga and chess is that certain pieces are confined to certain parts of the board.

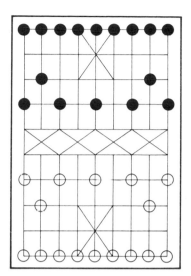

8: *The board of the modern form of chess in China.*

The group of people in the background are playing the Chinese River Game, in this scene by the Japanese artist Hokusai (1760–1849).

The range is most severely limited for the General and the Counsellor, whilst the Elephant can move only in its own half of the board.

The River Game was and is popular, despite the fact that the educated classes tended to despise it and to prefer Go as being more refined and difficult. Chaturanga, and later chess, could make no headway against Go; but, as I have already surmised, it is probable either that the River Game was strongly influenced by chaturanga or else that it derived from the Indian game.

The extent to which the Chinese Empire contrived to cut itself off from the barbarians outside its civilized confines is strongly indicated in the fact that chess as we know it failed to penetrate its borders. It was only when the Communist régime was established after World War II and while it remained a friendly ally of the Soviet Union, that chess began to percolate from Moscow to Peking. There was talk of forming a Chinese Chess Federation which would apply for membership in the World Chess Federation, and Soviet masters and teachers were despatched to Peking. But, alas, the Chinese soon decided that the Soviet State had become a hotbed of 'imperialist reaction'. Back went the masters to Moscow, and the wall once again kept out the modern game of chess.

Recently, however, there have been signs of a welcome relaxation in this respect. In 1974 the first championship tournament of the Peoples' Republic of China was held in Peking, and the Chinese Chess Federation has applied for affiliation to the World Chess Federation. If indeed the game does become popular there, then there are dazzling prospects for the addition to the ranks of chess-players of, at first, some hundreds of millions of enthusiastic beginners, and, in the near future, of thousands upon thousands of masters and grandmasters.

I must leave Chinese chess with the remark that it still presents many intriguing problems to the historian. No doubt in the course of time, when archaeologists have disinterred the rich mines of information which must exist throughout that huge land, we shall be furnished with sufficient evidence to solve most of these problems.

It was only natural that chaturanga should also spread from north-west India to Tibet, and the name of chess in Tibet, Chandaraki, looks very much like a derivative from the Sanskrit. But the game also spread to lands occupied by the Mongols, although this appears to have been, as one might indeed have expected, at a rather later date. The names by which the game was known in the vast stretches of northern Asia inhabited by the various Mongolian tribes are nearer to the Persian 'chatrang' and the Arabic 'shatranj'. Shatara and shatir, for example, both seem closer to the Persian and early Arabic names for chaturanga, than to the Sanskrit.

There is, however, no written record, and the pieces that have been found are too varied and, in many cases, too remote from what we tend to regard as chesspieces for there to be anything like certitude in this matter. It is unlikely, to say the least, that chess came to northern Russia by these routes, as was once maintained by Russian historians.

As I indicated at the beginning of this chapter, by far the most important expansion of chess from India, important that is from the point of view of its further history and popularization, was the spread of the game into Persia.

The fact that Persia produced a great poetic literature means that in one way we are lucky, for there are frequent references to chess. But they can, alas, be misleading. The most famous and the one with which we all become acquainted in our schooldays is, of course, Edward FitzGerald's translation of the *Rubaiyat* of Omar Khayyam:

> 'Tis all a Chequer-board of Nights and Days
> Where Destiny with Men for Pieces plays;
> Hither and thither moves, and mates, and slays
> And one by one back in the Closet lays.

It seems that FitzGerald was dissatisfied with his first treatment of this passage since he produced two more versions in later editions of his translation, finishing with these lines:

> But helpless Pieces of the Game he plays
> Upon this Chequer-board of Nights and Days;
> Hither and thither moves and checks and slays,
> And one by one back in the Closet lays.

My good old friend Norman Knight says, in that most interesting anthology, *Chess Pieces*, that he is assured that what follows is a literal translation of the best Persian text:

To speak plain language and not in parables, we are the pieces and Heaven plays the game. We are played together in a baby-game upon the chess-board of existence, and one by one return to the box of non-existence.

FitzGerald's most famous translation, the first I have given, is the one which carries the most conviction and is the most striking. It also, however, demonstrates that it is deceptive to rely upon the *Rubaiyat* for any authentic description of early chess in Persia. Khayyam was too far removed from the facts: he was writing in the eleventh century and the events with which we are concerned happened some four hundred years earlier. What the passage from the *Rubaiyat* and many others like it do prove is the lasting popularity of the game in Persia, and they are valuable evidence to that extent.

Persian literature of Omar Khayyam's time continually used the game as an illustration and a parable of the happenings in real life. Thus Unsuri, a poet who was his contemporary, wishing to praise the success of his patron, Mahmud of Ghazni, in warfare and diplomacy, wrote of him:

The monarch played chess with a thousand kings for the kingdom. And to each king he gave checkmate in a different way.

An even greater poet than either of these, Firdausi, relates in his national epic, the *Shāh-nāmah,* how chess was invented, in the beautiful and sad legend of Gav and Talkhand. The two were half-brothers whose widowed mother was ruler of a kingdom in north-west India. When they came of age they quarrelled as to which was to be king, Talkhand being the fiercer in the dispute and Gav, milder and more defensive. Already we see the makings of a game of chess, with the one side taking the initiative with the White pieces and the other defending with Black.

Eventually it came to open warfare, and Talkhand was heavily defeated. He rallied hidden forces, which were again beaten in a second battle. He himself was killed, even though Gav had given strict orders that his life was to be spared (the King cannot be captured). The Queen-mother, inconsolable, in the depth of despair, blamed Gav for the death of her other son. So Gav held a council of the wisest men in the kingdom and asked them to devise some simulacrum of a battle that would show his mother how events actually had gone. It took them the whole night to invent chess, which is about eleven hours and fifty-nine minutes more than the usual popular limit of time ascribed to the game's invention.

Oddly enough, the board contained 100 squares, the two additional squares in each row being necessitated by the addition of a couple of Camels. These could move three squares at a time, but otherwise the movements of the pieces did not differ from those in chatrang. Nor did the general lines of play. Eventually the side that was defeated saw its Shah (King) die of fatigue and thirst (mated).

Gav showed the game to the Queen who studied it without a stop. She could find no solution and eventually died. That is how chess was invented according to the Persians.

This legend clearly indicates that chatrang is a war game. Here, as in so many instances in the history of chess, the bare facts are clothed in an aesthetic and colourful way. Firdausi embroidered even the facts themselves, since the earlier story, the *Chatrang-nāmak* to which I have referred, lacks the poetic Talkhand-Gav conflict and merely describes how chatrang came to Persia from India. The Khusraw mentioned there was Nushirwan, who reigned in Persia from 531 to 578 AD. This seems a little early if chaturanga was invented in north-west India only in the latter half of the sixth century. But of course we are still dealing with legend here, the *Chatrang-nāmak* probably having been written about two centuries after this Shah's reign.

Some confirmation of this date is furnished by a reference to chatrang in a romance, the *Kārnāmak,* written in about 600 AD about Artaxerxes (Artakhshir) the founder of the Sassanian dynasty, which commenced in the third century AD. This relates how Artakhshir excelled in ball-play, in horsemanship, in chatrang, in hunting and in other accomplishments. Since the *Kārnāmak* is generally supposed to have been written round about 300 years after Artaxerxes lived, the idea that he played chatrang is a pleasant, romantic but mythical conception. Its mention in 600 AD, however, does show a certain recognition of the game at the beginning of the seventh century as a kingly pursuit.

No earlier reference to chess (taking it that chatrang was the equivalent) has been found in literature. The Sanskrit references, as given in my first chapter, are about half a century later, though presumably they apply to an earlier period. The game itself, the pieces, their names, placing and function are all described in the *Chatrang-nāmak* and later in the *Shāh-nāmah*.

The chaturanga Rāja became the Shah (modern King) and already we can see how today's word, 'checkmate', was derived. When you attacked the Shah you pointed out the assault to the adversary by saying 'Shah', since it was incumbent upon him to extricate his Shah from attack forthwith. When, however, this was impossible, the Shah was said to be 'mat', an adjective meaning 'defeated' or 'helpless'. So 'Shah-mat' equals 'checkmate'. It is interesting to observe that later on the word 'mate' was to intensify in meaning so that one finds it being used in Middle-English and even in Elizabethan literature to mean 'killed'.

The Minister became Farzin (modern Queen), a Persian word meaning a wise man and hence a counsellor. The Farzin was placed on Q1 like its chaturanga predecessor and, like the Minister, was a piece of feeble powers.

The Elephant was called Pīl, but here there is some mystery as the word Pīl is not Persian, nor is it known where it comes from. One suggestion has been that it emanates from a tribe somewhere between Persia and India. The Persians would have had to borrow the word for elephant in any case, just as we have had to do, since the animal is not native to Persia.

The normal word for horse in Persian is Asp, and this was the name for the modern Knight.

The Chariot became Rukh (modern Rook), and here we are again in troubled waters that have become muddied with a large number of guesses. These range from a camel to a hero via 'an elephant bearing a tower on its back'. Obviously this last interpretation is merely a description of the sort of piece that was made in later and modern Indian sets. Camel is pure guess-work, possibly based on the fact that this animal appears in variants of the game. Rukh was used by Firdausi to describe a hero, but this is merely a poetic recognition of a chariot-driver as one who 'rides the whirlwind and directs the storm'.

Whatever Rukh meant in contexts other than chatrang, there can be no doubt, as Murray says, that the chess term Rukh meant Chariot. Later on there is some evidence that the Moors, when they came to Spain, used the word to mean chariot; but this, to my mind, is a piece of analogy from chess to life rather than the other way round. Still it supports the chess use and meaning of the word.

The Foot-soldier became Piyādah (modern Pawn), and this was derived from 'pai' which is Persian for 'foot'.

The game of chatrang flourished under the Sassanian empire; but it received an even greater impetus when the Persian empire fell to Arab invaders.

Before taking up the story in the next chapter, I must first dispose of one myth that seems perennial, and then deal with an interesting side-venture of the game. The myth is that chess, chatrang or chaturanga were played in ancient Greek and Roman times. For this there does not exist the slightest vestige of proof. No reference to the game is found in classical literature and no chess-pieces survive from those periods or places. So, sadly one has to dismiss the idea of Ulysses having been a great positional master or of Achilles as a bold combinational player.

But the Greeks did take chatrang up for all that and it became the Greek 'zatrikion'. Only it was not to Troy nor to ancient Athens that the game came but to Byzantium. When exactly it reached the Byzantine Empire is not known, but the assumption is that since the Greek word is nearer the Persian than the Arabic the period would have been some time in the eighth century at the latest. It is known too that Nicephorus, Emperor of Byzantium in 802 AD, was acquainted with the game.

Zatrikion fell into disrepute in Byzantium as a sort of Bohemian way of passing the time, stemming from Persian debauchery. We know that Horace regarded Persian luxury as a sort of refined lechery, and there exists a piece entitled *De arte Persica* which refers to 'slaves and games of bolgon [whatever that is] and chess and love of women'. Murray says that it would seem that 'chess is associated with other notorious features of Persian luxury'. When he adds that 'It has probably never been in worse company', however, he betrays a somewhat sheltered existence and a gap in his knowledge of chess and chessmasters. This is perhaps the reverse of *'Et ego in Arcadia'*.

Anyway, it is known that the Emperor Alexis Comnena, who reigned in Byzantium in the early twelfth century, loved to play zatrikion with his close friends. His daughter, Princess Anna Comnena, tells us in her *Alexiad* that he did this, and she adds that the game was 'discovered in the luxury of the Assyrians, and was brought to us.' For Assyrians read Persians.

This, unfortunately for the game, proved to be a turning point in its practice. The Emperor had, as the commander of his body-guard, a certain John Zonares, who appears to have got religion and exchanged his profession as a soldier for the vocation of a monk on

Mount Athos. From there he issued some canonic rules, or rather interpretations thereof, in which zatrikion (or chess) and its pursuit were classed as ways of debauchery. The relevant passage runs as follows:

> Inasmuch as some of the Bishops and clergy leave virtuous paths and play zatrikion or dice or drink to excess, the Rule ordains that such shall cease to do so or be excluded.

Not only are all types and grades of clergy forbidden to play the game according to this canon, but 'if laymen be given to chess-playing and drunkenness they shall be excluded.'

Whether this ecclesiastical blast was wholly successful in suppressing the game is not known. My guess is that it was still played sub rosa and might even have gained a little guilty popularity from being so condemned. When Constantinople fell in 1453 and the Byzantine Empire disappeared, perhaps some of the scholarly refugees who fled to Italy and prompted the Renaissance may also have inspired the upsurge in Italian chess with a contribution from zatrikion. But the Italian story is for a much later chapter.

chapter **3**

The game becomes shatranj

Barely half a century after chatrang came to Persia a new explosion of peoples occurred that was to change the history of the world, to create a new civilization, to promote and encourage a remarkable blossoming of the arts and sciences and, as a natural consequence of this last development, to provide a fresh and lasting impetus to the game, both as regards its practice and its expansion throughout the known world. Under the influence and the incitement of the teachings of Mahomet, the Arabs burst into an immense proselytizing activity which overthrew old empires and created a new one.

Among other empires to which they put an end was the Sassanian rule of Persia. It was the Caliph Omar, the second in the line of the four famous orthodox caliphs, who achieved this round about the middle of the seventh century. His successor, Caliph Ali ben Abu Talib, seems to have been the first Arab ruler to have come in contact with the game. Ali, who was Mahomet's son-in-law, 'once chanced to pass some people who were playing at shatranj (chess), and asked them, "What images are these upon which you are gazing so intently?", for they were quite new to him, having only lately been introduced from Persia, and the pawns were soldiers, and the Elephants and Horses were depicted according to the custom of the Persians.'

It is interesting to note how dominant was the dread of the influence of the graven image in the minds of the Semitic peoples (there is a close parallel here with the Judaic laws). The prophet's son-in-law would have been well aware of Mahomet's disapproval of such things and it is perhaps fortunate that he knew nothing of the game, for otherwise his teachings might have expressly forbidden his followers to play it.

This incident seems to have been authentic; but, since it was a war game, I cannot credit a story which says that Omar approved of the game as being quite in order. He is supposed to have asked what shatranj was and to have been told practically the same tale that I have narrated in Chapter 2 as the legend of Gav and Talkhand. This is all much too pat to have any more import than simply to show how wide-spread both the game and the legend were.

In any event, the existence of these legends, and many others in Arabic literature, demonstrate what a firm hold the game took on

An illustration from an ancient Persian manuscript, a 'Treatise on Chess'.

the Arabic world. Shatranj quite superseded the older game of nard (backgammon), though it never drove it out completely. As far as one can tell from written records, the Arabs were the first people to study the game scientifically, and this one might have expected from so talented a race.

In some ways it might be regarded as fortunate for chess that this was so, since the Arabs, with irresistible force, carved their way through great nations and carried the game with them wherever they conquered and colonized. But, as I have already pointed out, chess moves hand in hand, as it were, with the progress of civilizations. It tends to flourish where there is a high level of intellectual cultivation, so it is not really a question of fortune. No doubt this is a flattering theory for the chess enthusiast to hug to his bosom, but I hope to prove in this book that the experience of 1,500 years supports this idea.

Two perhaps kindred pursuits were taught to the rest of the world by the Arabs—mathematics and chess, and, if you are tempted to accuse me of placing chess in too high a company, before you do so, consider the Arabic legend of the invention of chess, which centres round the mythical philosopher, Sassa (or Sissa). One can easily see that his name has some connection with the word, Shah, and thus even with the word, chess.

Sassa, in order to distract an Indian King, Balhait (or possibly Shahraim—the story gives both names), from the lure of backgammon, invented chess. Overjoyed with the game and being of a lavish disposition, Balhait offered Sassa a choice of the most precious objects in his kingdom. The philosopher protested mildly that he was a modest man with modest desires. Not for him jewels, wealth or lands; all he wanted was a little corn. But, feeling that his reward should have some connection with the game he had just invented, he suggested an ingenious method for determining the exact quantity of grain.

There was no need for weighing-scales or calculations of any kind. Just place one grain on the first square of the chess-board. Double that quantity on the next square, double that on the third square and so on until all sixty-four squares were covered. Agreeably surprised at the lightness of Sassa's demands, the King, who usually found philosophers (especially those of an inventive turn of mind) rather more greedy than ordinary claimants, gave orders that this should be done.

Alas for his orders! His granaries were quite exhausted long before the sixty-fourth square was reached. Lodge, in his *Easy Mathematics,* has calculated that the amount involved, some 18,446,744,073,709,551,615 grains, would have been enough to lay a blanket 38.4 feet deep over the whole of England. It becomes abundantly clear from this touchingly innocent (on Balhait's part, at any rate) mathematical legend that for the Arabs chess and mathematics did go hand in hand.

Nathaniel Bland, an orientalist of the last century, who committed suicide in 1865, surmised that Sassa and Xerxes were the same name, and he may well have been right in his assumption. But though Xerxes was certainly a philosophic emperor he could hardly have been the same man, since he had the misfortune of living many centuries before chess was invented.

I should perhaps mention here that I came across Bland's name in a curious and almost sinister connection while I was doing research for this book. It was in the Royal Asiatic Society in London, and I was studying some beautiful illustrations of the work of Firdausi in a fifteenth-century folio when I ran into a mystery. There seemed neither rhyme nor reason for the positions of the pieces in the diagrams on these illustrations. Firstly I discovered that, instead of going up and down the page as they do in a modern diagram, the pieces went from side to side. Next, and this was much more remarkable, the pieces had been transposed on to the diagrams by a mirror effect.

Somebody else before me had also been puzzled. In fact, he had gone so far as to scratch out some of the pieces and put in some of his own—a barbarous action, considering the beauty of the illustrations. It was clear that this had been done at a much later date than the fifteenth century. I wondered if it had been in the 1850s, for it was then that Bland read a paper on the Persian folio to the Royal Asiatic Society after having borrowed it from the library. Could he have been the criminal? Or could it have been a certain learned professor of Oriental languages at London University who also borrowed the folio and then returned it with comments in which he attacked Bland's conclusions and restored, so he said, the illustrations to their correct order? Perhaps it was neither of these, but rather some subsequent scholar; we shall never know.

This much can be said for Bland—he was the author of some very pleasing translations of Arabic chess literature. Take the following piece from an early eleventh-century Arabic manuscript entitled *Yawakit ul Mawakit*:

> O thou whose cynic sneers express
> The censure of our favourite chess,
> Know that its skill is science' self,
> Its play distraction from distress.
> It soothes the anxious lover's care,
> It weans the drunkard from excess;
> It counsels warriors in their art,
> When dangers threat, and perils press;
> And yields us, when we need them most,
> Companions in our loneliness.

Whether chess has weaned many drunkards from excess I venture to doubt, if personal observation is anything to go by; but the sentiment expressed in the last few lines is valid, and I have known an extraordinarily large number of editors to whom the first line would apply.

The author of this poem was Ibn Al-Mutazz, the son of a Caliph Al-Mutazz, who was so keen a chessplayer that he would brook no interruption to a game, no matter what the reason. Once a messenger arrived bearing not only the welcome news that his chief rival, Al-Mustain, had been defeated but also the vanquished man's severed head. Al-Mutazz took no notice, but continued playing until he had finished the game. Sir Francis Drake with his game of bowls was hardly more nonchalant.

It was just as well that the caliphs favoured the game since, as in the courts of Byzantium, chess came under heavy attack from religion. One of the troubles was this business of the graven image to which I have already referred. But perhaps this was an excuse for something deeper. Wrapped up in the religious mind was the thought that no one should be intensely absorbed in and dedicated to a mere game. Chessplayers were not even giving up to Caesar the things that were Caesar's. They were sacrificing their time to an unknown god with a frivolous objective. This attitude persisted through the ages and is still held in certain circles.

Just as the Byzantine, John Zonares, laid down canonic rules condemning the practice of the game, so the Moslem religious lawgivers forbade it. If those who were less strict condoned it, then it was only if no one played for money (again how often history has repeated itself) and if the game did not lead to debauchery, oaths and blasphemy.

The caliphs and the learned seem to have overridden or ignored these religious attacks. I particularly like the urbane story of one of the later caliphs, Ummayyad Hisham, who reigned in the middle of the eighth century. He was playing chess one day when a visitor from Syria was announced. At once he commanded a slave to fling a cloth over the chess-board and when the visitor had been allowed to enter, he questioned him to see what he knew of the Moslem religion. Being a Syrian and therefore a Christian he was entirely devoid of all knowledge of the Moslem religion. Much relieved, the caliph gave orders that the chess-board be uncovered and resumed playing, for, he said, 'There is nothing forbidden to the uneducated.' Presumably, he did this with his tongue in his cheek; but As-Suli, who tells this story, puts it forward as evidence of the legitimacy of the game of chess.

It seems that chess, however, was not considered so evil as backgammon (nard), presumably because not so much money changed hands. When an earlier Caliph, Yazid I ben Mu'awiya, committed a hideous murder of a holy imam, it was observed by a contemporary religious historian that it was quite in order to curse the Caliph, bearing in mind that he was a nard-player.

By the time the caliphs had departed from Persia and made Baghdad the centre of their empire, chess, though still under some religious suspicion, had become a recognized courtly pursuit, a game for statesmen and the learned and a source of civilized pleasure. Although the Caliph Al-Mahdi, who ruled towards the end of the eighth century, paid lip service to the religious attitude towards chess in a letter to the people of Mecca in which he desired them to abandon 'the assembly of fools for nard, dicing, archery, chess and all vanities that lead astray', he still kept in his service at court a poet, Abu Hafs, who was known as 'the chess-player' for his expertise at chess, which included, it seems, the ability to play blindfold.

Al-Mahdi's son, the famous Harun al-Rashid, who appears so often in *The Arabian Nights' Entertainments,* was so devoted to chess that he gave pensions to the good chessplayers in his service. Amongst the stories in the *Thousand and One Nights* is the tale of his buying a slave-girl who was a fine chessplayer, losing to her three times and rewarding her by granting the life of her lover.

One could pile instance upon instance of the popularity of chess in Arabian courts during the ninth and tenth centuries, but it is time to consider what exactly shatranj was and how it was played in this rapidly-developing stage of the game. Perhaps the best description of the game, of its quality and of its purpose, is to be found not in Arabic, but in the Hebrew writings of a Rabbi BonSenior Abu Yachia who lived towards the end of the tenth century. His poetic account was published by one of the earliest English chess historians, Thomas Hyde, in the late seventeenth century. The opening sketch runs as follows:

In the beginning of the reign, the armies stand before thee.
Thine eyes shall see the King in his glory.
Behold, he standeth at the head of all his hosts; he shall cry, yea, he shall shout aloud; he shall do mightily against his enemies. By the strength of his hand and in his power, he is established in his stronghold, the fourth post, which is his place of encampment in the beginning of his reign.

The origin of chess, according to the Persian poet Firdausi's Shāh-nāmah—the battle of Gav and Talkhand.

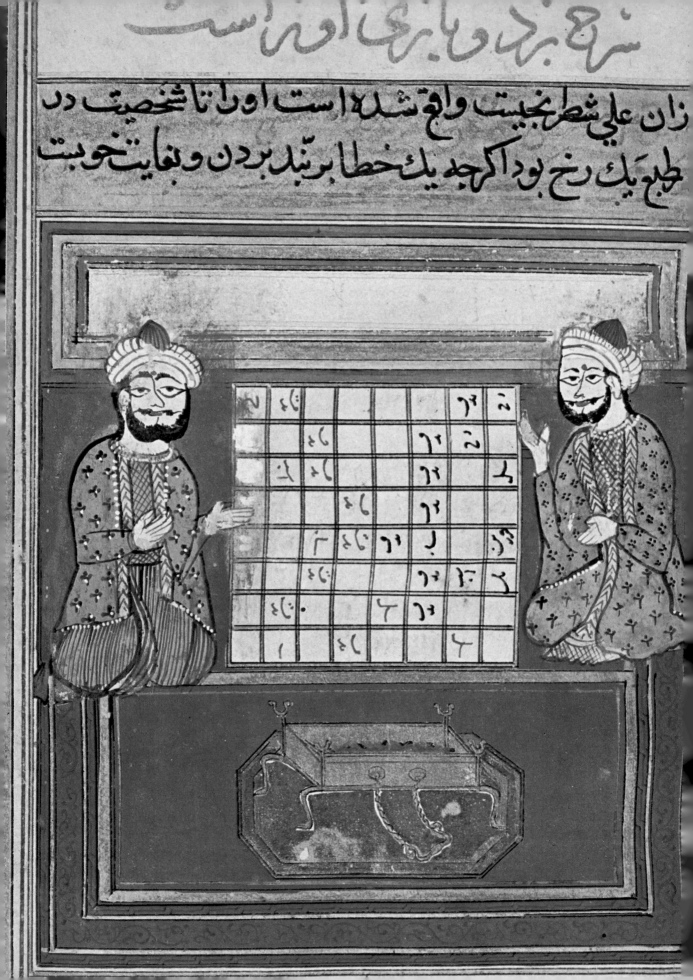

شرح برد و ماری او اوست

زان علی شطرنجیست واقع شده است او را تا شخصیت در
طبع یک رخ بود اگرچه یک خطا برند بردن و بنهایت خوبت

The finely carved ivory King of an antique Indian chess set from Delhi.

The Queen doth stand at his right hand; he looketh upon her with favour.

Nigh unto them are two Horsemen mounted upon fed horses; at their right and at their left is an Elephant, and a War-car on either side.

These are the generals and officers, such as have ability to stand. Facing these in full array, stand two opposing lines of warriors.

The same are the mighty men which were of old. Such are their positions, and the standards of their camps, according to their families, according to their fathers' houses.

When the King marcheth from place to place in his dominion, there is but one law for him, whether his course be flank-wise or straight; all that he desireth he doeth; but his heart is not ambitious to extend his range in battle, lest he should die in the war.

The Elephants advance three paces without divergence, in oblique direction, bent in their path on victory, and they turn not aside. Behold them tramping forth, and whither they go, they work utter desolation.

Another position illustrated in the Persian 'Treatise on Chess'. The manuscript is undated and survives only in fragments.

And the Horsemen set themselves in array at the gate. Each hath his sword girt at his side. The glory of the snorting is terrible. They pace one stage straight across the field, and take another step in an oblique direction, before they halt in face of the enemy.

Before the War-cars lies but a straight path, their movement being the same on their four sides. They turn not when they go. They march along the whole length of the path which is before them. If they prevail by strength, none assaileth them; but should the commanders or servants of the hostile King stand before them, gone is their power to pass. Nor by their multitude, nor by their wealth can they deviate from the course already taken. Notwithstanding the great strength of this officer, one of the lowest rank of the enemy may suddenly capture him, when he deemeth himself in a place of safety.

When the war rageth, the King avoideth standing at the extremity of the battle-field, far from his troops; and thither he attempteth not to go, nor is he seen there, nor found there, unless one of his warriors stand before him, as a shield and as a safeguard to conceal his person from all men. If he arise again and walk abroad upon his staff, after he hath been seen, he waxeth in his wrath; he goeth and hideth himself behind a wall or fortress, and he fleeth and escapeth from the battle.

This and more from the learned rabbi is surprisingly modern in its conception. Already there are signs of a change in the game, but his description contains enough of the Moslem form to be representative of the earlier period too.

One respect in which shatranj differed vitally from the modern game was that the board was unchequered. Whereas in chess today one tells the beginner that he should place his King on the coloured square opposite to the colour of his King, and his Queen on the square coloured the same as its own colour, no such distinction was possible in the Moslem game. Obviously, too, there was no placing of the board with the white square on one's right. Thus, there seems to have been no initial fixed place for the King or Queen (or perhaps I should rather write, for the Shah or the Firz—the Minister). The player who was regarded as the higher ranked of the two would pick one of the two centre squares on his bottom rank for his King, whereupon his opponent would place his own King opposite. The other pieces were placed, however, as in modern chess, and the original set-up could be either of the two shown here (Diagrams 9 and 10).

Opponents played alternately as in modern chess, and some moves (the King, Knight, Rook and pawn) were as those in today's game. So the Shah (King) moved one square at a time and could not go into check, i.e. to a place attacked by the enemy. Castling was not yet invented and, when the Shah was attacked, the attacker had to cry Shah, a rule that was to endure right up to modern times. If the aggressor attacked another piece he had to mention that too. When the Shah was so placed that it could not escape attack it was Shah-mat (the King is helpless). This was checkmate and the game was won for whoever delivered it. Equally, if a Shah was 'zaid' (stalemate) the game was lost. As in chatrang, one could also win by denuding the enemy of all his forces.

The Firz, or Minister (Queen) was the same weak piece that it

9 and 10: The two possible ways of setting up the pieces for shatranj.

had been in chatrang and could only move one square diagonally.

The Fil, or Elephant (Bishop) was also like its Persian predecessor and moved two squares, jumping over the first. It moved diagonally and to that modified extent foreshadowed the modern Bishop.

The Faras, or Horse (Knight) and the Rukh or Chariot (Rook) moved like their modern equivalents.

The Baidaq, or Foot-soldier (pawn) moved like a modern pawn, except that it could not move two squares at a time initially. On attaining the eighth rank it was promoted to a Firz.

It can be seen that there was little difference in the rules between shatranj and chatrang. Shatranj remained a slow game in which the two sides took a long time to come to grips. There were combinations, but the emphasis lay on subtlety rather than incisiveness. That the game was still capable of being played with great virtuosity is evidenced by the rise of some celebrated great players, as we shall see in our next chapter.

Where shatranj did differ from chatrang (as far as can be ascertained, in view of the paucity of genuine material on the Persian phase) was that scientific principles were applied in the Moslem game, and much closer study was given to position play. Possibly this was assisted by the introduction of the algebraic system of notation. By a rather odd chance, this system was to be reintroduced to the world—and with success to Europe—in the early eighteenth century, as will be seen in a later chapter.

Since, when discussing the style of play and giving examples, I think it only just to use the algebraic system, I include herewith a brief description of that system for those unacquainted with it:

The files are lettered from left to right with the first eight letters of the alphabet, a to h, and the ranks are numbered from bottom to top, 1 to 8, as shown in Diagram 11. Thus, each square is indicated by one letter and one number. This has the advantage over the descriptive system, both of brevity and of lack of ambiguity. For example, a2 could be QR2 or QR7 in descriptive, depending upon whether you are looking at it from White's or Black's point of view.

Piece moves (i.e. moves with pieces other than pawns) are indicated by the initial letters of the piece and the square of arrival of the piece. In cases of possible ambiguity the departure square is also indicated. In Pawn moves it is not necessary to indicate the nature of the piece. Thus c3 in Diagram 11 would mean P-QB3 in descriptive notation. Captures are indicated by : at the end of the move and are not indicated in pawn moves.

It should not be thought that the algebraic notation was used universally in shatranj. In fact, for some time it was employed only in problems and it made its way chiefly through putting problems in written form, an exercise which became very popular. As an illustration I give the most popular shatranj problem of all, known as Dilaram's problem (Diagram 12).

The first story to have accompanied this problem concerned a player whose favourite wife was called Dilaram (Heart's Ease). Opposed by a very strong adversary, he wagered Dilaram as a stake. He had the White pieces (or rather the Red, as they were in those days) and seemed in a bad way, for Black was threatening mate on the move. Dilaram, with a quick sight of the board but very little respect for the rules of the game, cried out, 'Sacrifice your two Rooks but not me.' Her husband saw the point and won as

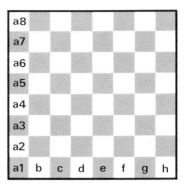

11: Indicating the squares by the algebraic system.

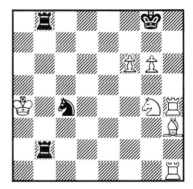

12: White to play and mate in six moves.

follows: 1. Rh8+, Kh8. 2. Bf5+, Rh2 3. Rh2:+, Kg8 4. Rh8+, Kh8 5. g7+, Kg8 6. Nh6 mate. (Since I imagine my readers will be more used to the modern names of the pieces I have not used their shatranj names.)

The story and the problem appeared again and again and survived into the Middle Ages in Europe. Originally an Arabic affair, it made its appearance in its last and perhaps wittiest form in an Urdu work by Durgaprasada. This time the protagonist became the Mogul Emperor, Shah Jehan, and instead of one wife it was a choice of which of four he would surrender from his harem. He got into the same mess as the Arabic gentleman, though his opponent was supposedly a Persian prince. Mate seemed inevitable and he turned to each lady in turn to see which he should sacrifice.

The first wife, Jahan (World) Begum, said, 'Thou art a king of the world; then let not the *world* go from thy hands, for the king cannot do without the world.'

The next one, Hayat (Existence) Begum, said, 'The world is pleasant, but *existence* is essential. When existence is at an end, what is the use of having the world?'

The third, Fana (Destruction) Begum, said, 'The world, existence, and all other things are inconstant. *Destruction* should be thy requirement, for destruction is the ultimate state of all things.'

Lastly, his favourite wife, Dilaram, who, being a good chess-player and hence scarcely supplied with moral sentiments, asked to see the position. When she did, it became apparent to her that Shah Jehan had an ingenious win. History does not relate how long she spent on the problem, but she too broke all the rules of chess and said, 'Give away two Rooks, O King, but do not give away thy Dilaram. Advance the Elephant (Bishop) and the pawn, and the Knight gives checkmate.'

It would seem from the Dilaram problem and from many other indications in Arabic literature that woman in that period were distinctly more formidable chessplayers than they have been either before or since. Consider the following extract from the *Arabian Nights* as translated by Sir Richard Burton. It comes from the forty-ninth night:

> When the lady saw Sharrkan, she stood up to him in honour and, taking his hand, seated him by her side and asked, 'O son of King Omar bin al-Nu'uman, hast thou any cunning in the game of chess?'
>
> 'Yes,' he answered, 'but do not thou with me as said the poet,

I speak and longing love upties and unties me;
Till with her honey-dew of inner lips she plies me:
I brought the chess-board and my liefest lover plays me
With white and black, but black-cum-white ne'er satisfies me:
'Twas as if King for Castle I were fain to place me
Till wilful loss of game atwixt two queens surprise me:
And if I seek to read intent in eyes that eye me
Oh man! that glance askance with hint of wish defies me.'

Then she brought the chess-board and played with him; but Sharrkan, instead of looking at her moves, kept gazing at her fair mouth, and putting Knight in place of Elephant, and Elephant in stead of Knight. She laughed and said to him, 'If thy play be after this fashion, thou knowest naught of the game.'

'This is only our first,' replied he, 'judge not by this bout.' When she beat him he replaced the pieces in position and played again with her; but she beat him a second time, a third, a fourth and a fifth. So she turned to him and said, 'Thou art beaten in everything'; and he replied, 'O my lady, how should one playing with the like of thee avoid being beaten?' Then she bade bring food, and they ate and washed their hands; after which the wine was set before them and they drank.

chapter 4

Shatranj develops its theorists and great masters

It was the Arabs who made the first scientific study of the game, that is, as far as we know and as far as we have written evidence. Before the Arabs, there were indeed descriptions of the method of play and references of diverse kinds in the literature of both the Persians and the Indians. But these allusions and descriptions, where they are not fanciful and almost folk-lorish, are merely humdrum and entirely without any indication that such a thing as theory even exists. It might well be that the Persians and the Indians had analysed the principles of the game before the Arabs; if so, their studies have been lost in the obscurity of time. The fact that they have left no trace, whereas there is more than ample evidence of the Arabs' activities, compels me to believe that such theory as had existed before the Moslem expansion of the game was feeble and elementary.

In any case the pattern of history is quite clear. Just as the Arabs were the great popularizers of scientific mathematical knowledge, so were they also the innovators of scientific study in what we now call chess and they termed shatranj. One cannot but marvel at the intellectual energy of a people who flourished more than a thousand years ago and yet set the style for theoretical analysis which, with the natural differences that occurred as the game developed and changed, has endured all that time.

Of course there had to be differences over the generations—some of them enormous. I have already pointed these out in previous chapters, so I limit myself here to restating that shatranj, the old Moslem game, was far slower than today's chess, since the powers of the pieces, in particular those of the Queen and the Bishop, were much less, and since a number of devices designed to make the game more dynamic had not yet been invented. Nevertheless, the method of study, both of theory and practice, was surprisingly similar. This is either a tribute to the good sense and clarity of mind of the ninth-century Arab or else a condemnation of our own conservatism of thought. Self-respect drives one to the former conclusion.

Then, as now, they divided play into the opening, the middle-game and the ending. Then, as now, they concentrated on the development of pieces in the opening; considered strategy and tactics in the middle-game, and worked out mating possibilities in the ending. I have but one proviso here. They do not seem to have detected the subtleties that exist in the end-game to anything like the extent one would have expected from such a race of savants. The reasons for this omission are obscure. After all, the most difficult and subtle ending in modern end-game theory is undoubtedly that of the Rook and pawn. That should not have differed so much, since the Rook's moves were the same as now and there was little difference in the pawn moves. Possibly the comparative weakness of the other pieces—in particular the fact that when the pawn reached the eighth rank it had to be exchanged for the Queen, one of the weakest pieces on the board—militated against interest in the end-game.

By and large, their study of the end-game was confined to working out how to mate in a specified number of moves, that is to say, to setting problems which they termed 'mansubat'. This meant 'something that has been arranged', a rather better definition of a problem than ours. Their problems were, however, intensely practical. The subtle and poetic refinements of the modern problemist were undreamt of then. Their arranged positions were such as might appear on the board after a somewhat intricate middle-game had occurred. Very little that could be deemed artificial appears in their mansubat, and such poetry as exists is also that which is inherent in the game itself. They did consider the more elementary features of the ending as comprised in the interaction of piece against piece, but it was all on a low level. The world had to wait for Lucena some centuries later before the real subtleties and difficulties of end-game play were discussed.

Where one does find something approaching the art of modern end-game study is in those positions that have been taken from practical play over the board. Take, for example, the following mansuba from the collection of al-Adli, the first great Arabic player and writer. He was the acknowledged champion during the reign of the Caliph Mutawakkil in the latter half of the ninth century, until he was defeated by an even greater player, ar-Razi (Diagram 13).

This position is a basic one in any modern end-game text-book in the section dealing with Rook versus Knight. Since the moves of these particular pieces have not changed at all, it forms a perfect parallel. Al-Adli gives the solution: 1. Rh5,Kb8 2. Kc6,Nd8+ 3. Kd7,Nb7 4. Rb5,K any 5. Kc7, winning the Knight.

Manifestly, it is insufficient, as was apparent to al-Adli's successors. Rather more than half a century later, as-Suli, who became recognized as the best player the Arabs ever produced and who was also an eminent writer on the game, added the following solution to the same mansuba:

1. Ra1+,Kb8 2. Kc6,Nd8+ 3. Kd7,Nb7 4. Ra3,Nc5+ 5. Kc6,Ne6 6. Ra5,Nc7 7. Re5,Na6 8. Re8+, and wins.

Later writers added still more.

It is apparent from the works of as-Suli that, wherever possible, he revised and supplemented those of al-Adli in a spirit of un-Christian charity (as was only natural), but examples of similar procedures are not lacking among authors today or at any time during the thousand years after these great Arabic writers lived.

But the point I set out to make was that this position was in fact taken from actual play. It occurred in a game between Rabrab and Abu'n Na'am, two distinguished players who preceded al-Adli by

13: White to play and win.

14: White to play and win.

half a century, and belonged to a set of grandmasters in the court of Al-Ma'mun, the son of Harun al-Rashid. I have purposely referred to them as grandmasters since they were known in Arabic as 'aliyat', which means of the highest class. The other two great players of this period, Jabir al-Kufi and Abdalghaffar-al-Ansari, together with Rabrab, provoked the caliph's famous lament in 819, 'How strange that I, who rule the world from the Indus in the east to Andalusia in the west, cannot manage thirty-two chessmen on a board two cubits square.'

Great as all these players were, it was al-Adli, who followed them, to whom goes the credit for formulating and working out their ideas on shatranj in book form. A versatile man, he also wrote a book on nard (backgammon). The Dilaram mansuba, which I gave in the previous chapter, seems to have appeared first in his collection; the pretty story attached to it came later.

Al-Adli also included the following pleasing problem, which is akin to the Dilaram conundrum in idea (Diagram 14). The solution is 1. Nh5+,Rh5: 2. Rb6:+,Kb6: 3. Re6 mate.

It is when the Arabic writers deal with the opening stages of the game that one sees the greatest disparity between them and modern theorists. Since the pawns could move only one square at a time, in contrast to the two that today's pawns can move initially, and, since the powers of Queen, Bishop and King were so much less in shatranj than in chess, it followed that nothing violently dynamic could take place in the early stages. During the first dozen moves each player could proceed as though he were alone on the board, for he need fear neither molestation nor interference from his opponent.

But if he could do as he liked, how should he do? It is clear that this posed grave problems for the ordinary player, and it was precisely these problems which the great players and writers whom I have mentioned set out to solve. No doubt working from practical experience, they evolved certain set positions which, after the first ten or twelve moves, would provide players with the best opportunities for deploying and using their troops in the middle-game. So their opening analyses started not with move 1, 2, 3 or even anything up to the early teens, but were deferred till later.

Each grandmaster and writer had his preferred starting point which sprang from a particular collocation of pieces and a particular pawn skeleton or structure. In accordance with whatever master he followed, the ordinary player made the moves that brought him to the appropriate point of departure. Until then, he was like the gentleman in the Gilbert and Sullivan opera who 'never thought of thinking for himself at all'. Does this all seem much too routine and unimaginative? If so, just consider those modern lines in the Ruy Lopez, where you might as well say to your adversary, 'let's start at move 18 on page 154, column 12, of Master X's standard work on the openings.'

Opening positions were given cunningly suitable names by their inventors. Players were expected to commit these to memory and to make their own way to the position which, when you come to think of it, is superior to the modern method of teaching the player to learn by heart all the opening moves, whether he understands them or not.

Interesting and typical was the 'Sayyal', the Torrent, introduced and practised by Abu Sharara the elder. It was called the Torrent

A King on the Indian model, an example of Arabic work in ivory dating from around the eighth century.

because the f pawn (the KBP) was deemed to be the most attacking pawn, capable of being thrust forward with the force of a torrent. In fact, it became known as the Torrent pawn and, as will be seen when I come to deal with the opening, it really was an unusually dynamic move for so slow a game. The Sayyal was given in al-Adli's book, among others; as-Suli, who also included it in his writings, rightly looked upon it with favour as a speedy and effective opening. But it was his disciple, al-Lajlaj (the Stammerer), who genuinely analysed this opening (and others) in almost modern fashion.

His work starts in the usual Moslem manner, with an invocation to God and Mahomet for help. Then suddenly and with an almost blinding flash of percipience, he draws open the curtain and reveals a new scene and a new world of analysis. He says that while his predecessors have shown which are the best openings and have also taught, through problems, how the pieces move, no one has bothered to tell the player how to use these openings. The advanced thinking

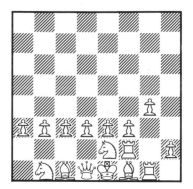

15: The Sayyal (the Torrent).

of this remark is shown by the fact that even nowadays there is a strong tendency among experts to write about openings without telling their readers how these should be employed in the middle-game.

Alas for al-Lajlaj, he was more than a thousand years ahead of his time, and he met, therefore, with as little support as he would have today. Not until the coming of Philidor in the eighteenth century was anyone again to write about the game with such comprehension and clarity. Al-Lajlaj was himself conscious of being a pioneer, for he recorded that he had no forerunners in his researches; but he stated modestly and generously that it was only thanks to the instruction he had obtained from long discussions with as-Suli that he was able to write the work. He seems to have had no immediate followers, and genuine research on opening theory had to wait until the game became Europeanized.

Al-Lajlaj's analysis of the Torrent Opening and its consequences (see below) illustrates how a keen mind can vitalize what had become routine and mechanical. Abu Sharara the elder reached the following position after twelve moves and claimed it constituted a good basis for operations in the middle-game (Diagram 15). Obviously, this can be achieved in a number of ways. Bearing in mind the lines of analysis al-Lajlaj gives, I suggest the following as plausible, at any rate. Remember that in shatranj the pawns could move only one square initially; that the Queen (or Firz) was a feeble piece with a move confined to one square diagonally; that the Bishop (or Fil) was limited to moving two squares diagonally, leaping over the intervening square, and that finally there was no castling. Considering all that, you might even feel some surprise that one could get to the middle-game after a mere twelve moves: 1. g3,g6 2. g4,f6 3. e3,e6 4. f3,d6 5. d3,c6 6. c3,b6 7. b3,a6 8. a3,g5 9. Ra2,Ra7 10. Rf2,Rf7 11. Ne2,Ne7 12.Rg1.

And now we have the Sayyal position. A little explanation is perhaps in order. As a general rule, the Arab masters liked to attack on the flanks, since this enabled them to bring the most powerful piece, the Rook, into speedy action. For the same reason all the pawns are advanced one square as soon as possible.

The g pawn is advanced to g4 so as to form a support for the Torrent pawn, the f pawn, and this will come out more clearly when I give one of al-Lajlaj's lines of analysis. It must go to g4 on the second move, because if it delays for only one move then Black can prevent the whole opening by playing 3..,f5.

Once the Sayyal position is reached, White can continue with a thrust of the Torrent pawn with 13. f4; or he may form quite a different plan starting with Ng3 and further development. The main objective has, however, been achieved with the development of the two major pieces.

Al-Lajlaj was not content with this rather stereotyped process, but devised a number of lines in which the action was much sharper and almost modernly dynamic while still keeping within the main idea of the Torrent attack. One example is the following game which starts off as though it were going to pursue the ordinary Sayyal lines but breaks new ground at an early stage:

1. g3,g6 2. g4,f6 3. e3,e6 4. Ne2,d6 5. Rg1,c6 6.f3,b6 7. f4,a6 8. f5,ef: (8..,e5 looks better) 9. gf5:,gf5: (and here 9..,g5 was safer) 10. Bh3,Ne7 11. Rf1,Rg8 12. Ng3,Rg5 13. Bf5:,h6

14. Bh3,Nd7 15. d3,d5 16. c3,Qc7 17. b3,Ra7 18. c4,Bd6 (remember, the Bishop can leap over one square and its contents) 19. Nc3,Be6 20. cd:, 21. d4,Bf8 (a somewhat feeble pointless move, but his position is already inferior) 22. Rf2, (over-cautious; 22. e4 looks very strong) 22. .,Qd6 23. b4,Rc7 24. Kd2,b5 25. Ba3,Nb6 26. Bc5,Nc6 27. a3,Kf7 28. Qc2,Bc4 29. Raf1,Rg6 30. Nh5,Ke8 (if 30. ., Nd7 31. Nd5:) 31. Nf6:+,Kd8 32. Nf6d5:, Rb7 33. Rf8:+,Kd7 34. Bf5+,Ke6 35. Nf4 mate.

Note that this rather pleasing finish is achieved by combining the forces of the two strongest pieces of shatranj, the Rook and the Knight (Faras), a concept which also becomes manifest when one studies the problems of that period.

Another opening position of which both as-Suli and Lajlaj strongly approved was the Mujannah (the flank attack). This, like the Sayyal, was reached in twelve moves, probably as follows: 1. f3,f6 2. f4,f5 3. Nf3,Nf6 4. g3,g6 5. c3,c6 6. c4,c5 7. Nc3,Nc6 8. b3,b6 9. e3,e6 10. d3,d6 11. Rb1,Rb8 12. Rg1,Rg8 (Diagram 16).

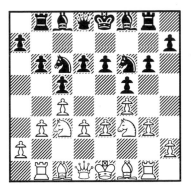

16: The Mujannah.

Looking at this position, I found it familiar and remembered that in my youth there was a player, H. H. Cole, who was fond of this kind of set-up, which I christened the Vortex Opening. He even played something like it against me in a British Championship, and on that occasion it did seem strange to me. I did not then realize that this was a subconscious return to a game a thousand years older than the one we were playing.

Other openings which established themselves in shatranj took more moves to reach their set position and are therefore that much less effective. One that seems to me to have merit, however, is the Mu'aqrab (the strongly-built) (Diagram 17). This was the favoured opening of a certain Fam-al-hut and is given in al-Adli's work. As-Suli did not think much of it and used it as a peg on which to hang a disparaging remark about al-Adli: 'Of these eight openings none are weaker than these two, Mu'aqrab and al-Mashaikhi (the sheikh's opening), and yet I consider them better than the remaining openings which al-Adli gave and which I omit.' To me the Mu'aqrab looks exactly like its title and I would have thought it admirably suited to shatranj since it renders the Rooks mobile while providing ample playing space for the other pieces.

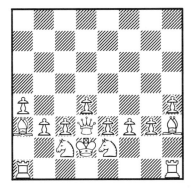

17: The Mu'agrab.

Another workmanlike opening which, like the Mu'aqrab, took nineteen moves to mature is the Muraddad (the moves to and fro, a reference to the to-ing and fro-ing of the Knights). Two of the grandmasters, Jabir and Rabrab, preferred it. Of all the shatranj openings it appears most to resemble positions that arise in modern chess (Diagram 18).

Shatranj, though still quite far away from chess, nevertheless possessed more kinship with today's play than did its predecessors chaturanga and chatrang. In fact, under the influence of that renowned chess scholar, H. J. R. Murray, a resurgence of interest occurred in this remarkable game. When I was in Moscow some twenty years ago I bought a book *Shatranj,* by Orbeli and Trever, published in Leningrad in 1936. Although most of it is devoted to the myths of chess history, there are some good illustrations which the writers seem to have taken from the works of Firdausi.

It was the appearance in 1913 of H. J. R. Murray's *History of Chess* which turned the attention of some of the leading British players

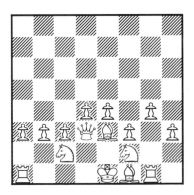

18: The Muraddad.

towards shatranj. Herbert Jacobs and G. A. Thomas (as Sir George then was) played a short match under the Moslem rules at the City of London Chess Club. *The Times* of 5 March 1914 carried a long article on shatranj, together with the score of one of the games. This game, with notes by the winner, was published in the *British Chess Magazine* for that year and I give it here. Readers may like to compare it in quality with the genuine older article I have already presented.

White: H. Jacobs.   Black: G. A. Thomas.

1. P-Q3,P-QB3 2. P-Q4,P-QKt3 3. P-K3,P-QB4 4. P-Q5,Kt-KB3 5. Kt-QB3,Kt-R3 6. P-K4,P-K3 7. PxP,QPxP 8. P-B3,Q-K2 9. P-QR3,K-Q2 10. B-K3,K-B3 11. Q-K2,Kt-B2 12. P-QR4, B-KR3 13. Q-Q3,B-R3 14. KKt-K2,Q-Q3 15. K-B2,Q-K4 16. P-QKt3,KR-Q1 17. P-KKt3,R-Q2 18. Kt-Q1,QR-Q1 19. Kt-Kt2,Kt-R4 20. B-R3,P-Kt3 21. KR-QKt1,P-B3 22. B-KB1,P-B4 23. P-QKt4,PxKtP 24. Kt-Q1,PxP 25. PxP, (25. QxP, would give Black time to protect his QKtP, as White would have to protect his Kt at Q1 before playing RxP.) 25. .,Q-Q5 26. RxP,Kt-B3 27. K-Kt2,P-K4 28. Kt-B2, (forgetting that his B is undefended. The blunder, however, does not count for much, the value of a B being so small.) 28. .,QxB 29. Kt-R3, B-KB1 30. Kt-Kt5,Q-Q5 31. Kt-KB3,R-K1 32. R-Kt3,Kt-K3 (A weak move which allows White to start an attack.) 33. P-B3,Kt-B4 34. R-Kt2,Q-K6 (He would probably do better to play 34. .,QxP. The Queen cannot be extricated from K6.) 35. P-R5,P-QKt4 36. Kt-B1,B-B5 37. Kt-Kt3, (The position of White's Queen and Bishop illustrates one of the peculiarities of the medieval game. They form a practically impassable barrier, since they cannot be attacked except by Rook or Knight, and, as even a Knight is worth much more than both Q and B, Black can never afford to take the Queen.) 37. .,B-Q3 38. R-K1,Q-B5 39. PxQ,BxP 40. KtxKt,KxKt 41. P-R3,R-Q3 42. R(K1)-Kt1, P-QR3 43. Kt-K1,Kt-Kt1 44. K-B3,R-KB1 45. K-K3,Kt-K2 46. Q-B2,R(Q3)-KB3 47. B-Q3,Kt-B3 (Black must lose something, but this move turns out very badly. R-QKt1 was perhaps best.) 48. BxP,KtxP 49. B-Q3,B-R3 50. R-R1,Kt-B3 (50. .,R-B7 threatening 51. .,R-K7 mate, was probably Black's best line of play. If then 51. RxKt ch, then K-B3 (best, if K-Q3 52. R-Q5 ch,) 52. RxKP,R-K7 ch 53. K-Q4,RxKt.) 51. Q-Kt3,R-QKt1 52. R-R4,B-K3 53. RxP,R-B2 54. B-Kt1,B-QB1 (A blunder, losing the Knight and the game.) 55. Kt-Q3 ch,K-Kt4 56. RxKt,KxR 57. KtxP ch,K-Q3 58. KtxR ch,K-K2 59. KtxB, (White might have saved himself trouble by not capturing the B. His Kt is now imprisoned for some time.) 59. .,B-K3 60. B-Q3,K-B3 61. K-B4, K-Kt2 62. K-Kt5,R-QB1 63. R-KB2,R-B4 ch 64. B-B5,RxP 65. BxP,R-Kt6 ch 66. K-R4,RxQ 67. Kt-B7,R-Kt5 68. Kt-Kt5, K-R3 69. R-B7,B-B1 (Black might as well have resigned here. The position is hopeless.) 70. R-K7,R-R5 71. K-Kt4,R-R4 72. P-R4,R-R3 73. B-B5,PxB ch 74. KxP,K-R4 75. R-K8,KxP 76. RxB,R-R4 ch 77. P-K5,R-R8 78. R-B3,R-B8 ch 79. Kt-B3 ch, K-Kt6 80. K-K4,R-QR8 81. P-K6,K-Kt5 82. K-K5, R-R4 ch 83. K-Q6,R-R3 ch 84. K-K7,K-B4 85. R-B5 ch,K-Kt3 86. R-Kt5 ch,K-R3 87. K-B6,R-R5 88. R-KB5,R-KKt5 89. Kt-K5,R-KR5 90. P-K7,K-R2 91. P-K8=Q,R-R3 ch 92. K-B7,R-R3 93. Q-Q7,R-R3 94. Kt-Kt4 and Black resigns.

chapter 5

The game comes to Europe

The history I have been tracing so far is that of an Asiatic game which flourished as an Asiatic game into the sixteenth and seventeenth centuries. Shatranj waxed and waned in just the same way and at the same tempo as did the great Moslem culture which commenced with Mahomet and started to decline somewhere in the sixteenth century, possibly with the defeat of the Turks outside Vienna by Jan Sobieski.

One shatranj grandmaster, a member of the court of Timur, the Mogul Emperor, who died in 1405, bore a name that has become hallowed in the history of pantomime—none other than Aladdin himself. He was a lawyer whose full name was Ala'addin at-Tabrizi. So outstanding was he (he could successfully give odds to the other leading players, a pawn to one and a Knight to another), that he became known as Ali Shatranji, which I take to mean Ali *the* chess-player. I have seen in the Royal Asiatic Society's library in London a beautifully-illustrated manuscript containing a number of problems, which is reputed to date from the fifteenth century and is supposedly by him. In the preface he tells us a little of his chess career:

> I have passed my life since the age of fifteen among all the masters of chess of my time, and since that period till now, when I have arrived at middle age, I have travelled through Iraq, Khurasan and Transoxiana, and I have there met with many a master in this art, and I have played with all of them, and through the favour of him who is Adorable and Most High I have come off victorious.

I like the modestly religious touch in the last sentence, though I fear this modesty is merely the sort of gesture the superstitious make in touching wood to avert bad luck.

He was also a great blindfold player and confesses without urging, 'I have carried on four different games with as many adversaries without seeing the board, while I conversed freely with my friends all along, and through the Divine favour I conquered them all.'

The last writer on shatranj seems to have been B. Sukaikir, who came from Damascus and died in Aleppo in 1579. He tells of a blind player he knew in Damascus who had played against the Sultan

Sulaiman in Stamboul. During the game the sultan cheated, removing one of his opponent's pieces when, presumably, it was not his turn to move. 'Well', said the blind man, 'since you have done this my only recourse is to accept the situation and play as well as I can, but had it been anyone else then I would have appealed to the sultan for justice.' How the sultan reacted to this dignified rebuke Sukaikir does not say; it is to be hoped he generously spared his opponent the bastinado.

But now, let us revert to the ninth and tenth centuries, when shatranj was at its highest peak. The game, though comparatively young, was too lusty an infant to be confined to one continent. Its spread was inevitable, and the means, the traditional ones—trade and war. It was thus that shatranj came to Europe.

I have mentioned in an earlier chapter (Chapter 2) the theory that Russia received the game much earlier than the rest of Europe, via the tribes of central Asia, an assertion which it is so far impossible either to confirm or to disprove. If it were true, then what she received would have been chaturanga and not shatranj, and here I am concerned solely with the arrival of shatranj in Europe. How important this advent was will appear in the next chapter, when I discuss the great changes that took place after it had established itself there. Seemingly it needed the consideration of fresh minds to revivify a game which was in danger of ossifying itself; the fixing of set opening positions, for instance, was a bar to originality. The world has Europe to thank for discovering the means for creating a renaissance in chess as well as in the arts.

The Arabs, being a warlike race with a religious message to convey to the rest of the world, became formidable expansionists. One of their most important moves was that by the Moors across the small strip of the Mediterranean into Spain and the nearby Narbonne area of France. By early in the eighth century, the Moorish caliphs had already established themselves in Granada, Cordova and Seville. Memorials to their admirable rule can still be seen in the great gardens and buildings of the Alhambra and in similar complexes in Cordova and Seville. Just as they cultivated the land with new methods of scientific irrigation, so they cultivated the mind with algebra and chess. The very name by which the Spanish call chess, 'ajedrez', is Arabic. How near it is to the original can be realized when one knows that it used to be pronounced ash-adres and that the Arabic for chess is 'ash-shatranj'.

An even closer relic of shatranj is to be found in the Spanish word for Bishop, which is 'Alfil'. This is in fact al Fil, the Elephant. How this Elephant became a Bishop seems to lie in the proximity of the King's Bishop to the King. It was therefore regarded as a counsellor to the King and, in early medieval times, the King's natural advisor was a dignitary of the church. Europeans could make nothing of the word, Fil, as they had not seen an elephant since the days of Hannibal.

It is only fitting that the first authentic reference to chess in Europe (other than that concerning Arab players and the Arab game) is to be found in Spain. In the will of Ermengaud I, Count of Urgel, which is to be found in a twelfth-century church at Seu de Urgel in Catalonia, the Count commands his executors to give his set of chessmen to the Convent of St Giles 'for the work of the church'. The Count was killed in a battle against the Moors at Cordova in 1010, and although his will is dated as of 1000, Murray surmises that this was a mistake and that it was drawn up in 1010, just before the battle.

The chessmen, like other sets of the period which were also destined to become heirlooms, were valuable in that they were made of rock-crystal. I have seen beautiful rock-crystal chessmen in Cordova and in a village not far from Seville called Arcos de la Frontera. (The word 'frontera', means frontier and the border concerned is that which divided the Spanish from the Moors during the Moorish occupation.) The Convent of St Giles is in Nîmes, in Southern France, and the family of the Counts of Urgel, a village on the border between Spain and France, made many bequests to it, including a second rock-crystal chess-set. This one was bequeathed by Countess Ermessind, a sister-in-law of Ermengaud, in a will dated 1058.

As I will show in a later chapter, chess became very popular with the kings of Spain and with their courtiers and the country was destined to become one of the two great centres of chess in the world. The other was to be Italy, and the story of how chess arrived there is a little more complicated. The Arabs never succeeded in conquering or even in establishing settlements on the Italian mainland. But during their ninth-century expansion, they overran the islands of the western Mediterranean and even occupied Sicily. It was another marauding, conquering race, the Vikings (or Normans as they were then known), who took Sicily from the Saracens.

It is probable that chess came to Italy mostly through the merchants who traded with the Arabs from such prosperous ports as Venice and Genoa. The Venetians in particular had much to do with the eastern trade (remember Shakespeare's Moor of Venice?). It is also likely that the fame of the excellent Moorish schools in Seville and Cordova lured many Italian students to study there and to bring home with them the 'vicious' habit of playing chess.

I write 'vicious' because the first reference to the game in Italy vilifies it as an impious sport. This condemnation is contained in a

Rock-crystal chess pieces from the eleventh century showing Islamic influence; they are in the Museo Diocesano, Lerida, Spain.

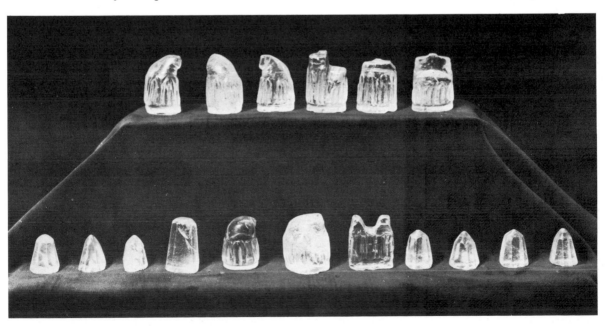

Ivory pieces with traces of gilding, made in southern Italy in the late eleventh century. From left to right: pawn, King, Vizier (Queen), and finally Elephant (the modern Bishop).

bitter rebuke from the Cardinal Petrus Damiani to the venerable Bishop of Florence for indulging in the vanity of chess. The account is to be found in a letter dated 1061 from the cardinal to Pope Alexander II, in which he goes so far as to say that the sport is disgusting in a priest and to report that he inflicted upon the Bishop a penance commensurate with the serious nature of his sin. Alexander was Pope-elect when this letter was written, and this has led some commentators to speculate that the contretemps had occurred earlier, and that the Bishop in question was no less a person than Gerard who was himself elected Pope in 1058, reigning as Nicholas II. Hence he was the predecessor of Alexander II, who was elected in 1062.

Entertaining though this clerical passage at arms is in retrospect, it may, nevertheless, have had a pejorative effect on the progress of chess in Europe for quite a time. If, as was apparent, it was a game of the intellect and yet suspect in canonical eyes, then it was logical to conclude that there must be something sulphurous and devilish about it. It already suffered from the handicap that it was indulged in by unChristian Arabs who dealt in such black-magic subjects as algebra and mathematics. So for many years, as far as the church was concerned, the game was practised either surreptitiously or in those parts of Christendom where the authorities were comparatively emancipated.

Chess seems to have been equated by many religious authorities with dice. Thus, Odo Sully, the celebrated Bishop of Paris (died 1208) decreed, '*Ne clerici in suis domibus habeant scaccos, aleas vel decios*'. (Clergy shall not have either chess or dice in their abodes.) In England in the thirteenth century, Henry III instructed his clergy to 'Leave diceing and chesseing undone, on pain of durance vile.'

Chess in Persia—another position given in the 'Treatise on Chess'.

سیاه بردو باری ببرماورا است

این منصوبه ان حاجی نظام سبزالی است د نظر ندارد

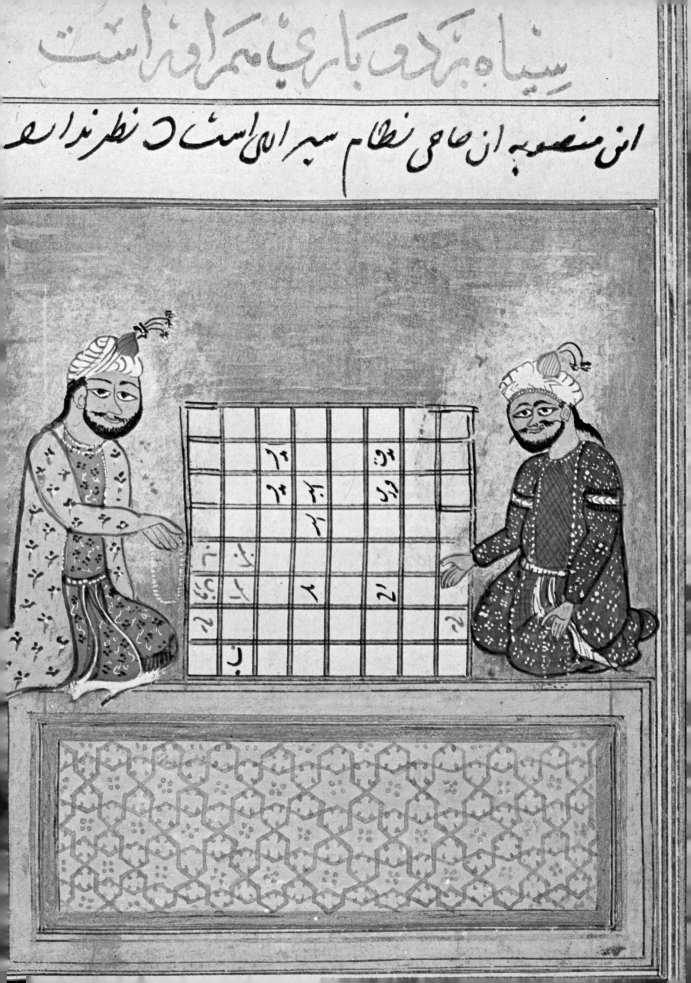

که از صافی عشق عکس پذیر بود و چون جام جهان نمای همه چیز بر وی نمود بر سه

ایوان حسن افتاد و عکس دوم حاصل شد از آنجا برق شوقش درخشان گردند

بر کشت و شیفته حضرت شیخ مجدالدین بغدادی کشت و چون معلوم کرد که او

شطرنج است از آن روی که اول تانیس و بعد از آن تشویق و اخمه

در عرصه انس پیا دؤ راند تا اسپی زندشهات شد و حضرت شیخ عراقی

درکتاب ده فصل آورده آنجا که فرموده مثنوی

بودح نجم الکا بر کبه ی	یکی از عاشقان جمال ترا
آن قسرین دل و کزین احد	آن معین شریعت احمد
آفتاب معانی اسرار	بود در جسم خ الجح اخبار

And in 1291, Archbishop Peckham concentrated his attack on the grave wickedness of playing chess in the Priory of Coxford, Norfolk, as follows:

> The Prior and Canons, one and all, had been led astray by an evilly-disposed person named Robert de Hunstaneston, who had actually taught them to play chess, which heinous vice was to be banished, even if it came to three days and nights on bread and water.

To some extent all this had a limiting effect on the layers of society which might play chess with impunity. The one representative of what we would call nowadays the middle class, the clergy, being forbidden to take part, it became and remained for many years a privileged pastime of kings and noblemen. True, these kings and these noblemen could employ what one might call 'professionals', selecting them from the more talented members of classes lower than theirs. But the professionals, once selected, either became classless or lesser breeds without the law, just as court jesters were licensed to deride and make fun of people above their station. It took the eighteenth century with its rise of the middle classes and the ensuing French Revolution, and even more the English Industrial Revolution, to sweep away class barriers.

However, I am anticipating the course of chess history and must return to the eleventh century. Still, remember that when I write about the popularity of the game and its expansion in medieval and even in early modern times, I am on the whole referring to its acceptance among the upper classes. For the remarkable Ströbeck exception see Chapter 8.

Prejudice and superstition notwithstanding, the game spread. From Spain it went to one part of France; from Italy it went to another part of France and also to Switzerland and southern Germany. From France it went to England. But I must reserve these extended developments for the next chapter and consider here how the game reached eastern and northern Europe.

Ignoring the earlier speculations on the possibility of chaturanga having appeared in Russia, I come to the more easily proved matter of the arrival of shatranj in what is now part of Russia, but what was then the Princedom or Dukedom of Kiev. Of the three possible ways in which it could have been imported, one, the invasion by the Mongols in the thirteenth and fourteenth centuries, can be ruled out forthwith. Their incursion was far from being a medium for the expression of chess. They came to plunder and destroy and not to civilize nor even to colonize. In any case, there is evidence that the Russians were playing chess before their arrival.

The second possibility, that it was introduced through the influence of Byzantium (you will remember reading in Chapter 2 that zatrikion was played there as early as the eighth century) is discounted by Savenkov, and the Russian writer is supported in this by Murray, though the latter does admit the possibility that Byzantium formed a link in a trade chain, the third way the game might have entered.

Despite the authority of these historians, I must beg to differ. It is known that Oleg the Wise, the second in the Varangian dynasty of princes who ruled Kiev from the ninth century, waged war success-

An Islamic miniature from the eighteenth century: Nagm Ad-Din Kurba playing chess with his pupil Magd ad-Din Bagdadi.

fully on the Byzantine Empire, took portions of it and, by 907, had so shaken it that it was glad to come to terms with him—to convert him into a friendly ally from a formidable foe. From then on there was much intercourse between the two empires and I am sure that this was one way in which the game spread into Russia.

Murray argues that the Russian church, in condemning the game in the twelfth century, referred to it as shakmate and not as zatrikion or variations thereof. Byzantium must, therefore, he says, be excluded as a source of chess for Russia, since shakmate clearly derives from the Persian or Arabic shah-mat. So it does, but why should not the game have come from two parallel sources—from both Byzantium and from the Arabs?

This brings me to the third possible means—by way of trade. The Russian merchants would have traversed the length of the River Volga, then, after paying a toll, would have proceeded along the Caspian until eventually they took to the land and went by camel to Baghdad. Hoards of Arabic coins from the ninth and tenth centuries, which have been discovered in the Dnieper basin near Kiev, prove this trade route existed.

So the game spread and flourished throughout Russia, despite diatribes on the part of the religious authorities (or possibly because of them). As time went on it grew so popular that it became a household word. There is little wonder that, with such a tradition, the Russians should have produced so many splendid players then and subsequently. The tsars all seem to have played chess with tremendous enthusiasm. Ivan Grozny (Ivan the Terrible) died just when he was about to commence a game. The account given by Horsey in his diary of a visit to Moscow is wonderfully evocative of the scene:

> Brought forth, setts him down upon his bead; calls Rodovone Boerken a gentilman whome he favored to bringe the chess board. He setts his men (all savinge the kinge, which by no means he could not make stand in his place with the rest upon the plain board): his chieff favorect and Boris Federowich Goddonove and others about him. The Emperor in his lose gown, shirtt and lynen hose, faints and falls backward. Great owtcrie and sturr; one sent for Aqua vita, another to the oppatheke for marigold and rose water, and to call his gostlie father and the phizicions. In the mean he was strangled and stark dead.

Note the baleful omen about his failure to get his King standing upright. Certainly Ivan was more in need of his 'gostlie father' than most men, if even one-tenth of the crimes he is supposed to have committed are taken into account. But he was a keen chessplayer, so, no doubt, much will be forgiven him. Boris Godounov also appears to have been a chess enthusiast, for Horsey wrote in the same diary a few pages later, 'The lord Boris Federowich sent for me at eavening, whom I found playenge at chess with a prince of the blood, Knez Ivan Glinscoie.' Jerome Horsey, who went to Moscow in 1573 as a clerk in the service of the Russian Company, was later knighted for his Services by Queen Elizabeth.

The names given to the pieces in Russia throw an interesting light on the history of the game there. The King is Korol (pronounced Karol) and is named after Charlemagne (Carolus Magnus or Karl the Great). This is not because Charlemagne was a chessplayer, but rather because he exerted so irresistible a mystique over Europe that he was regarded as the epitome of kingship. Numerous legends have arisen about Charlemagne as a chessplayer, but there is not one tittle of evidence to show that he could play, and what indications there are seem to point the other way. For one thing his dates, 742 to 814, are rather too early for the advent of chess in western Europe. Although admittedly he did do battle with the Moors in Spain, his circumstance was entirely different from that of the resident Spaniards. On the famous occasion which ended with the ambush and destruction of his rear-guard at Roncesvalles, he had merely been called in to lend a helping hand against the Emir of Cordova. Another negative point is that his chronicler, Eginhard, makes no reference to chess in his *Vita Caroli Magni*; since he credits him with every other skill in all the arts and pastimes pertaining to knightly chivalry, this omission is doubly significant.

Regrettably, the chess-pieces which are supposed to have been Charlemagne's—the celebrated King in the *Bibliothèque Nationale* in Paris and other pieces there which have obviously no connection with this King, and those in the Dom treasury at Osnabruck—were all made many centuries after his time. The King in Paris is clearly of Indian origin, and Antonius Van der Linde, author of the first great historical chess work, *Geschichte und Litteratur des Schachspiels*, 1874, dated it as sixteenth century. The other pieces there are Nordic, and believed to be from the fourteenth century. Although the Osnabruck chessmen are earlier, they are not earlier than the twelfth century.

To return to the Russian names for the pieces: The Queen remained Firz, as in shatranj. Nor was there any real change in the

These eleventh century pieces— Bishop, Knight and pawn—show the Viking influence on Arabic chess. The pieces are abstract Arabic basic forms with Nordic modifications.

Bishop. It was and still is called 'Slon' which means elephant and is a literal translation of the shatranj Fil. The Knight and the pawn too remained unchanged, becoming respectively Kon (Horse) and Pieshka (Foot-soldier). But there was a remarkable transformation in the most powerful piece, the Rook, which in shatranj was a Chariot (Rukh). It became in Russia 'Ladya' (a boat). Why this occurred is not clear. It also happened in other lands where there were broad rivers and much swamp land (Bengal, Siam and Java) and where in consequence the boat or ship was a necessary arm of war. Savenkov theorized that in Russia it was because of the boats or sledges used on the rivers and plains in the Moscow area during the sixteenth century.

Another possibility has occurred to me. The Varangian dynasty which penetrated Russia in the ninth century was in reality a Viking dynasty whose chief war arm was undoubtedly the warship. It is plausible, at any rate, to suppose that this was the reason for substituting the Boat for the Chariot.

I will deal with the influence of the Vikings in spreading chess throughout Europe in the next chapter. Possibly there is some connection between what I have just written and the spread of chess into Scandinavia, for there may still have been some intercourse in trade and other matters between the Varangian rulers of Kiev and their place of origin. One should not, however, push this too far. Certainly Olaus Magnus in his *Historia de Gentibus Septentrionalibus,* which dates from 1555, gives us a pretty story of the Goths, Swedes and Vandals:

> It was a custom amongst the most illustrious Goths and Swedes, when they would honestly marry their daughters that in order to prove the disposition of their suitors that came to them and to know their passions especially, they used to play with such suitors at Chess and Tables. For at these games their anger, love, peevishnesse, covetousnesse, dulnesse, idlenesse, and many more pranks, passions, and motions of their minds, and the forces and properties of their fortunes are used to be seen; as whether the wooer be rudely disposed, that he will indiscreetly rejoyce, and suddenly triumph when he wins; or whether when he is wronged, he can patiently endure it, and wisely put it off.

What little is known about the Goths, a Germanic tribe who invaded the eastern and western Empires during the third to the fifth centuries, and disappeared as a people in the sixth, hardly supports the story that they could have played chess. All that we have in writing is a portion of the Gospel of St Mark, which Bishop Wulfila translated from the Greek before chess was invented, and some tomb inscriptions. Perhaps Olaus Magnus was deceived by such names as Gothenburg and Gothland into believing that the Goths went to Sweden.

chapter 6

Early medieval times
the spread to Western Europe

Basically the game spread to western Europe and became popularized there by a sort of two-pronged attack; the Moors in Spain and southern France established it in the south-west and the Vikings in the north-west. This meant that each influence had some effect on what might be termed central-western Europe, but here too trade, literary and cultural forces were at work carrying the game from Italy into the centre. The importance of this expansion into and within the west lies in a circumstance to which I have already referred, the relationship between the advancement of chess and the advancement of civilization. The reasons are not far to seek. With civilization comes leisure and with leisure comes the urge to use one's wits in a playful, albeit logical, manner.

Thus, though early medieval times did not exactly constitute a wholly civilized period in mankind's history (semi-brutal sports were indulged in, and literature and the arts confined to the upper classes and to such shreds of the middle classes as then existed), the first real stirrings and progress in modern civilization were then to be found in western Europe. True, the Moors had their own civilization, as can be seen from the relics of their rule in Spain. But it seemed to derive fresh impetus and colour from contact with the west. Despite the inevitable enmity between the conquered and the occupying forces, there was a sort of mutual leavening of spirit or perhaps, to change the metaphor, a sparkle deriving from the clash of keen blades. This was certainly to the benefit of chess insofar as the game became almost a vital part in the training of a young warrior-knight.

A good example is the relationship between the Moorish poet-king, Al-Mutamid, who reigned over Seville from 1040 to 1090, and the Spanish. This was in the days when the Moorish powers were waning and those of the Spanish kings were waxing. Eventually Al-Mutamid was beaten in battle by Alfonso VI, King of León and Castile, and sent into exile to Aghmat in the Atlas Mountains of North Africa. Upon his death in 1091 a fellow poet, Ibn-al-Sabbana, commemorated him in a charming epitaph with some references to chess from which one can draw the delicate assumption that he was perhaps better regarded for his chess powers than his capacities for reigning.

Chess in medieval Europe—a break in the jousting?

All things have their time
All wishes their predestined end.
Chameleon-coloured fortune
Shows many a varied face
We are chess-men in her hands
And the King may fall to a lowly Pawn
Take no care for this world
Or the men who live in it
For now the world is left
Without men worthy of the name.

The nature of Al-Sabbana's lament is old but nevertheless true and affecting.

It would seem that Al-Mutamid was not only interested in chess but had the good sense to employ an outstanding chessmaster, Ibn-Ammar, who was also a poet and, what is more, a master in the matter of diplomatic warfare.

In 1078, Alfonso VI determined to destroy the Moorish sway over Seville. He advanced with a large army and laid siege to the city, vowing that he would never quit the spot till he had captured that most beautiful of capitals (as it then was). All seemed lost since the poet-king's forces were quite insufficient to deal with Alfonso's. But Ibn-Ammar, his vizier, knowing Alfonso's interest in chess, had constructed a marvellously beautiful chess-set. The pieces were made of aloe, ebony and sandalwood and the board, which was just as ornate, would have satisfied even Bobby Fischer, who was so particular about this when he played at Reykjavik nearly 900 years later with the same determination to destroy his enemy that Alfonso entertained.

Carrying this wondrous set, Ibn-Ammar betook himself to Alfonso's camp under flag of truce and asked to have audience. The king, partly lured by the marvel of the set itself, and partly spurred by the challenge (he was both covetous and a sportsman) agreed to a game of chess. If he won, he would receive the magnificent board and chess pieces. If he lost, then he had to grant the vizier one wish. History (or what then passed for history) relates, however, that Alfonso, aware of the prowess of his Moorish adversary, accepted the bet with some reluctance. He was horribly beaten and, like many millions of players before and since, became very angry. But the wager had been made in the presence of all his courtiers and he had no alternative but to grant the vizier's wish, which was to raise the siege and allow Al-Mutamid to reign for a few more years. Alfonso was, however, given the chess-set anyway, and in view of that, it seems a little harsh and hypocritical that, on his return home, he doubled the tribute that Al-Mutamid was due to pay.

Eventually the Moors were all driven from Spain, but they left behind a store of knowledge on the game which was to make Spain the leading country in chess for three centuries. The Spaniards were eminently and unusually literate and, in consequence, it is in Spain that we find the earliest European works on chess. The most cele-brated and the oldest to come down to us in its entirety was that written by the King, Alfonso el Sabio (Alfonso the Wise), in 1283. 'Written by' Alfonso is perhaps the wrong way to put it. It is in fact a work prepared in accordance with his instructions about indoor games such as backgammon, games with dice, an enlarged form of chess, astronomical chess and, of course, chess itself, which is clearly the most important part of the work as it comes first and is given the most space.

When I was in Madrid in 1956 I spent some time studying the manuscript which is in the Escorial a little way outside the capital. It is remarkably beautiful and the monk (or monks) who actually wrote it must have done the work with loving care. It consists of ninety-eight leaves, oblong in shape, and is bound in sheepskin. There is no title on the front, but written on the back is '*Juegos de axedrez, dados y tablas*' (games of chess, dice and boards). On the fly-leaf there is a longer title, '*Juegos diversos de axedrez, dados, y tablas con sus explicationes, ordenados por mandado del rey don Alfonso el sabio*' (various games of chess, dice and boards with their explanations arranged according to the instructions of the king don Alfonso the wise).

His instructions must have been very lucidly framed, for careful explanations are given as to how to play each game. From these it is clear that there had as yet been hardly any change from the Moslem game of chess except for one interesting and significant circum-stance. A large section of the chapter on orthodox chess is devoted to problems of the sort I have described as mansubas in the chapter on chatrang. Fourteen of the 103 problems presented however have a much more modern spirit. While still employing more or less the same rules of movement, they break them quite wildly in ways that

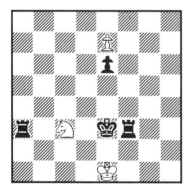

19, 20 and 21: Three problems from Alfonso the Wise's manuscript.

presage the future. In some cases even, promoted Queens leap three squares. Compared to the mansubas, these are miniature problems with mate in a definite number of moves, usually far fewer than the number required to win in a mansuba. It is Murray's supposition that one of the monks came across a collection of European problems and added them to the old-fashioned Moslem ones. This is undoubtedly correct, unless Alfonso was exercising his wisdom in rather an advanced way.

I give three problems to show that if Alfonso the Wise was indeed the author, then he would have done quite well in fairy chess nowadays. In Diagram 19 the task is Black to play and mate in three moves with the pawn on d4 and the solution is: 1. Kc3; 2. Ktb2 ch and 3. Pd3 mate. If you get the impression that the wise king (if this problem was set by Alfonso) is using a sledgehammer to crack a nutshell, then remember that in this instance the Queen is still a feeble force capable of moving one square only, and remember too that the Bishop can only leap over the Queen and not capture it. In Diagram 20 Black mates in three moves. The solution is: 1. Rxe3,c5 ch; 2. Ke6,Ke8; 3. Rc8 mate. Quite a neat end-game, despite, or perhaps because of, the disparity in strength. In Diagram 21 there are different conditions: Black mates in three on d2, each piece moving once. And the solution: 1. Rxc3; 2. Kf2 and 3. Rf3d3 mate.

None of these is over-subtle and this applies to all the problems given in the manuscript, but many show a care for the aesthetics of the game which is somewhat unusual in chess of the period.

Some explanations as to the variants of chess given in the work are worthwhile since they are attractive and again give signs of future things to come. Firstly, enlarged chess, or 'great chess' as it is called in the Spanish original: The origin of this variant, which may or may not be played with dice, is ascribed by Alfonso to India. There are twelve pieces on the back rank, which are lettered a to l. The Rooks are on a1 and l1 and move exactly like our Rooks. On b1 and k1 there are Lions which leap vertically or horizontally to the fourth square. On c1 and j1 there are Unicorns with a first move that of a Knight (without the possibility of making a capture), but subsequently that of our Bishop. On d1 and i1 there are Giraffes. They can leap diagonally to the opposite corner of a rectangle five squares by two, and hence change the colour of their square every time they move. On e1 and h1 there are Crocodiles and these move like our Bishops. The King stands on f1 and moves to any adjacent square, but can also leap to a third square on its first move only. (Is this possibly a forerunner of castling?) On g1 there is a very powerful piece, the Gryphon, with its move that of one step diagonally and thereafter any number of squares vertically or horizontally. This is a heavily-orchestrated game much faster than the Moslem form of chess.

Four-handed chess had similarities with modern four-handed chess. It was called *Acedrex de los quatro tiempos* (chess for the four seasons). Unlike modern four-handed, though, a normal-size board was used, with each player having a King, Rook, Knight, Bishop and four Pawns, these being placed in the respective corners of the board. There was no official partnership, but possibly an involuntary or tacit one. The player who was the season Spring, also represented the element of air, the colour of green and the humour of blood.

Summer was fire, red and choler; Autumn was earth, black and melancholy, and Winter was water, white and phlegm.

Astronomical chess was based on the signs of the Zodiac, and the board consisted of a number of concentric rings, each of which was the orbit of a star in the Ptolemaic system. Appropriately, it was played with dice and it does not seem to have survived the advent of Copernicus and Galileo.

I have spent some time and space on Alfonso's manuscript because it is of great importance as our earliest work on chess. It is also most beautifully illustrated by a series of miniature paintings, each of which appears in the enlarged first letter of a chapter or a section. Another aspect that makes it highly interesting is that it uses chess as a sort of parable to say how Knights, Kings etc. should behave in real life.

When it comes to parables, however, the really formative work on the subject in relation to chess was the *Liber de moribus hominum et officiis nobilium* of Jacobus de Cessolis. This, while having less really to do with the game than Alfonso's did, exerted considerably more influence on the world. It was translated into many languages and eventually achieved the distinction of being the second book ever to be printed in the English language (religious books apart).

Jacopo Cessolis, to give him his Italian name, was an exact contemporary of Alfonso the Wise and he represented the Lombard school of chess, which at that time was dominant in Italy. Not that he would have very much relished such a description. He was a thirteenth-century Dominican friar who based his celebrated morality on sermons that he preached. But the fact that he used chess as a kind of stepping-stone from which to consider the moralities of real life is an indication of the status the game had attained by the last quarter of the thirteenth century in Italy. This was most significant in the progress of chess, for, as we shall see in ensuing chapters, Italy became at first just as important as Spain, and later, even more important.

The game had been introduced into Italy by a number of routes, by the Saracens and by traders, as I mentioned in the previous chapter. There must also have been some Viking influence since the Normans (Vikings in origin), conquered Sicily in early medieval times and established a kingdom there that lasted for some time; and there certainly would have been close contact between Sicily and the mainland of Italy.

As I have said, Lombardy was Italy's leading chess centre, and that de Cessolis was a Lombard is apparent not only from his allusions to the area in his *Liber de moribus hominum* (or *Ludus Scacchorum,* as it is commonly known) but also from his description of the rules, which is peculiarly Italian and specifically from Lombardy.

There are some vital changes in his rules from those of the Moslem school. A remarkable—almost startling—foreshadowing of the practice of castling appears in the King being allowed on its first move to advance from one to four squares, providing that it does not go through check. Other signs of modernity were the facts that stalemate counted as a draw, and that the pawn could advance two squares on its first move. It did not, however, at this stage have the right to capture en passant. Again, as in the modern rules, a player who was left with the King alone was not necessarily lost. Earlier rules had awarded the game to the player who 'bared' the enemy King. A combination Lombard rule that failed to survive was that an unmoved King and Queen could make a joint move as their first move, this counting as only one move.

Significant though these facts are when considering the progress of chess from something like shatrang to our modern game, at the time by far the major part of and point of the work were its parables and moralities. This is borne out in William Caxton's translation, which was made not from the original Latin, but from a French translation by Jehan de Vignay, a friar who was *'hospitalier de l'ordre du Haut-Pas (de l'ordre de St Jacques)',* and who himself translated it from de Cassolis about the middle of the fourteenth century under the title, *Le livre des eschecs moralisé en françois.*

The *Ludus Scacchorum* is planned firmly and neatly and Caxton's table of contents is perhaps the most colourful and, to modern eyes, most readable part of the whole work:

> This booke conteyneth iiii traytees/
> The first traytee is of the Invencion of this playe of the chesse/ and conteyneth iii chapitres
> The first chapitre is under what kynge this play was founden
> The ii chapitre/ who fonde this playe
> The iii chapitre/ treteth of iii causes why hit was made and founden
> The second traytee treteth of the chesse men/ and conteyneth v chapitres
> The first chapitre treteth of the form of a kynge and of such thinges as apperteyn to a kynge
> The . ii . chapitre treteth of ye quene & her forme & maners
> The . iii . chapitre of the forme of the alphins and her offices and maners
> The . iiii . chapitre is of the knyght and of his offices
> The . v . is of the rooks and of their maners and offices
> The thirde traytee is of the offices of the comyn peple And hath viii . chapitres
> The first chapitre is of the labourers & tilinge of the erthe
> The . ii . of smythis and other werkes in yron & metall
> The . iii . . is of marchantes and makers of cloth & notaries
> The . iiii . is of marchantes and chaungers
> The . v . is of phisicyens and cirugiens and apotecaries
> The . vi . is of tauerners and hostelers
> The . vii . is of ye gardes of the citees & tollers & customers
> The . viii . is of ribauldes disepleyars and currours
> The . iiii . traytee meuyng and yssue of them And hath . viii . chapitres
> The first is of the eschequer
> The seconde of the yssue and progression of the kynge
> The thirde of the yssue of the quene
> The fourth is of the yssue of the alphyns
> The fifth is of the yssue of the knyghtes
> The sixth chapitre of the yssue of the rooks
> The seuenth is of the meuynge & yssue of the comyn peple
> And the eyght and laste chapitre is of the epilegacion.
> And of the recapitulacion of all these forsaid chapitres.

By 'alphyns' Cessolis means Bishops; 'alfin' was the medieval word for Bishop, and the relationship to 'alfil' is obvious.

A picture from 'The Game of Chesse' (Ludus Scacchorum) translated and printed by Caxton in the fifteenth century. This was one of the first wood engravings executed in England. Here we see the King and the philosopher playing chess.

What made the work so popular and wide-spread in its appeal? It was partly its construction and the ingenious way in which the author equated the chess-pieces with figures of real life. The itemization of the pawns and their various parallels reads like a description of trade unions; and it is interesting to see that he classes notaries with merchants and sellers of cloth, all presumably having been respected members of the lower middle classes in the early medieval epoch. But the chief attraction must surely have been the vast number of stories and anecdotes with which the work is stuffed. It is rather like a semi-religious and pseudo-historical gossip column. Characteristic is the account of the invention of chess; the style and content would be welcomed by present-day Fleet Street as eminently suitable for the popular press.

The game, says Cessolis, was invented during the reign of Evilmerodach, the son of Nebuchadnezzar. Why should he have chosen this Chaldean king, apart from the baleful and Edgar-Allan-Poe-like sonority of his name? Let Jacopo explain:

In lyke wyse (he has been describing the reign of the emperor Nero) was somtyme a kynge in babiloine that was named Evilmerodach a Jolye man with oute Justice and so cruell that he dyde dohewe his faders body in three honderd pieces/And gaf hit to ete and deuour to thre honderd birdes that men call wultres. . . . Under this kynge than Evilmerodach was this game and playe of the chesse founden.

After this colourful and auspicious start, which paints a picture of Evilmerodach as a jolly man with a heart of gold as far as vultures were concerned, Cessolis thinks it time to dispel the fanciful lies which others have written about the origin of chess. Now he applies cold science:

> Trewe it is that some men wene that this playe was founden in the tyme of the bataylles & siege of troye But that is not soo cam to the playes of the caldees as dyomedes the greek sayth and reherceth That amonge the philosophrs was the most renomed playe amonge all other playes/ And after that/ cam this playe in the tyme of Alixandre the grete in to Egipte And so unto all the parties toward the south/ And the cause wherfore thys playe was so renomed shall be sayd in the thirde chapitre.

In the next chapter he says that the inventor of the game was a philosopher of the Orient who was called Exerxes by the Chaldeans and Philometer by the Greeks 'which is as moche to saye in english as he that loveth Justice and mesure.' His first reason for inventing it was 'to correcte and repreve the kynge'. For this purpose he baited his moral hook cunningly. Evilmerodach, much taken with the beauty of the game, desired the philosopher to teach him how to play; but Exerxes refused and the king then asked him why he had invented it. In a couple of pages the philosopher explains that it was a kind of moral and mental discipline.

It should be observed that this legend of chess having been invented at the siege of Troy was strongly held up to the nineteenth century, and to this day there are people who believe that Alexander the Great was a chessplayer of some merit.

Cessolis lavished much ingenuity on interpreting Biblical texts to give his chess history some authentic (because religious) verisimilitude. He quotes 'blessed Saint Jerome', for instance, as having said that the great city of Babylon was square in every quarter and that the chess-board thus represented the city in which the game was invented. The philosopher ordered that a table should be constructed of sixty-four squares, like a chess-board. Its border was higher than the area covered by the squares, to represent the wall of the city, and one of the corners was a tower, the tower of Babylon —hence the Rook.

De Cessolis's work was a useful antidote to the attacks made on the game by ecclesiastics, to which I have referred in an earlier chapter. It derives its virtue and force from the most outrageous use of what in a less respectable author one would call a tissue of lies or, at best, an embroidery of anecdotes.

Though the most popular and seminal, the *Ludus Scacchorum* was not the earliest writing of its kind. The first was a short Latin work entitled *Ouaedam moralitas de scaccario;* in some manuscripts it has the sub-title, *per (or secundum) Innocentium papam (or tertium).* This can be translated as 'A morality of chess, according to Pope Innocent III'. Murray has called it neatly, *The Innocent Morality,* but he doubts very much that Pope Innocent was the author, and prefers to ascribe it to Johannes Gallensis, otherwise known as John of Waleys (John of Wales). Whoever was the author, and, of course, it might have been neither, it would seem that Innocent, powerful though he was, was destined to have trouble with men named John, for it was with England's King John that he was on such bad terms during his reign as Pope, between 1198 and 1216. Now, nearly a thousand years later, his fame—as a chess expert at any rate—appears to be being denied by another John, from Wales.

The work uses the idea of morality from quite a different angle, almost opposite, from Cessolis. Like his, however, it is precisely worked out, and it also gives an insight into the nature of the moves and of the chess-board in the early thirteenth century. Murray has paraphrased this as follows:

The world resembles a chess-board which is chequered white and black, the colours showing the two conditions of life and death, or praise and blame. The chessmen are men of the world who have a common birth, occupy different stations and hold different titles in this life, who contend together, and finally have a common fate which levels all ranks. The King often lies under the other pieces in the bag.

The King's move and powers of capture are in all directions, because the King's will is law.

The Queen's move is aslant only, because women are so greedy that they will take nothing except by rapine and injustice.

The Rook stands for the itinerant justices who travel over the whole realm, and their move is always straight, because the judge must deal justly.

The Knight's move is compounded of a straight move and an oblique one; the former betokens his legal power of collecting rents, &c, the latter his extortions and wrong-doings.

The Aufins are prelates wearing horns (but not like those that Moses had when he descended from Sinai). They move and take obliquely because nearly every Bishop misuses his office through cupidity.

The Pawns are poor men. Their move is straight, except when they take anything: so also the poor man does well so long as he keeps from ambition. After the Pawn is promoted he becomes a Fers and moves obliquely, which shows how hard it is for a poor man to deal rightly when he is raised above his proper station.

In this game the Devil says 'Check!' when a man falls into sin; and unless he quickly covers the check by turning to repentance, the Devil says 'Mate!' and carries him off to hell, whence is no escape. For the Devil has as many kinds of temptations to catch different types of men, as the hunter has dogs to catch different types of animals.

It is interesting to note that the moves as described are still those of the earliest type of European chess, but that now the chess-board definitely consists of alternate black and white squares, whereas earlier there had been no differentiation in colour.

Leaving the game well established in Italy, we can trace its influence upon neighbouring countries to the north—on southern Germany, Austria and France. The various moralities were translated into German and French (hence the version from which Caxton translated his work), and even into Czech in Bohemia. A little later, too, France developed its own literature of chess, or rather, literature in which chess figured; but that will be dealt with in the ensuing chapter.

The earliest reference to chess in southern Germany is not, however, contained in a morality, but in a Latin poem entitled *Ruodlieb*, dating from early in the eleventh century. It was found in a monastery at Tegernsee in Upper Bavaria and refers to negotiations for a peace treaty between two kings. It is supposed to be based on an actual meeting between the King of France and the German emperor at a conference in 1022. An emissary of one king goes to the court of the other with peace proposals and plays first against the viceroy at what is clearly chess—*Ludus Scacchorum*. He is obviously much better than the viceroy and loses only when, out of a sense of diplomatic politeness, he contrives to do so purposely. Then he meets the king and, playing him repeatedly for a wager, wins a great deal of money from him.

Either the monastery at Tegernsee was a permanent centre for chess, or else, more probably, a monk named Metellus picked up the reference to chess in the *Ruodlieb* some hundred years later and introduced it into a story in the Charlemagne cycle. For this monk tells a romantic story of how the son of Pepin the Short, King of France, repeatedly loses to the hero of the tale, a young Bavarian noble. Incensed at the humiliation of losing and confident that his father will protect him, the son picks up a Rook and deals the Bavarian a mortal blow. This has been held by some chess historians, notably Duncan Forbes, in his *History of Chess,* 1860, as proof that chess was played as early as the eighth century in the Carlovingian court; but it is purely fable, and the terms in which it is written betray an almost utter ignorance both of chess and of Charlemagne. Nevertheless, one way and another, Tegernsee does seem to have had a long tradition of chess.

Slightly later, but probably still in the eleventh century (Murray dates it as such) is the Einsiedeln poem, so called because it was found in a monastery at Einsiedeln in Switzerland. It is entitled *Versus de scachis,* which is exactly what it is, as it describes the board and the pieces in some detail. It is interesting to note that, although the names of some of the pieces have become those of a state in Germany and its nobility, the Fierz is now called a Queen (Regina). Also, since this was apparently about the time that the chequered board was being introduced, the poem says that the board is sometimes chequered. Clearly this was written at a transitional stage in the game. The poet also emphasizes the fact that no betting or use of the dice is involved, presumably wishing to demonstrate to the clerics the high ethics of chess. Bishops are not yet known as such:

Fourteenth or fifteenth century pieces (left to right): Rook, Knight and Bishop—from Vreta Kloster (a Cistercian Nunnery) in Östergötland, Sweden.

they are Comes (Counts), and later the use of the word Curvus (the Aged One) makes its appearance; but it is clearly the old form of Bishop since it moves diagonally to the third square and cannot change the colour of its square.

Leaving the south for the north of Europe one comes to the influence of the Vikings, who were far and away the greatest travellers of early medieval Europe and have indeed good claims to having been the greatest voyagers of all time. They circled the known globe both as warriors and as traders. In this latter capacity they were also great civilizers, that is to say, furtherers of the arts and crafts which go to make up a civilized society. Here again we have another link between the game and civilization, for the Vikings spread the light of chess wherever they went.

They introduced the game into the Netherlands, northern France, England, Ireland and Scotland and, most outstandingly, into Iceland. Anyone who has visited Iceland knows how popular chess is there, and its hold on the people is rooted in a long-standing tradition that goes right back to the time when chess was introduced into western Europe. The great literature of the sagas is full of references to the game. Perhaps the most striking is that passage about King Knut (Canute) and Jarl Ulf and the infamous match at Roskilde on St Michael's day, 1027, which ended in murder. The account, which is part of the *Heimskringla* and is supposed to have been written by Snorre Sturlason in about 1230, is considered by historians to have some basis in fact. Knut, it is said, used the game as a pretext to get rid of a leader of a faction of nobility that was becoming too powerful. It is a fine story:

King Knut saw that the kings of Norway and Sweden had sailed eastwards along the coast with their army. He straightway sent men up on land and ordered them to ride day and night on the landways, and follow the movement of the king's army. Some spies went away when the others came back. Then King Knut had tidings each day about their journey and his spies were in the king's army. And when he learnt that a great part of the army had left them, he sailed back with his army to Zealand and lay with the whole force in the Sound; part lay off Zealand and part off Scania.

King Knut then rode up to Roskilde, the day before Michaelmas, with a great troop of men, for there his kinsman, Ulf the Jarl, had made a great feast for him. The jarl was eager to entertain him and was very happy, but the king was silent and not at all friendly. The jarl talked to him and sought topics of conversation which he thought the king would like best, but the king answered little. Then the jarl asked him if he would play chess. He said 'yes' to that, and they then took out the chessmen and played. Ulf the Jarl was quick in his words and daring both in speech and in all other things; he was an active man in his land and a great warrior; about him a long saga is told. Ulf the Jarl was the mightiest man in Denmark next after the king. Ulf the Jarl's sister was Gyda whom the Jarl Gudine Ulvnadson had wed; their sons were Harold, King of England, Tosti the Jarl, Valtjov the Jarl, Morukare the Jarl and Swein the Jarl, and their daughter was Gyda who was wed to Jarvard the Good, King of England.

And when King Knut and Ulf the Jarl were playing chess, the

king made a bad move and the jarl then took a Knight from him. The king put his men back and said he should play another move. The jarl grew angry and threw down the chess-board; he stood up and went away. Then said the king: 'Runnest thou off, Ulf the coward?' The jarl turned round near the door and said: 'Farther wouldst thou have run in the Holy River if thou hadst been able. Thou didst not call me Ulf the Coward when I came to thy help when the Swedes were beating you like dogs.'

There upon the jarl left and went to sleep. A little after the king went to bed. Next morning when the king was clad, he said to his shoe-lad: 'Go thou to Ulf the Jarl and slay him.' The lad went, was away some time, and then came back. Then said the king: 'Hast thou slain the jarl?' He answered: 'I have not slain him for he was gone to St Luke's Church.' There was a man of Norse stock, called Ivor the White, who was at that time in King Knut's bodyguard and slept in the king's house. To him the king said: 'Go thou and slay the jarl.' Ivor went to the church into the choir and there he struck a sword through the jarl, whereby Ulf the Jarl met his bane. Ivor then went to the king with the bloody sword in his hand. The king asked: 'Hast thou slain the jarl?' Ivor answered: 'I have slain him now.'

'Thou hast done well then,' said the king. But after the jarl had been slain, the monks had the church locked. This was told the king, who then sent a man to the monks, bidding them unlock the church and sing Mass, and they did as the king bade. And when the king came to the church, he granted it great lands so that it became a big lordship and this church has since grown greatly. King Knut rode out afterwards to his ships, and there he lay a long time in the autumn with a great host.

According to the sagas, taking moves back seems to have led to a lot of trouble in Icelandic chess. In *Thorgil's Saga,* a grand-nephew of Snorre Sturlason, a youth named Thorgil Bod Varsson, was playing chess with Samur Magnusson and refused to let him take

Swedish walrus-tooth pieces from the thirteenth century. Left to right: pawn (?), Bishop, Queen.

este es otro iuego departido en que ha ueyn   del cauallo blanco. (E pues lo meior es que
tar q quatro trebeios que han a seer enta   tome el rey blanco el peon prieto: que esta
latre assi como esta en la figura del en   en la tcera casa te so taque. (El segundo

*The oldest and most celebrated
European work on chess still to
survive is that by the Spanish
King Alfonso the Wise, dating
from the late thirteenth century.*

ego cõ el rey blãco ꝗ esta ẽ la segũda ca
sa del rey pero ponerlol ẽ la segũda casa ....:

uo blãco. z este es el departimiẽto deste
uego. z esta es la figura dell entablamie
to.

Este es otꝛ uego departido ẽ ꝗ a xxiiij trebeios
ꝗ an a seer entablados como esta ẽ esta fi
gura deste entablamiẽto. z iuegã se assi:
Os blãcos iuegã pꝛio z dã mate
al rey ꝗto ẽ viij uezes delos se

El ij iuego dar la iaꝗ cõ ell otꝛ cauallo
blãco ẽ la segũda casa del alfil ꝗto. z cã
ta el rey ꝗto. ẽ la otꝛ segũda casa de su alfil
El tcero iuego dar la iaꝗ cõ el cauallo bla
co ẽ la casa del alfil ꝗto z ente el rey

tomãdo el alfil blãco que esta en
la tercera casa del aliferza blãca · C
si los prietos entren de dar xaque ca ·÷

Este es otro iuego departido en q̃ a veynt
e un trebeio q̃ an a seer entabla de assi
como estan en la figura del entablamiẽ

xaque prieto en la casa del cauallo vla
co z entama el rey blãco · en la su se
gunda casa · C El segundo iuego dar

On this page and opposite, two positions from King Alfonso the Wise's Juegos de axedrez, dados y tablas *(Games of chess, dice and boards).*

Alfonso the Wise's work on chess, from 1283, contains instructions about many indoor games, including backgammon, enlarged chess or 'great chess', astronomical chess, and, of course, chess itself.

back a move which had put a Knight en prise. The inevitable and unethical spectator intervened and suggested that Thorgil should not make such a fuss, but should allow his opponent to put the Knight back on its original square. Whereupon Thorgil, quite enraged, swept the pieces into the bag and struck Samur a mighty blow with it, making his ear bleed. Samur might have counted himself lucky not to have had his brains knocked out.

It is to the Vikings in Iceland that we probably owe the oldest chess-set known to be still in existence. In 1831 a labourer was digging in a sand-bank at the Bay of Uig on the west coast of the Isle of Lewis, in the outer Hebrides, when he found a cache of seventy-eight chessmen in a stone chamber some fifteen feet below the bank's top. They consisted of eight Kings, eight Queens, sixteen Bishops, fifteen Knights, twelve Rooks and nineteen pawns. Sixty-seven of these are in the British Museum, and the remaining eleven are in the National Museum at Edinburgh. The pieces are made of morse (walrus) ivory, and they are beautifully and imaginatively carved, with each (except the pawns, which for the most part are mere counters on octagonal bases) having its own striking expression. Their colours are natural ivory and a lovely rich deep red. The tallest of them, the King, is nearly four inches high (about nine and a half centimetres). The smallest, the pawns, vary in size but are on average two inches high.

Despite the immense length of time they lay concealed in their cave, they are wonderfully preserved and the detail, of which there is a great deal, is hardly disturbed or broken. The King is seated on his throne with a drawn sword in his hands, a broad beard and a marked air of authority on his face. There is some elaborate carving on the back of the throne, which has at its base a winged dragon. The Queen is definitely feminine and is, therefore, no longer the Firz or Fierz, the vizier and advisor to the King, as in the shatranj form of the game. She has her right hand lifted to her face, and this gives her a pathetic air of sorrow. In her left hand she holds a horn, probably a drinking horn (I have seen such in Iceland). She is also seated on a throne, but although the back of hers is also richly carved, it is without the winged dragon. There is some decoration on the bottom of her robe which is lacking from the King's. The Bishops, also seated on thrones, are almost as impressive and authoritative-looking as the King himself. In the left hand each holds a crozier and the right is a little uplifted, as though delivering an admonition or a sermon. The Knights are mounted warriors, each with a spear in the right hand and a shield with a cross on it on the left arm. Their horses are stylized with detailed heads and tails, diminutive hindquarters and no middles. The Rooks are helmeted warriors on foot, each with a drawn and upright sword in the right hand and a shield on the left.

It is the Rooks which really betray the origin of the pieces. According to most authorities, they were made in Iceland in the twelfth century and taken to the Isle of Lewis by the Vikings. Had they been of English manufacture, as some suppose, then they would have been towers or castles. (I once gave a simultaneous display in which I used replicas of the Isle of Lewis chessmen and I found the Rooks confusing, since in some ways they resembled our modern Bishops.) Whoever carved these chessmen was a master craftsman, for they are among the most attractive I know.

A walrus-tooth Rook, made in Scandinavia at the end of the twelfth century.

75

But what was the intention of whoever buried them deep in the sand-bank? Were they the booty of mere robbery? Did the Viking trader who brought them from Iceland merely put them in a safe place pending despatch to the British mainland? Or were they treasure which someone had bought legitimately and stored away in a sort of permanent deposit? All of these are merely suppositions and can be neither proved nor disproved. From the fact that the stone chamber was apparently constructed especially to contain the chessmen, I tend to favour the last guess. Such a hiding-place was as near to being a safe-deposit box as anything that could be obtained in medieval times.

The presence of the chessmen on the fringes of the British Isles tends to show that the Vikings were involved in the progress of chess there. Remember that King Canute (or Knut, if one regards him as a Danish king) was also King of England and that he is supposed to have learned to play on a pilgrimage to Rome in 1027. If he and his courtiers did play chess in England, the impetus to take the hobby up must have been strong, amongst the nobility at any rate.

The usual theory is that chess came to England with the Norman Conquest in 1066; even this, I suppose, could be interpreted as a Viking influence since the Normans were in fact Vikings who had settled in northern France. But there is some evidence that chess was played in England even before the Normans arrived. This is cited in the writings of Alexander Neckam, and in the so called Winchester Poem. Neckam has a chapter on chess, *De scaccis*, in his great philosophical work *De Naturis Rerum,* which he wrote towards the end of the twelfth century. The Winchester Poem, which dates from about the first half of the same century, is entirely about chess and how it is played. In both works the description of the men and the game appears to indicate that it was played before the Norman Conquest.

It is only logical that the Vikings should have left firmer cultural traces than did any other peoples on the sea-coasts of Ireland, Scotland and north-east England, for we know that is where they settled. Unfortunately, no reference to the game survives in the writings of the time. This is not surprising, however, since the monks, the chief preservers of literature in medieval days, seem to have been particularly rigorous in excising all references to any leisure activities which might have incurred the charge of yielding to the pleasures of the flesh. Hence, no Anglo-Saxon love poetry has survived, and I believe that this also explains the absence of chess poetry of that period.

There are indeed references to chess as having been played in Ireland in incredibly ancient times; but these are either to be found much later (in the fifteenth and sixteenth centuries) or else are based on a mistaken identification of the game. In the *British Chess Magazine* of December, 1933, there is an article on chess in ancient Ireland by P. T. McGinley, who was then president of the Colmville Chess Club in Dublin. After quite rightly saying, 'There is no good account of chess coming down to us in Irish history', he then adds (mistakenly I believe), 'The old historical or legendary romances are full of references to the game' and quotes a selection of them which, he says, 'cannot fail to interest chess players'.

One is from the *Tain Bo Chuallgne* (first century BC).

This was the way in which the King Conchubhar spent his time ever since he has taken on him the government of the province. He divides the day into three parts. The first third part he spends in superintending the noble youths of the province at the games of military exercise and ball hurling. The second third he spends in playing Brandabh (Draughts) and Fidhcheall (Chess); and the last third in eating and drinking, until sleep seizes on the company, professors of music and amusements entertaining them at the same time.

When Conchubhar's nephew, Cuchulain, visits his uncle at Emhain Macha for the first time, he gets into mischief with some of the lordlings of the court and in a fury of pursuit upsets the chess-board at which the king and his chief executive officer, Fergus Mac Roich, were playing. Naturally, he does not smooth things for himself with his uncle.

In another tale of Pagan times, Midir, the De Danaan man of Bri Leith, takes a fancy to Etain, queen of the High-king Eochaid Aireamth of Tara, and wins her from him by a brilliant game of chess. The following colloquy took place between the High-king and Midir:

'What is your name?' said Eochaid. 'It is not illustrious—Midir of Bri Leith,' answered he. 'What brought you here?' said Eochaid. 'To play chess with you,' said he. 'I am very good at chess-playing,' said Eochaid. 'I will test that,' said Midir. 'The queen is asleep,' said Eochaid, 'and the house (Grianan) in which the Fidchcall (chess-board) is belongs to her.'
'I have a Fidcheall here myself, which is not worse than it' (just as good as yours, Sir King), said Midir.

That was true; indeed, he had a silver chess-board and golden men ornamented all over with precious stones, and Fearbolgs (pawns) of plated wire of Credhumba.

Then we have the incident in the famous romance of Dairmuid and Grainne (third century AD), still in pagan times. Dairmuid O'Duibne, fleeing from the vengeance of Fionn, takes shelter in a quicken tree. But Fionn and his Fianna, who are pursuing, camp beneath the tree. Having washed and supped, Fionn and his son, Oisin the poet, sit down to a quiet game of chess. Old Fionn, with his thumb of knowledge, is getting the better of Oisin. The son is just about to make a 'howler' of a move when Dairmuid, who has been quietly watching from above in the tree, sees a better move and drops a rowanberry on the piece that *should* be moved.

In all their wanderings through the green plains of Erin, the Fianna carried with them their Fidchealls to sharpen their wits and beguile their weariness. The number and value of those chess-boards was extraordinary—if we can believe the tales.

Another ancient tale, this one referred to at about the time of the Incarnation, has the following passage:

Cuchulain landed upon the island and came to a house with pillars of Findruine (white metal) in which he saw three times fifty couches, with a Fidcheall, a Brandabh and a Timpan hung over each of them.

The Dialogue of the Ancient Men, printed in the *Book of Lismore,* has the following:

> (Certain Tuatha de Danaan chiefs came to see a hurling match at Assaroe, and) there was brought to them a Fidcheall for every six of them: a Brannabh for every five: and a Timpan for every ten: and a Cruit (harp) for every hundred: and a vigorous Cuisleanna (fluter) for every nine.

An old law tract enumerates the duties and pleasures of a king:

> There are now seven occupations in the law of a king—viz., Sunday at ale-drinking, for he is not a lawful Flaith who does not distribute ale every Sunday: Monday at legislation for the government of the tribe: Tuesday at chess: Wednesday seeing greyhounds coursing: Thursday at the pleasures of love: Friday at horse-racing: Saturday at judgment.

McGinley adds, 'I have probably given you quotations enough to show the national standing of chess in Ireland in the old days; but none of these references, nor any I have seen, touches upon the laws of the game or how it was played.'

All these tales, except perhaps the last, which probably came much later, belong to what one might term the pre-history of chess. If indeed the Irish were playing the game long before it was invented in north-west India, it would be the kind of perverse anachronism that really belongs to science fiction. The answer is that Fidcheall is not chess at all. A letter that appears immediately following the article in the *British Chess Magazine* hazards the guess that Fidcheall, which is the same as an ancient Welsh game, 'Gwydbwyll', is a survival of the Roman game of 'Latrunculi' which was brought to Britain during the Roman occupation. There is the possibility, too, that it could have been backgammon which, as I have said, is older than chess and might fit in with the earlier dates.

It may be appropriate here to deal with the names and nature of the chess-pieces during this period of history. The changes (and the retentions) were all in accord with the set-up in medieval society. This is convenient, since whenever there is some doubt as to the reason for a change one can fall back upon what one might term a social explanation.

There was obviously no reason to change the nature of the principal piece, the Shah, which became a King everywhere in Europe (with the exception of Russia, as I pointed out in the previous chapter). But the transformation from Fierz or Fers to Queen is highly interesting and has been the occasion of much ingenuity and even fanciful reasoning. It is, after all, quite a long way from a vizier, a prime minister or a chief counsellor to the consort of the King—the Queen, who may or may not be his counsellor but who often has powers as great as his own. The simple and probably correct answer is that in medieval times real-life queens did indeed sit side-by-side with kings, just as on the chess-board. One additional complication was that the word 'Fers' was used contemporaneously with the word 'Queen'.

Thus, as late as 1369, Geoffrey Chaucer included the following charming passage in his poem, *The Boke of the Duchesse:*

> At the ches with me she gan to playe;
> With hir false draughtes divers
> She stal on me and took my fers:
> And when I sawgh my fers awaye,
> Allas, I couthe no lenger playe,
> But saide, 'Fare wel, sweete, ywis,
> And fare wel al that evere ther is!'
> Therwith Fortune saide, 'Chek here!'
> And mate in the midpoint of the chekkere,
> With a poune errant! Allas,
> Ful craftier to playe she was
> Than Athalus that made the game
> First of the ches—so was his name.
> But God wolde I hadde ones or twies
> Ycond and knowe the juparties
> That coude the Greek Pyctagores
> I sholde have played the bet at ches,
> And kept my fers therby.

All of us who have ever lost Queens must sympathize with Chaucer's distress at losing his Fers. Even worse happened to him, for he was checkmated in the middle of the board by a stray pawn. What he is saying at the end is that, had he known the mathematical chances as well as Pythagoras, he would have played better and been able to keep his Queen. One interesting point that arises out of this is that, by the time Chaucer was writing, the Queen had become so powerful that its loss was equivalent to the loss of the game. There is a second point—that chess had by then become an important courtly accomplishment, since Chaucer himself was not only a major poet, but also a high-ranking courtier and diplomat.

A pleasingly fanciful explanation as to how Fierz became Queen was given by Fréret in a piece entitled *Origine du jeu des échecs* (Origin of the game of chess), which he read to the French Academy in 1719. He thought that French players, not understanding what Fierge (Fierz) meant, had confused it with *vierge,* and that this, by a natural transition, became the Virgin Mary, Queen of heaven. This idea would not appear so whimsical in French, since the word for a Queen at chess is 'Dame', and the concept of the Virgin Mary as the Queen (Dame) of heaven comes naturally to the French. Consider the *ballade* that François Villon wrote in the fifteenth century at the request of his mother, a prayer to Our Lady which begins, '*Dame du ciel*' (Queen of heaven). And consider too his even more famous *ballade des Dames du Temps jadis,* which begins with these words:

> *Dites-moi ou n'en quel pays*
> *Est Flora la belle Romaine;*
> (Tell me where, in what country,
> Is Flora, the beautiful maid of Rome;)

Its penultimate stanza reads as follows:

> *Et Jeanne, la bonne Lorraine*
> *Qu'Anglois brulerent a Rouen;*
> *Ou sont-ils, ou, Vierge souveraine?*
> *Mais ou sont les neiges d'antan!*

(And Joan, the good maid of Lorraine,
Whom the English burnt at Rouen;
Where are they, where, sovereign Virgin?
But where are the snows of yester-year!)

I have quoted this not merely for the reference to the Vierge souveraine, but also for that to Joan of Arc, for this brings me to a recent suggestion by Dr Silbermann that the Fers became a Queen under the influence of her story. It, too, is an attractive theory, but on the whole I believe that the simple explanation I gave earlier is the likeliest. It is also perhaps more in keeping with my theme that chess and social movements (in this case, the organization of medieval government) go hand in hand.

The most drastic change took place with the Elephant, which eventually became a Bishop in most countries. Europeans could make nothing of 'Fil' or 'Al-fil', except for the Spaniards who were so strongly under Moorish influence that they have retained the word 'Alfil' for Bishop to this very day. The French and the English converted the mysterious 'Alfil' to the equally mysterious 'Alfin' or 'Aufin'. How then did an Elephant become a Bishop? Again one has recourse to medieval government. These were the pieces placed closest to royalty and might therefore be deemed to be their advisers. In medieval times it was the clergy who counselled the king. Moreover the shape of an elephant's head, with its dip in the middle, might have been confused with the shape of a mitre. Eventually, later in the Middle Ages, Alfin or Aufin became Bishop in English. But in France the remarkable story was not yet at an end; there it finished up by becoming a 'fou' (a fool or jester). Possibly this resulted from genuine confusion between a Bishop's mitre and crozier and a fool's cap and bauble. Or else it might have come from a deliberate satirization of religion, as exemplified in the crowning of a fool at religious carnivals in Paris.

The original Horse was converted quite naturally to a Knight in most European languages (though not in Spanish, for example, where it remained a Horse). As can be seen in the Isle of Lewis chessmen, it became a mounted warrior in medieval times, but has reverted to a Horse in more recent times.

The Arabic Chariot (Rukh) was, like the Elephant, incomprehensible to Europeans who simply adapted the sound of the word to Rook or variants such as Roc, Roche, Roque etc. Later, it was to become a Castle or Tower and hence the French Tour, the Spanish Torre and the German Turm.

Though a long way away from the Arabic (Baidaq) in name, the Pawn is the exact equivalent of the Arabic original. It was a Foot-soldier when the game began and has remained such ever since.

chapter **7**

Late medieval
and early modern times
the game becomes dynamic

It is no exaggeration to say that this period, and in particular the fifteenth century, ranks as the most important in the history of the game, next, one supposes, to the date of its invention in north-west India in the sixth century AD. Indeed, in some ways it is even more important, since it is certain that chess would never have become genuinely popular had the old slow method of play not changed for something with a faster tempo.

I find it amazing that for a thousand years players were content with rules and moves that were stultifyingly slow. It is perhaps a comment on the essential tedium of life for so many people that the game was played at all. One can't help thinking a wild thought—that if television had been invented in the sixth century, nobody might have bothered to play chess at all.

The game suffered from the conventions and circumstances of the time in which it developed, starting as a war game based on military arms which were essentially slow. Once, however, new forces of warfare, as well as of science and the arts, were set in motion—that is to say, with the coming of the Renaissance—a vast change revivified the game's spirit almost as speedily as if it had been touched by a magic wand. Curiously enough, chess became not only more dynamic but also more subtle. It is a fallacy to think that because a game is slow in its operation it is therefore necessarily refined in its thought processes. The reverse is also true. Speed does not preclude, but rather encourages, subtlety of thought. Murray has remarked apropos this change from the older form to the modern that, 'Whether chess has actually gained as an intellectual and strategical game is doubtful' (*A History of Chess,* p. 777). This to me shows a failure to appreciate the point. The older rules inhibited the formulation of strategy; the modernization of the game has added immensely to its intellectual possibilities.

Since it was in Italy that the Renaissance flowered, it was natural that it should have been Italian chessplayers, stimulated by the revivification of the arts and the sciences, who were chiefly responsible for the changes in the game. These were devoted to making it more dynamic, to converting what had been in origin the chaturanga tortoise to the modern hare. For this purpose all the pieces, with the solitary exception of the Knight, had their powers of movement

A German ivory knight from the early sixteenth century.

notably increased. Why the Knight was left out of this acceleratory process it is difficult to determine. Perhaps it was felt that its curious, almost crablike movement, together with its powers of leaping over pieces, constituted a sufficiently piquant element that needed no enhancing. The consequence has been that beginners and less experienced players have always regarded the piece as a mysterious chessman with Asiatic or Oriental connections—which, in a way, it has. A further consequence has been that (and now I write from the point of view of the practical player) extra attention has had to be given to the Knight to bring it into action.

Note that when I discuss the speeding up of the game, I am really referring to an increase in the scope of action of the pieces. The greater the space a piece can control the quicker it is to get into action. Thus, whenever I refer to a speeding up of play, I am basically considering the increase in the amount of space involved by the change.

Remarkably, these changes were for the most part concentrated in the brief period of the latter half of the fifteenth century. Murray asserts that it was an even briefer period—only a quarter of a century, from 1475 to 1500. But I find this difficult to credit. Even so, whether it was twenty-five years or fifty years, it is still astonishing that such major changes should have occurred in so short a time. Normally, drastic changes come by evolution rather than by revolution, and it is a tribute to the impact of the Renaissance on the medieval world that such immense transformations could have been wrought so quickly.

Change had already occurred prior to this period, as I mentioned in the last chapter. In addition to the small leaps that were given to the Queen and the Bishop, the pawn could be moved two squares on its first move (or one, of course, according to the player's choice). But the option of taking off en passant came first in the late fifteenth century. The Spanish writer, Lucena, in his *Arte de axedres,* published in 1497, mentions taking en passant in describing the pawn's move:

> *Los peones primaramente pueden el primer lance hagar a una casa o a dos despues a una siemprey por barra y prenden por esquina: y pueden passar que quiere dezir que estando el peon del otro en contrario podeys passar vuestro peon otra casa mas adelante dela casa del encuentro quedando enla eleccion del otro dexar lo passar o prender lo.*

(The Pawns firstly can on the first move go one square or two, but afterwards only one, moving vertically and capturing diagonally: they can 'passar batalla', which means that if an opponent's Pawn stands facing yours, your Pawn can go on another square beyond the square of contact, it being left to the choice of your opponent to allow it to pass him or to capture it.)

Lucena goes on to say that a pawn is promoted to a Queen when it reaches the eighth rank and that it can give check at that point without moving. Then comes an interesting variant in which he says that if you play the way he does, the pawn, on being promoted to a Queen can, on its first subsequent move, take and give check as both Queen and Knight. He also describes how a King may on its first move leap three squares but cannot do this if in check or if it passed over or onto a square that is under check. Clearly this is the forerunner of castling, but in fact uniform castling took about another century to come into regular practice.

The power of advancing a Pawn two squares on its first move would have had little effect had it not been for the two most important changes that now occurred. The Queen and Bishop were both given their modern powers, and the fact that the Bishop lost its ability to leap meant little in contrast to this immense increase in strength for both pieces. The Queen became by far the strongest piece on the board and the Bishop became a formidable one. This accentuation of strength and the consequent violent increase in the tempo of the game did not escape notice at the time, as is apparent from the names given the new type of play. The Italians termed it *scacci alla rabiosa,* 'mad chess', and the French, *eschecs de la dame enragée,* 'chess of the maddened Queen'.

It is clear that this revitalized game arose in Italy, since players came from abroad to Rome to learn of the developments. Lucena, for instance, states in his book that he went there to gather material for writing about the new form and its rules. Moreover, the French term, which came later than the Italian, is obviously a translation of *rabiosa.* In 1536, Christian Egenolff published a fresh edition in Frankfurt-am-Main of a book by Mennel called *Schachzabel.* This gave the rules of the old game, and Egenolff added a description of the modern one under the heading, *Ein ander art das Schachspil zu ziehen/so mann nennet Current oder das welsch Schachspiel.* This means, 'Another way of playing chess which is known as the Current or Italian game.' It seems, oddly enough, that 'welsch' here is equivalent to Italian.

From Italy the new game spread first to France and Spain, and then to Germany and England. It is known that the modern form had already made its way to England in the first half of the sixteenth century. There is a pretty poem by Henry Howard, Earl of Surrey, in *Tottel's Miscellany* (published in 1557), which refers to a game of chess that must have been played under the new rules which gave such power to the Queen. Entitled *To the lady that scorned her lover,* it describes how he parries a check from the lady and sees how he himself can give check while at the same time attacking the Queen (Ferse). Since the unfortunate earl was executed in 1547, the poem makes it clear that England knew the new game at least as early as that. His is a parable in a rather different style from the moralities:

> Although I had a check
> To give the mate is hard.
> For I have found a neck
> To kepe my men in gard.
> And you that hardy are
> To give so great assay
> Unto a man of warre
> To drive his men away,
> I rede you, take good hede,
> And marke this foolish verse:
> For I will so provide
> That I will have your ferse
> And when your ferse is had,
> And all youre warre is donne:
> Then shall yourself be glad

To ende that you begon.
For yf by chance I winne
Your person in the feeld:
Too late then come you in
Your selfe to me to yeld.
For I will use my power
As captain full of might
And such I will devour,
As use to shew me spight.
And for because you gave
Me checke in such degree,
This vantage loe I have—
Now checke and garde to the!
Defend it if you may:
Stand stiffe, in thine estate,
For sure I will assay
If I can give the mate.

'For I have found a neck to kepe my men in gard' means that he has been able to cover the check and protect his men. It is interesting to see that when he attacks the Queen and gives check he thinks himself obliged to warn his opponent that he is attacking the Queen ('Now checke and garde to the'). This was still the practice in England until the twentieth century.

In Howard's time chess was a game of status, played in royal courts and by the nobility. Naturally one must take all these tales of kings and chess with many grains of salt. For one thing, there is, as I have already pointed out, an obvious parallel to be drawn between kings and queens in real life and those on the chess-board. It pleases mankind to see pieces of wood come to life and behave like flesh and blood. For another, it is a natural tendency for us to attribute to anyone who is a leader of men, in whatever sphere, a penchant for diverting his leisure hours in a more or less intellectual way. Countless are the number of potentates, emperors, statesmen, warriors, composers, scientists, painters and artists of all kinds who have been wrongly classed as fine and fervent chessplayers.

I know of only one great painter who was also a fine chessplayer—Marcel Duchamp, and amongst composers I can name only Prokofiev. As for scientists, I was in Moscow when Gagarin made his celebrated voyage to outer space, and I asked a friend of mine, Maiselis, a well known expert in King and pawn endings, 'Does Gagarin play chess?' The reply was, 'I don't know if he does now . . . but he will.' In Russia, as elsewhere, fame seems to equate with playing chess.

The attribution of expertise in the game to Alexander the Great and to Charlemagne is less than plausible. True, Napoleon played chess, but he was a weak player who became extremely irritated when he lost. Fortunately for themselves his companions and courtiers knew this and behaved discreetly at the chess-board. King John was supposed to have been playing chess in 1213 when he should have been relieving Rouen, and Thomas-a-Becket was supposed to have been a fine chessplayer. But then, King John has always had a bad press, and Becket a good one.

Edward I really does seem to have been a keen chessplayer, although he might well have been put off the game by an incident that could have been fatal. Nicholas Trivet narrates in his Annales '*Adolescens cum milite quodam in camera testudinata ludo acaccarii occupatus*' that as a young man he was playing chess against a soldier in a room with a tiled roof, that he suddenly left the room and that then an immense rock fell on the very spot where he had been sitting: '*lapisque immensae magnitudinis, qui sedentem conquassasset, in eodem loco ceciderit.*' That the incident did not quash Edward's enthusiasm is apparent from the wardrobe accounts for the years 1299 to 1300, which show that he possessed two valuable chess-sets: '*Una familia pro scaccario de jaspido et cristallo, in uno coffro. Una familia de ebore pro ludendo ad scaccarium.*' (A set of chessmen in jasper and crystal in a coffer. A set of ebony for playing chess.)

In similar vein we learn from an inventory of the effects of Charles the Bold, Duke of Burgundy (1467 to 1477) that he had no less than seven chess-sets and boards of great value. Among the best was '*Ung eschequier d'argent d'un coste et de l'autre coste armoye des armes de MS., garni d'eschetz de cristal.*' (A chess-board silver on one side and with the armorial bearings of the Duke on the other, with chess-pieces of crystal.)

Then, too, there are all those stories of kings who quarrelled with their opponents after losing at chess. I have already given a sample with King Knut as the hero (or the villain according to taste), but there are many others. Robert Burton, who, in his *Anatomy of Melancholy* (1621) already went so far as to give a possible reason for the invention of chess—'invented (some say) by the general of an army in a famine to keepe his souldiers from mutiny'—included this anecdote about William the Conqueror:

William the Conqueror in his younger years while playing at chess with the prince of France, lost a mate, and was so provoked thereat, that he knocked the chess-board about his adversary's pate, which was a cause afterwards of much enmity between them.

On similar lines but with a more genuine ring of truth is the following story from the *Dictionnaire d'Anecdotes* (1783): Ferrand, Count of Flanders, having been taken prisoner by Philip Augustus at the Battle of Bovines, his wife, who might have obtained his release, left him to languish a long time in prison (from 1213 to 1226). They hated each other and their hatred proceeded from playing at chess together; the husband could never forgive his wife for constantly beating him at chess; and she could never resolve to suffer him to win a game.

The medieval French romances, and their translators and imitators in England and Germany, are full of accounts of heroes, kings and nobles, who were addicted to chess and were either saved by their prowess or perished through playing the game. Some of these tales were mythical; others concerned real historical figures but, separated from reality by the distance of time (such as those about Alexander the Great and Charlemagne), might as well have been mythical for all the truth there was in the statements that they played chess. Some were about real figures who may possibly have played, but whose involvement with the game was obviously most fancifully presented.

Chief of these was Richard Coeur de Lion who was supposed to have learnt chess from the Saracens on his Crusades (but he was

Chess-players depicted in the border of the Romance of Alexander, *dating from around 1340.*

never accused of abandoning the siege of a city in favour of playing chess, as was his brother John). According to a Middle English romance (*Richard Coeur de Lyon,* c.1300), Lion-Heart was an excellent player:

> The messengers then hyed hard
> Till they came to Kyng Richard.
> They found Kyng Richard at play
> At the chess in his galeye;
> The Earl of Richmond with him playd,
> And Richard won all that he layd.

In this poem, Richard seems to have derived profit from wagers.

In a French thirteenth-century romance of the Charlemagne cycle, entitled *Renaud de Montaubon,* he made more violent use of his skill with the pieces. Caxton translated the work under the title, '*The Right Pleasant and Goodlie Historie of the Foure Sonnes of Aymon*' (published 1489). I quote a passage which would make a fine scenario for a film of violence—perhaps all the more so because Caxton mistranslated the French text through his ignorance of the names of some of the chess-pieces. The position is that Richard is the captive of Renaud de Montaubon, who has a gibbet erected on which he proposes to hang his prisoner.

> After that the ladder was ryghted to the gybet above upon the hyghe gate Ardeyne, Reynawde called two of his folke and sayd to theym, 'Galantes, goo fet me the duke Rycharde, for I wylle that he be hanged incontynente;' 'Syre' sayd they 'we shall doo your commandement.'
>
> And they wente on the chambre where the noble duke of Normandy was, and founde hym playing atte the ches with Yonnet the sone of Reynawd, and thenne these men take hym, and sayd 'Syre duke, com forth! for Reynawde hathe commaunded that ye shall be hanged incontynent.'
>
> Whan the duke Rycharde of Normandy herde these felawes speke thus to hym, he looked upon theym over the shoder and wolde not answer to theym, but sayd, 'My fair Yonnet, haste

you for to playe, for it is tyme that we goo to dyner.' And whan these galantes sawe that Rycharde of Normandy answered noo words unto theym, they began to take hym on every side, and said to hym, 'Aryse up, duke Rycharde, for in dyspyte of Charlemagn that loved you so moche, ye shall be hanged now!'

When the duke Rycharde saw that these serjountes had hym thus by the arme, and held in his hand a lady of yvery, wherwyth he wold have gyven a mate to Yonnet, he wythdrewe his arme, and gaft to one of the serjountes such a stroke wyth it in to ye forhede that made him tomble over and over at his fete and then he toke a roke and smote another wythall upon his hede that he all to broste it to the broste, and after that he smote another of theim wythe his fiste so grete a stroke that he break his necke, and felle dead to therthe. And when the other sawe theym felawes thus arayd, they began to runne awaye. And whan Rycharde saw theym goo, he cryed to theim: 'The rybawdes goddys curse have you: come not here again.' And whan he had said soo, he sayd to Yonnet, that was all abasshed; 'Playe well, my childe, for ye shall be mated, I trowe there truantes were droken, that thus wolde have had me awage, but I have well gyven theim their parte'.

And whan Yonnet herde him saye so, he durste not speke aganst it by cause he sawe hymselfe soo sore an angred, but played wyth his roke that he sholde not be mated, but he myght not save the mate. Whan the duke Rycharde had mated Yonnet, he called a yoman that was there, and sayd to hym, 'Goo, take then carles that lien here deed, and caste theim oute at the wyndowes.' The yoman dyde incontynente his commaundement. For he durst do noo thying there aganst, for doubte he sholde have fare as the other that he had seen slayen in his presence.

Now it should be observed that the 'lady of yvery' which Richard held in his hand and with which he struck the first sergeant was in fact a white Queen. The French text said that he held in his hand *'une fierte blanche de fin ivoire'* (a Fierte or Fers—Queen—white of fine ivory), and that *'L'un feri d'une fierte qui grans est et quarée'* (he struck the first with a Queen that was great and square). He hit the second with a Rook all right, but he used a Bishop on the third, not his fist: *'a pris .i. aufin qui la teste ot doree'* (he took an Aufin with a gilded head). Remember that the medieval term for Bishop was Aufin.

In contrast to all this violence is the following gentle extract from a French romance, *Eliduc,* written about the year 1300 by Marie de France:

> The King, arising from high table
> Went to his daughter's chambers
> To play at his beloved chess
> With an invited foreign guest.
> His daughter sitting next to him,
> Was eager to learn chess, t'would seem.
> Eliduc came, the King stopped play.

There is much about chess in one of the most famous romances of all, the *Roman de la Rose,* a fairly early thirteenth-century French work. It consists chiefly of a long and quite elaborate comparison between war and chess, but the passage that pleases me most is a joyous light-hearted treatment of chess which every bad loser should take to heart:

> . . . if Fair-Welcome comes your way,
> And you with him at chess should play,
> Or dice, or tables, or what not,
> Let him aye find that he hath got
> Advantage of you; when you lose,
> Laugh heartily, and ne'er refuse
> To play again, thereat will he
> Rejoice him most contentedly.
> My friends may freely enter here
> To dance and sing throughout the year,
> And live a joyous life and free,
> Whereof no sage need envious be,
> Nought passeth here but frolic play
> Wherewith to wile the time away,
> Light dances set to gleesome tunes,
> On viols, tambours, and bassoons,
> Sweet songs that savour amorousness,
> And games of tables, dice and chess,
> And many another for delight
> Of merry hearts. . . .

In a still earlier romance, *Huon of Bordeaux,* written about 1200, we find the kind of adventure which recurs constantly in chess legends—about the wandering hero who plays against a beautiful princess for her hand in marriage and who loses his head if he loses the game. In this one, Huon, who is disguised as a minstrel's servant, is asked by the king, Ivoryn, what his skills and accomplishments are, with the baleful warning that he must prove his prowess in everything in which he claims to be an expert. Among other things, he says, 'I can play at chess and tables as well as any other can do, nor did I ever meet man who could win off me unless I choose.' Here the king stops him, saying, Hold thee to this, for I shall prove whether what thou sayest be true or not.'

Huon goes on to boast that he 'can write well, . . . bear a shield and spear, and ride and gallop a horse . . . (and) can right well enter into ladies' chambers to embrace and kiss them, and to do them any service.' But it is at chess that Ivoryn chooses to have him 'essayed':

'. . . I have a fair daughter, with whom thou must play, on the condition that if she win, thou shalt lose thy head, and if thou canst mate her, I promise that thou shalt have her to wife for one day, and a hundred marks of gold beside.'

. . . While the King was making this bargain, a Paynim (a pagan) went into the ladies' chamber, and told (the princess) . . . 'Dame,' quoth he, 'I assure you that he that shall play against you is the fairest man that I ever saw, pity it is that he should.

'By Mahound,' quoth the lady, 'I hold my father wrong when he thinketh that I should suffer a man to die for winning a game of chess.' Then Ivoryn sent . . . for his daughter . . . (and) said: 'Daughter, thou must play at chess with this young varlet that

*From a miniature of 'The Three
Ages of Man', a manuscript of
the fifteenth century attributed to
Estienne Porchier: the scene is
one of the saloons in the castle
of Plessis-les-Tours in France, the
residence of Louis XI; the player
to the right resembles the King.*

thou seest here, so that if thou win he shall lose his head, and if he
win, I will that he shall have thee to wife for a day.'

'Father', quoth the lady, 'seeing it is your pleasure, it is right
that I do it whether I will or no.' Then she looked on Huon, whom
she found right fair, and she said to herself, 'By Mahound, for the
great beauty that I see in this young man, I would this game were
at an end, so that I were his wife this day.'

When the lady was come, their places were made ready, and
she and Huon sat down, while the King Ivoryn and his barons
sat down about him to see them play. Huon said to the King:
'Sir, I require you that no man should speak in our game, neither
for one party nor the other.'

. . . (The King) caused it to be cried through all the palace that
no man should be so bold as to speak one word, on pain of death.
Then the chessmen were made ready, and Huon said: 'Lady, what
game will you play at?'

'Friend,' quoth she, 'at the usual game, to be mated in a corner.'
. . . There were Paynims looking over Huon, but he . . . studied
only his game, which he began so that he lost some of his pawns.
In this he changed colour, and blushed as red as a rose. The
damsel perceived him and said: 'Friend, what are you thinking of;
you are nigh mated. Soon my father will strike off your head.'

'Dame,' quoth he, 'as yet the game is not done; great shame
shall your father have, when you are my wife, and I am but a
varlet to a poor minstrel.' When the barons heard Huon say this
they all began to laugh, but the lady was so taken with the love of
Huon . . . that she forgot all her play in thinking of him, and so
she lost the game . . .

Chess-players and spectators shown in a Flemish painting of the mid-fifteenth century.

When the King heard (this), he said to his daughter: 'Arise, cursed be the hour that you were born: great dishonour hast thou done to me, when thou hast mated so many great men, and now I see that a miserable varlet hath mated thee.'

'Sir,' quoth Huon, 'trouble not yourself for that cause. As for the wager that I have won, I am content to release it freely; let your daughter go into her chamber and sport with her damsels, and I shall go serve my master, the minstrel.'

'Friend,' quoth the King, 'if thou wilt shew me this courtesy, I shall give thee a hundred marks of money.'

'Sir,' quoth Huon, 'I am content with your pleasure.' The lady went her way sorrowful, and said to herself: 'Ah, false, faint heart, Mahound confound thee: If I had known that thou wouldst thus have refused my company, I would have mated thee, and then thou hadst lost thy head.'

It is extraordinary how long-lived this type of story is, and the last time I saw it, or something near it, was in a French film of the 1930s based on Pierre Benoit's novel *L'Atlantide*. In this case the hero lost, but was much distracted by the presence of the Princess's pet, a favourite leopard.

A parallel in real history—that is, if we can take Froissart's *Chronicle* for 1374 to be such—was the match at chess between King Edward III and the Countess of Salisbury. Strange how a love of chess ran in the family; it will be remembered that it was the king's distinguished ancestor, Edward I, who narrowly escaped being crushed by a rock while playing chess. The *Chronicle* runs as follows:

So he called for chess, and the lady had it brought in. Then the king asked the lady to play with him, and she consented gladly, for she made him all the good cheer that she might. And well was she bound thereto, for the king had done her a fair service in raising the siege of the Scots before the castle, and again she was

Another position from the thirteenth-century work on chess by King Alfonso the Wise.

Probably the work of the Vikings, some of the Isle of Lewis chessmen in the British Museum. Left to right: Rook, Knight, Rook. This set is the oldest known to be still in existence.

obliged because the king was her right and natural lord in fealty and homage. At the outset of the game of chess, the king, who wished that something of his might be won by the lady, challenged her, laughing, and said, 'Madam, what will your stake be at the game?' And she answered, 'And yours, sir?' Then the king set down on the board a fair ring that he wore with a large ruby. Then said the countess, 'Sir, sir, I have no ring so rich as yours is.'

'Madam,' said the king, 'that which you have, set it down, and consider not so narrowly.'

Then the countess to please the king drew from her finger a light ring of gold of no great worth. And they played at chess together, the lady with all the wit and skill she could, that the king might not hold her for too simple and ignorant; and the king played false, and would not play as well as he knew. And there was scarce pausing between the moves but the king looked so hard on the lady that she was all put out of countenance, and made mistakes in her play. And when the king saw that she had lost a rook or a knight or what not, he would lose also to restore the lady's game.

They played on till at last the king lost, and was checkmated with a bishop.'

The rest of the account is taken up by the king's gallant efforts to pay his wager. Although the lady refuses the ring, he says. 'The game has made it so, and if I had won be assured that I should have carried your ring away.' In the end he gives it to a damsel serving the countess.

When we come to the Tudors we find that they were all keen chessplayers. One inventory of Henry VIII's Wardrobe contains no less than a dozen chess-sets, many of considerable value; in another inventory, of a closet at Greenwich, there are more workaday sets. As one might have expected of Queen Elizabeth I, that most talented and cultured member of a talented family, she was also a keen and good player; she is known to have played chess with her Latin secretary, Roger Ascham, at the beginning of her reign. Her opposite numbers too in France and Spain were great patrons of chess: Philip of Spain was the patron of Ruy Lopez, and the Queen of France, Catherine de Medici, aspired to play against the formidable Italian master, Paolo Boi.

By Tudor times, playing chess was the expected accomplishment of a courtier and a gentleman. In the books written on the subject of the training of the upper classes, which became the fashion in the sixteenth century, much emphasis was laid on the game as mental training. Thus, for example, in Sir Thomas Elyot's *The Book named the Governour* (1531), the following is included:

The chesse, of all games wherein is no bodily exercise, is mooste to be commended; for therein is right subtle engine, wherby the wytte is made more sharpe and remembrance quickened. And it is the more commendable and also more commodiouse if the players have radde the moralization of the chess (the moralities to which I referred in the previous chapter), and when they playe do thinke upon hit; whiche bokes be in Englisshe. But they be very scarse, by cause fewe men do seeke in plaies for vertue or wisedome.

Baldassare Castiglione (1478 to 1529) in *The Book of the Courtier* is more restrained in his appreciation of chess. The Elizabethan translation by Thomas Hoby gives this dialogue:

The Lord Gasper answered: and what say you to the game at Chests?

It is truly an honest kind of entertainment and wittie, quoth Sir Fredericke. But me thinke it hath a faulte, which is, that a man may be too cunning at it, for who ever will·bee excellent in the play of Chests, I believe he must bestow much time about it, and apply it with so much studie, that a man may as soone learne some noble science, or compasse any other matter of importance, and yet in the ende in bestowing all that labour, hee knoweth no more but a game.

Therefore in this I believe there happeneth a verie rare thing, namely, that the meane is more commendable than the excellencie.

The Lord Gasper answered: there be many Spaniards excellent at it, and in many other games, which for all that bestow not much studie upon it, nor yet lay aside the compassing of other matters.

In the same book there is a remarkable account of a chess-playing ape, brought back by the Portuguese from the Indies who beats allcomers by 'some very cunning movements'. Little wonder that Castiglione advised moderation in the study of chess! The fact that he may have considered an over-addiction to the game as not quite appropriate for the perfect gentleman, however, did not deter nobles and courtiers in Tudor England and throughout western Europe from taking to it enthusiastically.

We know, for instance, that Sir Philip Sidney, who was acknowledged to be the finest gentleman of Europe, was a keen player. In 1934 the then head of the House of Sidney, Lord de L'Isle and Dudley, himself a keen player, gave permission for a big county match to be played in the thirteenth-century Baronial Hall at Penshurst Place in Kent, where, he said, Sir Philip had played chess nearly 400 years earlier. Sir Philip's knowledge of the game is shown in his work, *Defence of Poesie* (1595):

We see, or cannot play at chess but that we must give names to our chess-men; and yet, methinks he were a very partial champion of truth that would say we lied for giving a piece of wood the reverend title of bishop.

By then, of course, the word Aufin had long since given way to the modern Bishop.

chapter 8

The new game

The introduction of the changes described in the last chapter—the conversion of the old into the new, the transformation from medieval to modern—stopped the old game dead in its tracks. It was as if a slow tram had been left abandoned after being replaced by a speedy bus. In some isolated corners of Europe, the slower-paced game lingered on for a while, and outside Europe, in places nearer its origin (in India or where the Arab had brought shatranj), the old game lasted practically into the twentieth century. But in western Europe the modern form was practised everywhere by early in the sixteenth century.

It would seem too that the game had now reached its ideal form, since, with the exception of stalemate, there has been no ensuing change whatsoever in the main and basic rules. I may, of course, be a little too hasty in writing this, for the period of no change has thus far been a bare 500 years, whereas the game, with or without alterations, has a history of 1,500 years. So maybe we are due for some new change in the next 1,000 years. If there is to be one in the coming millennium, I hazard the guess that it will have something to do with computers, but that can be left to posterity.

This seems an appropriate place to deal with the question of stalemate. The changes here are far from clear, and they varied from country to country. In England in the seventeenth and eighteenth centuries the play who administered the stalemate was adjudged to have lost the game, but by the nineteenth century it had become a draw again. In France and Italy stalemate was always a draw, and in Spain at one time it was an inferior kind of win. From time to time there have been sporadic attempts, even by very strong players, to return to the rule that prevailed in the seventeenth and eighteenth centuries, but these have always failed to gain the approval of the general mass of players.

This too is the place to mention the extraordinary case of the village of Ströbeck, near the town of Halberstadt in Saxony. In this German village to this day everybody plays or knows how to play chess. It was here that the old game lingered on the longest, but an extraordinary variant known as the courier game was also played over approximately the same period as the medieval form.

The courier game, which goes back to the thirteenth century, was played on a rectangular board, twelve squares by eight, and each player had eight extra pieces to make up the two rows of twelve squares. On the second rank each had twelve pawns, and on the first rank each had two Couriers placed next to the Bishops and moving exactly like the modern Bishop. On the left half of the board, next to the Courier, was a Counsellor, or Man, which could move to any adjacent square; on the right half of the board next to the Bishop was a piece known as the Schleich, which could move to an adjacent square but only horizontally or vertically. This is obviously the slowest-moving piece on the board except for the pawn, and the reason for its name becomes apparent when one knows that the German for 'to creep' is schleichen. With the exception of the Rooks' pawns and the Queen's pawns, no pawn could move more than one square at the beginning of the game.

It must have been a stereotyped sort of game, since not only were the rules those of old chess, but it was obligatory to commence play by advancing the RPs and the QPs two squares and then playing Q-Q3. But it seems to have been popular, since Frederick William I of Prussia presented the villagers with a board and men for courier on a visit to Ströbeck in 1651. The board is still to be seen there, but not, alas, the men which were of silver, and were lent and never returned. The Berlin Museum possesses an excellent painting by Lucas von Leyden (1521), which depicts a game of courier chess in which a lady is playing a man and not doing very well if the satisfied air of her opponent is any criterion. One spectator is proffering advice to her, and another, more judicious, is endeavouring to persuade him to desist from interfering.

There are many legends as to how the intense interest in chess in Ströbeck originated and prospered. The one the Germans themselves favour tells of the imprisonment of a bishop (one who was not only a prelate, but also a ruling prince) in the prison of Ströbeck. Here a friendly jailer taught him how to play chess and on his

'Il giuoco di Scacchi' (The game of Chess), an early fifteenth century engraving executed by G. B. Leonetti after Anguiscola in 1555. Note that the knights have already become standardized in their modern shape.

Il giuoco di Scacchi

release, in gratitude, he had a special law passed which enabled every villager to play the game even though, as commoners, they would not normally have had this right. At Ströbeck they will show you where he was imprisoned and point out that the prison, now an inn, is built in the form of a Rook.

In 1744 Frederick the Great of Prussia, who was widely known for his interest in chess, visited the village and played there; and in 1823 a small foundation was created to enable the villagers to continue to play. For a long time Ströbeck produced no player of note, but two villagers did well in a German Championship that was recently held there.

Ströbeck apart, the modern game was in full swing by the beginning of the sixteenth century. But its advent had come earlier, coinciding with the invention of printing, which meant a considerable increase in the literature of the game. This by itself would have encouraged the growth of genuine theory in all its aspects. But more important was the dynamic nature of the modern game itself, which facilitated opening analysis. (It must have been very difficult to conceive opening strategy in the days when the players' pieces did not even make contact in the earlier part of the game.) Naturally enough, when these analyses started they were amateurish and almost feeble in both planning and execution. They cannot but appear so to modern eyes which have had the benefit of hundreds of years of research and practice by successions of great players and theorists.

The earliest printed book of analysis to be published was that by the Spaniard, Luis Ramirez de Lucena, in 1497. It was probably preceded, however, by a curious Catalan poem, which is in manuscript form, and uses a game as a parable of the courtship of Venus by Mars. The game was played between two Catalan players, Francisco de Castellvi and Narciso Vinoles, and there is also a commentary by the Abbot Fenollar, who was presumably the author of the work.

Chess pieces from South Germany, c. 1580. They are already ornate and baroque in style. They are made of majolica, semi-precious stones, pearls, and mother of pearl. Left to right: the Knights are two crouching monkeys, the Bishop is a peasant woman with garden shears, and fruit in her apron, and the King has a sickle and the Queen a turnip.

The game itself is reasonably played by White, but Black makes two errors on his seventh and, still worse, his nineteenth move. Incidentally, I use the terms White and Black since they are usual nowadays, but in the manuscript they are Red and Green.

White: Castellvi. Black: Viñoles. Centre Counter Defence.

1. P-K4,P-Q4; 2. PxP,QxP; 3. Kt-QB3,Q-Q1;
4. B-B4,Kt-KB3; 5. Kt-B3,B-Kt5; 6. P-KR3,BxKt;
7. QxB,P-K3; 8. QxP,QKt-Q2; 9. Kt-Kt5,R-B1;
10. KtxP,Kt-Kt3; 11. KtxR,KtxKt; 12. P-Q4,Kt-Q3;
13. B-Kt5 ch,KtxB; 14.QxKt ch,Kt-Q2; 15. P-Q5,PxP;
16. B-K3,B-Q3; 17. R-Q1,Q-B3; 18. RxP,Q-Kt3;
19. B-B4,BxB; 20. QxKt ch,K-B1; 21. Q-Q8 mate.

Speaking of theory and analysis, the phrase, *eschecs de la dame enragée*, which I mentioned in the previous chapter, came from a French morality in which the author includes a game; but it is not worth printing here, however, since it shows that he merely knows the moves of chess and no more. He thinks nothing of leaving the Queen en prise on the third move for White, and his lack of comprehension of the game is rather ironically (but unconsciously) expressed when he says, '*touttefoys l'invention est à moy estrange à cause que il s'appelle de la dame enragée. Et croy que c'est le tiltre que aucuns ont baillé qui estoient hommes indiscretz.*' (All the same, the idea is strange to me because it is called the maddened queen. And I think that this is a title given to it by some who were indiscreet.)

Lucena's celebrated Spanish work which is called *Repeticion de Amoresy Arte de Ajedrez,* is presumed to have been published in or by 1497, for, though no date is given in the book, there is an elaborate dedication to Don Juan, Prince of Spain (the son of Ferdinand and Isabella), who died in the autumn of that year. On the title page Lucena declares with some pride that he is the son of the most learned doctor and reverend protonotary, Don Juan Ramirez de Lucena, ambassador, and of the Council of our Lord Kings. The younger Lucena seems, at the time of writing, to have been a student 'at the illustrious university of the very noble city of Salamanca'. The book is rare; only five copies are known to be in existence, but in 1953 a facsimile edition of 250 was printed in Madrid. I fortunately possess one of these. If this edition is any criterion then the original was a handsomely printed volume.

This appears to be the first printed work of theory on chess, thoughWilliam Lewis, in his *Letters on Chess* by C. F. Vogt, claimed in 1834 that much of it was copied from an earlier work in Catalan by Vicent, entitled *Libre dels jochs partitis del scachs en nombre de 100, per Francesch Vicent. En Valencia, Lope de Roca, 1495* (Book of beautiful games of chess in the number of 100, by Francis Vicent. In Valencia, Lope de Roca, 1495). Since the Vicent book has been lost we shall never know what, if anything, Lucena copied, though it would seem from the title that there was no analysis of the openings as there is in Lucena.

It has also been surmised that Lucena was the author of an anonymous manuscript in Latin on the openings, which is in the library of Göttingen University and has become known as the Göttingen Manuscript. Whether this is indeed so, is hard to say. But Murray thinks that it is much superior to Lucena's Spanish work; however, after pointing out the differences, he comes, rather surprisingly, to the conclusion that the author is the same in both cases. I believe he underestimates the quality of the printed work. Admittedly, the opening analysis leaves much to be desired, but it should not be forgotten that we owe to Lucena some of the most important ideas on end-game play that have ever been invented or discovered.

After the dedication to Don Juan which is a rather diffuse display of classical erudition, Lucena gives a much more succinct treatment of the game itself. This is divided into twelve reglas, which originally means rules, but which should really be interpreted as sections or chapters. He starts, *'La primera regla es adotrinar a los que no saben nada en este juego'* (The first rule is to teach those who know nothing about the game) and then he goes on to give the rules of play, contrasting the new with the old and finishing with some amusing advice: 'If you play at night with only one candle, place it on your left hand, because it does not then so much disturb the sight; by daylight, place your adversary opposite the light, this being a great advantage to you.' Murray has rather simplified this in his translation, so as to make it look like cheating on Lucena's part. In a way, it is, but I think it would be better to class it as gamesmanship.

Murray does even worse with Lucena's final advice on the strategy of attack by merely giving 'Always break through on the Queen's wing, never on the King's wing.' An examination of the Spanish shows that this sentence is only part of a long paragraph in which the author explains that if you attack too recklessly and render your King vulnerable you can easily lose, whereas if you attack on the other side your own King will be in safety. Obviously he envisages an attack with the Pawns that can be undertaken without danger on the Queen's wing, but will be fraught with peril if executed on the King-side. There is much wisdom in this idea (cf. the losses that White may incur in some variations of the attack against the Sicilian Defence).

The remaining eleven rules are devoted to eleven openings, seven for White and four for Black, or rather seven for the player with the move and four for the defender, since it is apparent from the woodcuts which illustrate the work that Black has the first move. The notation in which all this is done is the most long-winded of descriptive. Take, for instance, the start of the second rule: *'La segunda regla es jugar del peon del rey a iiii casas, que se entiende contando de donde esta el rey'*. (The second rule is to play the King's Pawn four squares, which means counting from that on which the King stands).

I shall not attempt to give his analysis in this form, but will in fact use the descriptive. This will, I think, give a better picture of the notation employed. The algebraic did not make its appearance in western Europe till the coming of Stamma in the eighteenth century. Those unacquainted with one or other of the notations will find them both in the appendix of this book.

The first opening considered is what became known later as the Damiano Gambit:
1. P-K4,P-K4; 2. Kt-KB3,P-KB3; 3. KtxP, and now he gives both 3. .,Q-K2 and 3. .,PxKt, going rather badly astray in the latter variation.

The second opening is a Giuoco Piano which, however, he converts into a Ruy Lopez at the cost of a move. An interesting point is that at one moment in the analysis he gives R-KB1 and then on the next move K-Kt1, castling in the modern way, but *in two moves*.

The opening moves are: 1. P-K4,P-K4; 2. Kt-KB3,Kt-QB3;

3. B-B4,B-B4; 4. P-Q3,Kt-B3; 5. P-KR3,P-Q3; 6. B-QKt5.

The third opening has no name, deservedly so, but illustrates a horrible trap: 1. P-K4,P-K4; 2. P-Q3,P-QB3; 3. Kt-KB3,P-KR3; 4. KtxP??,Q-R4 ch and wins the Knight. I suppose one must not be too critical about this; Lucena is merely showing us how not to play. No doubt he saw such things in his first year at Salamanca University.

The next and fourth opening is a Petroff which was subsequently imitated, and a little improved, by Damiano, running: 1. P-K4,P-K4; 2. Kt-KB3,Kt-KB3; 3. KtxP,KtxP; 4. Q-K2 etc.

The fifth is a reasonable Centre Counter Defence: 1. P-K4,P-Q4; 2. PxP,QxP; 3. Kt-QB3.

In the sixth he says that if Black does not play either P-K4 or P-Q4 on his first move, White should play 2. P-Q4.

The seventh is a perfectly reasonable Bishop's Opening: 1. P-K4,P-K4; 2. B-B4,P-Q3; 3. P-QB3,Kt-QB3; 4. Kt-B3,B-K3; 5. BxB,PxB; 6. Q-Kt3,Q-B1; 7. Kt-Kt5,Kt-Q1; 8. P-Q4, followed by 9. B-K3, 10. QKt-Q2 and 11. 0-0-0 with the better game for White.

A page from Damiano's influential book entitled Questo libro e da imparare giocare a scachi et de le partiti; *it appeared in Rome in 1512.*

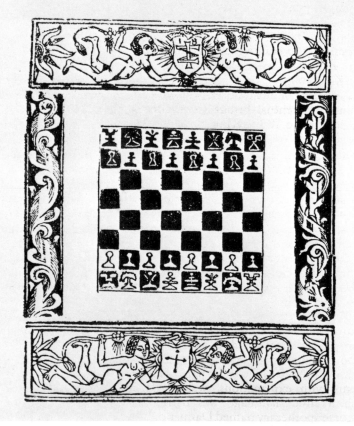

The eighth is a peculiar Ruy Lopez: 1. P-K4,P-K4; 2. Kt-KB3,Kt-QB3; 3. B-Kt5,KKt-K2; 4. BxKt,KtxB; 5. P-B3,P-Q4.

The ninth starts 1. P-K3, and the tenth is a rather indifferent Bishop's Opening.

The eleventh starts with a Queen's fianchetto (anticipating Larsen in our time) but then goes off the track into some very poor play.

Obviously this is far from perfect, but for a first venture with new rules it is still quite remarkable. Later theorists improved on his work, but it was Lucena who showed the way. Remember that he had nothing written to show him how to analyse; however, he does himself admit that he picked up much useful knowledge on voyages to Italy and France.

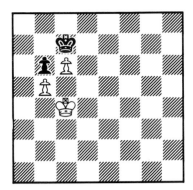

22 *and* 23: *Two positions from* Lucena's Repeticion de Amores y Arte de Ajedrez.

The remainder of the book consists of 150 positions, some of which are problems and others endings. Some of the problems are still based on the old rules. One wonders which of these he took from the Catalan Vicent, if any. This is important, for the chief virtue of Lucena, as I have already said, is that he gave us some of the basic verities of end-game play.

I give two illustrations. The first shows the idea of giving up a Pawn in the ending to avoid stalemate, and the second, even more valuable, is the notion of building a bridge for the King by a Rook move in a Rook and pawn ending. In the first:

White plays 1. K-Q5,K-B1; 2. P-B7, (but not 2. K-Q6,K-Q1; 3. P-B7 ch,K-B1; 4. K-B6 stalemate) 2. .,KxP; 3. K-K6,K-B1; 4. K-Q6,K-Kt2; 5. K-Q7, and White will eventually win the Pawn with a won Pawn ending (Diagram 22).

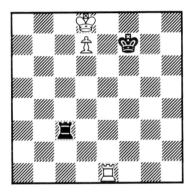

Diagram 23 is known as the Lucena position. The problem for White is how to extricate his King from in front of the Pawn without submitting to constant checks from Rook and without allowing the enemy King to approach the Pawn.

1. R-K4

The key-move. White's Rook still cuts off the enemy King while providing an eventual bridge (or shelter, depending on how you look at it) for the White King.

1.	R-B8
2. R-B4 ch	K-Kt2

If 2. .,K-K3; 3. K-K8

3. K-K7	R-K8 ch
4. K-Q6	R-Q8 ch
5. K-B6	R-B8 ch
6. K-Q5	R-Q8 ch
7. R-Q4	

This was the point of the Lucena move 1. R-K4. The checks are at an end and the Pawn must Queen.

Fifteen years after Lucena's book appeared, another author and theorist, profiting from the pioneer work of his predecessor, published a book that was to have greater influence on opening praxis. This appeared in 1512 in Rome, under the title *Questo libro e da imparare giocare a scachi et de le partiti*. It was the first and one of the most popular Italian works on chess theory and, while the first part was wholly in Italian, the latter part, which consisted of seventy-two problems with explanations, was partly in Italian and partly in Spanish. Neither language was native to the author; he was a Portuguese apothecary named Damiano. Little is known about him—

not his dates of birth and death, nor even his first name. But the book caught the public fancy much more than Lucena's. It ran through eight editions in the sixteenth century and continued on into the next century with unflagging popularity.

The book was short and to the point. The analysis too was short, even shorter than Lucena's, but it had the virtue of coming after the Spaniard's work, so that improvements could be made and mistakes deleted. One important addition by Damiano was White's 1. P-Q4, and he gave an analysis of the Queen's Gambit Accepted, showing what happens when Black tries to retain the Pawn by P-QKt4.

One reason why the book was so popular may have been that he included analyses of games at odds, which were now becoming the fashion and which were to remain so until the late nineteenth century. He also had some passages about blindfold play, which was regarded with great awe at the time. There are also some seventy-two problems and positions, hardly any of which according to Murray were Damiano's own invention. These problems too caught the public's fancy—in particular a smothered mate, which must have been a forerunner of what became known in the late eighteenth and early nineteenth centuries as Philidor's legacy.

One can only conclude that he fulfilled a need in his time and later, but from his analyses it is clear he was not a particularly good player and I think his reputation is inflated beyond its true worth.

About this time (in 1513, according to von der Lasa), a Latin poem on chess, *Scacchia Ludus,* was written by Marcus Hieronymous Vida, later Bishop of Alba, which was to have an astonishing success and also to have one little-foreseen consequence for the chess world. Vida, who was born in Cremona in 1490 and died in 1566, was twenty-three years old when he wrote what was rather a charming, mock-heroic piece about a contest at chess between Apollo and Mercury. How good he was as a player cannot be determined, but he had the idea, and indeed the necessity, of inventing classical names for the various pieces. One was Tower or Castle for the Rook (also Elephas, with the concept of an elephant bearing a tower on its back, which was already in Livy). The result was twofold: the Rook changed both its name and its shape. In every language save Russian it became Tower or Castle and many chess-sets, particularly those of the more ornate type, had Elephants for Rooks. This has caused some confusion inasmuch as Bishops originally had been Elephants.

Though he had written it years earlier, Vida did not publish the work until 1527, when he was thirty-seven years old. It had an immediate success and was translated into most European languages. *Scacchia Ludus* also became the model for similar poems for a couple of hundred years. Two English translations of note were made. One, published in 1597, has it as written by G.B. and this may be so in the sense that he may have translated it, since it says it was translated from the Italian. My Victorian replica also includes a section on how to play, but this is fairly perfunctory and the chief part of the book is the poem, which starts as follows:

> Fond shapes of warre and fained fight
> loe (heere) Wee doo report:
> Wee tell of Souldiers framde of Box,
> and Battailes fought in sport.

How boxen Princes strive for praise,
in colours black and white;
and how in partie coloured Armes
each one with other fight.

Compare this with the smoother and perhaps sweeter version by Oliver Goldsmith. The translation was not published in Goldsmith's lifetime but found among his papers after his death:

Armies of box that sportively engage
And mimic real battles in their rage,
Pleased recount; how smit with glory's charms,
Two mighty Monarchs met in adverse arms,
Sable and white; assist me to explore,
Ye Serian Nymphs, what ne'er was sung before.

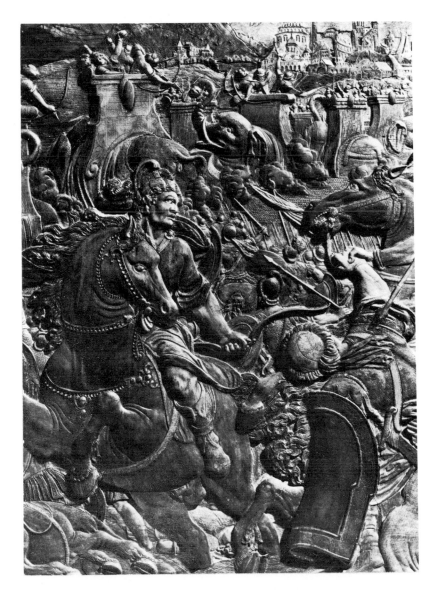

A section of an elaborately carved German chess board of the mid-seventeenth century, illustrating with great force that chess is a war game.

Then, still using Goldsmith's translation, the pieces are produced:

> But see, the mimic heroes tread the board;
> He said, and straightway from an urn he pour'd
> The sculptured box, that neatly seem'd to ape
> The graceful figure of a human shape:
> Equal the strength and number of each foe,
> Sixteen appear'd like jet, sixteen like snow.
> As their shape varies various is the name,
> Different their posts, nor is their strength the same.
> There might you see two Kings with equal pride
> Gird on their arms, their Consorts by their side;
> Here the Foot-warriors glowing after fame,
> There prancing Knights, and dexterous Archers came
> And Elephants, that on their backs sustain
> Vast towers of war, and fill and shake the plain.

The 'dexterous Archers' were Vida's idea of Bishops, and for some time under his influence quite a number of writers referred to this piece as an Archer. Note the reference to the Elephants with their towers, by which he means the Rooks. A little later we find him speaking of their 'castles', and then referring to the pawns as Foot-soldiers on the second rank:

> In either army on each distant wing
> Two mighty Elephants their castles bring,
> Bulwarks immense: and then at last combine
> Eight of the Foot to form the second line,
> The vanguard to the King and Queen; from far
> Prepared to open all the fate of war.

Vida's description of the moves of the pieces is in poetic terms, but clearly the rules are those of the modern game. First the Pawns:

> The Foot alone (so their harsh laws ordain)
> When they proceed can ne'er return again.
> But neither all rush on alike to prove
> The terror of their arms: the Foot must move
> Directly on, and but a single square;
> Yet may these heroes, when they first prepare
> To mix in combat on the bloody mead,
> Double their sally, and two steps proceed;
> But when they wound, their swords they subtly guide
> With aim oblique, and slanting pierce his side.

So the pawns can move two squares on their first move and capture diagonally. The Rooks are more direct:

> But the great Indian beasts, whose backs sustain
> Vast turrets arm'd, when on the redd'ning plain
> They join in all the terror of the fight,
> Forward or backward, to the left or right,
> Run furious, and impatient of confine
> Scour through the field, and threat the farthest line.

But they cannot move diagonally like Archers (Bishops):

> Yet must they ne'er obliquely aim their blows;
> That only manner is allow'd to those
> Whom Mars has favour'd most, who bend the stubborn
>   bows.
> These glancing sidewards in a straight career,
> Yet each confined to their respective sphere,
> Or white or black, can send th'unerring dart
> Wing'd with swift death to pierce through ev'ry part.

Vida shows a proper respect for the power of the Bishop and most delicately conveys the fact that the piece can never change the colour of its square. He then goes on to describe the Knight's and the Queen's moves, using the latter to illustrate the Knight's leap by differentiation:

> The fiery steed, regardless of the reins,
> Comes prancing on; but sullenly disdains
> The path direct, and boldly wheeling round,
> Leaps o'er a double space at ev'ry bound:
> And shifts from white or black to diff'rent
>   coloured ground.
> But the fierce Queen, whom dangers ne'er dismay,
> The strength and terror of the bloody day,
> In a straight line spreads her destruction wide,
> To left or right, before, behind, aside.
> Yet may she never with a circling course
> Sweep to the battle like the fretful Horse;
> But unconfined may at her pleasure stray,
> If neither friend nor foe block up the way;

Finally, there is an elaborate description of the King's move, of which the most important is this couplet:

> But when he changes from his first repose,
> Moves but one step, most awfully sedate,

He indicates that if the King is taken prisoner all is lost:

> While the King's safe, with resolution stern
> They clasp their arms; but should a sudden turn
> Make him a captive, instantly they yield,
> Resolved to share his fortune in the field.

The bulk of the poem, which contains 742 lines in the first edition and 658 in the second, is devoted to a description of the game between the two gods. At the end, when Apollo wins, he decides to bring the game to the earth. From the text it is apparent that Vida thought that chess originated in Italy:

> Soon after this, the heavenly victor brought
> The game on earth, and first th'Italians taught.
> For (as they say) fair Scacchis he spied
> Feeding her cygnets in the silver tide,

(Scacchis, the lovliest Seriad of the place)
And as she stray'd, took her to his embrace.
Then, to reward her for her virtue lost,
Gave her the men and chequer'd board emboss'd
With gold and silver curiously inlay'd;
And taught her how the game was to be play'd.
Ev'n now 'tis honour'd with her happy name;
And Rome and all the world admire the game.
All which the Seriads told me heretofore,
When my boy-notes amused the Serian shore.

So the modern game had acquired its poet, probably every whit as good as the poets of chaturanga, shatranj and the medieval game. It is fitting that he should have come from Italy, the land of the Renaissance.

But it was from Spain that the first great player of the modern game was to emerge, the famous Ruy Lopez de Segura, a Spanish priest. Perhaps the influence of the long years of Moorish occupation had prepared the ground there, and maybe Lucena's work was not so bad after all. In the earlier part of his career, Ruy Lopez was an amateur who devoted only his leisure hours to the game. Later, when he found it profitable, through the patronage of Philip II of Spain and others, he became what we would now call a professional chessplayer.

Unfortunately, we know little about the life of the man who, had such a title then been invented, would have rightfully been called the first world champion of modern chess. We do not even know when he was born or when he died. But it seems fairly certain that by 1560 he was Spain's leading player, or at any rate one of its leading players, and that he was so good that no one in Rome, at that time the centre of chess in Italy, could hold his own against him.

On the accession of Pope Pius IV many ecclesiastics visited Rome, including Ruy Lopez who, it seems went to secure confirmation of a promised benefice. While there, he played against the city's leading chessplayers, and was not impressed. This, he recorded in the book on chess which he published on his return to Spain (it appeared in 1561). He was equally disparaging about Damiano's book, which he appears to have read on his visit; he ascribed the Italians' lack of knowledge of the game to their dependence on so feeble a book. But he was not uncomplimentary about a player with whom he had several games, '*que se hazia llamar el muchacho de Roma; y esto estando en Roma al principio del pontificado del papa Pio 4 en el anno de 1560*' (who was called the boy of Rome, this being at the beginning of the pontificate of Pope Pio 4 in the year 1560).

This 'boy' was almost certainly Leonardo da Cutri, known as Il Puttino (the small or the young), and who was to become, along with Paolo Boi, one of Italy's best players. The opening of one of the games he and Ruy Lopez played has come down to us:
White: Ruy Lopez. Black: Giovanni Leonardo. Damiano Gambit
  1. P-K4,P-K4; 2. Kt-KB3,P-KB3; 3. KtxP,PxKt;
  4. Q-R5 ch,P-KKt3; 5. QxKP ch,Q-K2; 6. QxR,Kt-B3;
  7. P-Q4,K-B2; 8. B-B4 ch,P-Q4; 9. BxP ch,KtxB;
and here the moves end with the note that Ruy Lopez won the game, as indeed he ought to have done. Presumably he now played 10. QxP ch,B-Kt2; 11. B-R6. Nowadays we would play 11. 0-0,

but it is far from sure that castling (in one move at any rate) was in vogue by then. We also know now (and the Spaniards, but not the Italians, knew then) that 3. .,Q-K2 is better than PxKt. It is interesting to observe that 6. .,Kt-B3 is an improvement on Damiano's own analysis, though still insufficient.

Another trophy that Ruy Lopez brought back with him to Spain was the use of the word 'gambit', which, as he explains in his book, was derived from a slang word used in the sport of wrestling. 'Gamba' means leg and *gambitare* meant to set traps (presumably by tripping someone with the leg); so a brilliant and trappy opening is a gambit.

The book, which he published in the spring of 1561, was quite a large one, as works of theory went in those early days, and in some respects, though not all, it was an improvement on its predecessors. The first line is exceedingly strange, with, on the whole, more bad moves than good. It runs as follows:

1. P-K4,P-K4; 2. P-QB3,Kt-KB3; 3. Q-B2,B-B4;
4. P-KB4,BxKt; 5. RxB,PxP; 6. P-Q3,Kt-R4;
7. Q-B2,P-KKt4; 8. B-K2,Kt-Kt2; 9. P-KKt3,PxP;
10. QxKtP,P-KR3; 11. P-KR4,P-KB3; 12. P-K5,Kt-K3;
13. B-R5 ch,

and, says Ruy Lopez, White has the better game. Commentary is useless but it may be said that out of White's thirteen moves, three are good and out of Black's twelve, two are good.

But he does give some good analysis on the King's Bishop's Opening, the Lopez Gambit, the King's Gambit, and, most important of all, the Ruy Lopez, which he recommends for White in contradistinction to Damiano.

I give two of his lines:

1. P-K4,P-K4; 2. Kt-KB3,Kt-QB3; 3. B-Kt5,B-B4;
4. P-B3,PQ3; 5. P-Q4,PxP; 6. PxP,B-Kt5 ch; 7. Kt-B3,B-Q2;
8. B-Kt5,Kt-B3; 9. Q-Q3,Q-K2; 10. Kt-Q2,BxKt;
11. PxB, with the better game.

And now a modern, interesting variant of this defence:

1. P-K4,P-K4; 2. Kt-KB3,Kt-QB3; 3. B-Kt5,B-B4;
4. P-B3,KKt-K2; 5. P-Q4,PxP; 6. PxP,B-Kt5 ch;
7. Kt-B3,P-Q4; 8. PxP,QxP; with a good game.

It is amusing to see that among the opening moves he regards so bad as to be unworthy of consideration by a player of merit, though often practised by the beginner, are: 1. Kt-KB3, 1. P-QB4, 1. P-KB4, and 1. P-QKt3. What would Nimzowitsch and Larsen have said to this?.

The book prospered, and so did its author. He had rivals in Spanish chess but the nearest, Aldonso Ceron of Granada, was not so good. King Philip, as I have said, became his patron, and he was generous. Among his gifts was a Rook on a golden chain which Ruy Lopez was wont to wear round his neck. Although he never became a Bishop (George Walker, no doubt jocosely, called him a chess Bishop, but Walker was known for his jokes), he was given a rich benefice by the king. He is supposed to have visited Rome successfully again in 1573, though possibly with increasing years the task of defeating the Italians was harder. Presumably it was during this second visit that the famous Italian chess patron, Giacomo Buoncompagno, the Duke of Sora, presented him with a stipend of 2,000 crowns a year.

But he was growing older and his Italian rivals were growing stronger. In 1575, Leonardo da Cutri, no longer 'el muchacho de Roma', came to Madrid, accompanied by Giulio Cesare Polerio and Tomaso Caputo. These played matches against Ruy Lopez and Ceron and won decisively. The games were played in the palace with Philip II as spectator. A French painting of the eighteenth century which depicts the scene shows Leonardo turning away from the board with an unpleasant smile on his face and uplifted hands, as if to say, 'It was only too easy'. No wonder he eventually died of poison, administered, according to tradition, by a jealous rival.

A fragment of a game from the match between Leonardo and Ruy Lopez exists, and I give it here. It is of interest as showing an intermediate stage in castling when the King had the right to make a leap of three squares but not to interchange with the Rook.

White: Leonardo. Black: Lopez. Philidor Defence (before Philidor!)

1. P-K4,P-K4; 2. Kt-KB3,P-Q3; 3. B-B4,P-KB4;
4. P-Q3,B-K2; 5. Q-K2,P-B3; 6. P-KR3,P-B5;
7. P-KKt3,PxP; 8. PxP,K-QB2 (by a leap); 9. Kt-B3,Kt-B3;
and now we have only White's 10th, 11th and 12th moves which were P-QKt4,P-Kt5, and K-KKt2 (by a leap) with advantage to White.

Under the leadership of Leonardo da Cutri and Paolo Boi, dominance in European chess passed to Italy. The future was indeed with the Italian school since they believed in the rapid development of their pieces to take the utmost advantage of the changes in the rules as regards the powers of the pieces.

I have already touched upon the careers of these two great Italian players. They were both professionals (Leonardo at first studied law in Rome, but soon gave that up in favour of chess); and they were both colourful characters to whom, according to the stories that have been handed down, much happened. It is also certain that much of what has been handed down did *not* happen. Therefore, since some of their biographical material is suspect, I shall in writing about them have to make use of the phrase, 'supposed to be', a little more than I would like.

It is known that both went on to Lisbon after their Madrid visit, and that before they left, King Philip gave them liberal rewards, including a gift to Boi of official appointments in Sicily worth 500 crowns a year. Their biographer, Carrera, who is somewhat untrustworthy, did at least preserve a letter dated 22 August, 1575 in Madrid, in which the king commended Boi to his brother, Don Juan of Austria. One interesting fact about their Madrid visit is that the Spanish to this day regard it as having been the occasion of the first international tournament in the game's history. In fact, they referred to an international tournament in the Canary Islands in 1975 as the '400th anniversary tournament' of chess. It is clear, however, that what took place in Madrid in 1575, although it was an international meeting, was essentially only a series of matches. Had it been a genuine tournament, the Spaniards would also have played against each other, and the Italians would have done likewise. Such an idea never occurred to anybody until the London Tournament of 1851 was planned.

Leonardo, who had been called the wandering knight *(il Cavaliero errante)* by King Sebastian of Portugal on his visit there, eventually, after some wandering, returned to Italy and settled in Naples, which

French rock-crystal set of the fifteenth century.

became a strong centre of chess. He was made agent to the Prince of Bisignano, and it was at the prince's palace that he was poisoned by a jealous rival in about 1587. As will soon become apparent, the Borgias seem to have set a fine example in Italy, which was followed by chessplayers, at any rate.

It is said (and this is very suppositious) that while Leonardo was in Naples, news came to him that pirates had captured his brother and offered to release him for the bargain-price ransom of 200 crowns. He went to the rescue, found that the pirate captain was a keen chessplayer and, by winning a match against him, not only rescued his brother, but also walked off with a large money-wager. This seems doubtful, especially in the light of the story I am about to tell about what happened to Paolo Boi on his travels. That pirates ran riot in the Mediterranean then is, of course, a fact, and hence Charles V of Spain went to so much trouble to conquer Tunis and to establish the massive fort that can still be seen there. In any case, Leonardo, who was born in 1542, must have been about 45 when he died.

Meanwhile, Paolo Boi was having his own adventures. He, it seems, *was* captured by pirates on returning from Spain, but somehow or other he freed himself through his prowess at chess. Whether he played the same pirate captain (a gullible pirate more easily swayed even than those of Penzance; or whether, as another account has it, he was sold to a chess-playing Turk as a slave and then won a large sum of money by beating his master at the game, or whether the Boi story is an imitation of the Leonardo (or vice versa), one cannot determine.

Boi certainly travelled a great deal, going from Genoa to Milan, then to Venice and even to Hungary, where he played chess against the Turks on horseback. Eventually, after some twenty years, he returned to Sicily where he had been born. There he wandered again, supporting himself by playing chess. In 1598 he was invited to go to Naples, which, as I have already said, had become the chess centre. But he had not been long there before he was discovered dead in his lodgings. He had been poisoned. Three days earlier he had played chess against Alessandro Salvio and made a beautiful combination five moves deep that won his youthful opponent's Queen. But Salvio had seen two moves deeper than Boi and won the latter's Queen and the game. Resigning, Boi said, 'Youth can more than age; you are in the prime of life and I am seventy years old.'

Both Leonardo and Boi were practising grandmasters, but they wrote nothing and published nothing about the game. With their passing, Italy lost two great players, but they had, alas, in comparison with the leading Spaniards, made no contributions to theory. Their place was, however, taken by some theorists who were to make Italy celebrated in this respect.

Giulio Cesare Polerio, who had accompanied them on their visit to Madrid, was a mere compiler. But in Salvio and Gioachino Greco, who were operative in the early seventeenth century, Italy had players who were also copious writers and analysts. Salvio built up a centre in Naples which he eventually called a chess academy. His *Trattato* in 1604 contains not only the Salvio Gambit (or the King's Gambit), but also what was subsequently known as the Muzio Gambit, and both are analysed in a much superior way to that of his

An ivory chess piece—the King— from the Bargello, Florence.

'Chess players', painted by the Venetian Ludovici Caracci, in about 1590.

predecessors.

Even more important, in that he was also a very fine masterplayer, was Greco (1600–1634), who managed to pack a great deal both of playing and writing into his comparatively short life. Born in Celico in Calabria, and hence known as *Il Calabrese,* he came from a poor family and had little or no education. His manuscripts, of which he produced a large number, were, as a result, written in poor Italian. It was, in fact, outside Italy that he made his great reputation. At the age of twenty-one, he was in France, where he won 5,000 crowns playing at the court of the Duke of Lorraine. This he promptly lost to thieves on a journey to London, but he rehabilitated his fortunes by playing and beating all the best English masters. He returned to France in 1624, won more money there and then went to Spain where he was triumphant at the court of Philip IV. A Spanish nobleman took him to the West Indies where he died, leaving his fortune to the Jesuits.

His manuscripts were eventually published in one volume in Paris in 1669. The content is not so much analyses as a collection of brilliant games giving the essence of the Italian school's way of thought on the rapid use of the pieces. Although he popularized the Greco Counter-Gambit, he had a predecessor in this respect in Polario. His book, which has been published and republished down the ages (I own a copy that was published as late as 1900) is still entertaining.

With the passing of Greco, the last great Italian player disappeared and the last remote influences of the Renaissance were spent. Other countries, France in particular, and later England and Germany, were becoming important in the history of the game.

chapter *9*

The eighteenth century
the age of the savants

In the early half of the eighteenth century, the leading place in chess shifts from Italy to France, and then, in the latter half, to England. But it is not only a shift in place, it is also a movement from one class of society to another. A growing middle class begins to take over from the upper classes. Civilization—culture, the sciences and the arts—is no longer the privilege and domain of the court. While the courtier had earlier been held to be the carrier and the shield of the light of civilization, he now becomes almost a figure of fun to those who really carry on the light. We all know what Dr Johnson said about the letters of the Earl of Chesterfield to his son ('This man I thought had been a Lord among wits but, I find, he is only a wit among Lords!'). The contempt he was free to express in the eighteenth century would have been almost lèse-majesté in Elizabethan times.

Naturally, this process also involved a change of class in those who played chess, and just as naturally, it did not take place overnight. The seeds had been planted much earlier and the process was gradual. In England, for example, one can already see the signs as early as the seventeenth century in Stuart times; Francis Bacon, who for all his peerage was a genuine savant and scientist, was also a chessplayer who derived many a philosophic lesson from the game. Hence he wrote in his essay, *Of Boldness,* 'With bold men, upon like occasion, they stand at a stay, like a stake at chess, where it is no mate, but yet the game cannot stir.' And in his *Apologie,* he said, 'I know at chesse a Pawn before the King is ever much plaid upon.'

Oddly enough, James I of England, the wisest fool in Christendom, supports my theory in a negative way when he attacks chess:

> 'As for the Chesse, I think it over fond, because it is over wise and Philosophicke a folly: for where all such light playes are ordained to free mens heades for a time, from the fashious thoughts on their affaires; it by the contrarie filleth and troubleth mens heades, with as many fashious toyes of the play, as before it was filled with thoughts on his affaires.'

This is as much as to say that chess is not for the noble statesman or the wise politician, but for the scientist (which is what he implied in the word 'Philosophicke').

Another strange echo of this idea, but one put with a pleasing wit and an absence of the quality of putting his foot in it which characterized King James, is to be found in *Certain Personal Matters* by H. G. Wells some 280 years later:

> The passion for playing chess is one of the most unaccountable in the world. It slaps the theory of natural selection in the face. It is the most absorbing of occupations, the least satisfying of desires, an aimless excrescence upon life. It annihilates a man. You have, let us say, a promising politician, a rising artist, that you wish to destroy. Dagger or bomb are archaic, clumsy and unreliable—but teach him, inoculate him with chess.
>
> It is well, perhaps, that the right way of teaching chess is so little known, that consequently in most cases the plot fails in the performance, the dagger turns aside. Else we should all be chessplayers—there would be none left to do the business of the world. Our statesmen would sit with pocket boards while the country went to the devil.

To revert to the main path of my theme: By the beginning of the eighteenth century, both in France and in England, the time was ripe for the takeover of chess by scientists and men of literature. That the first flowering occurred in France rather than in England is due to the accident of genius. François André Philidor arose in France, but to tell the truth, his writings and methods of play had even greater influence in England than in his home country. In both London and Paris, the 'democratization' of the game was helped on its way by a comparatively small social development—the increase of coffeehouses and cafés. Before people in any number can play chess, they must have a suitable venue, and these gathering-places (many of them famous) provided this. In Paris the most celebrated place where men met to play chess, was the Café de la Régence. Here all

Interest aroused by a game in the Café de la Régence, the famous Parisian resort for chessplayers in the eighteenth century; an engraving after a sketch by Boilly.

the best French players were wont to assemble, as Denis Diderot recorded in the eighteenth century, in his novel *Le Neveu de Rameau*:

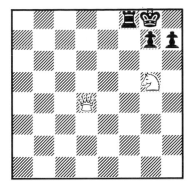

24: *The basic position of the smothered mate, or Philidor's legacy.*

If the weather is too cold or wet, I take shelter in the Café de la Régence. There I have my fun watching people playing at chess. Paris is the place in the world and the Café de la Régence the place in Paris where the game is best played; it is here that the profound Legal, subtle Philidor and the sound Mayot give battle to one another; there the most surprising moves can be seen, and the worst conversation can be heard: for, if one can be a wit and a great chessplayer like Legal, one can as well be a great chessplayer and a fool like Foubert and Mayot.

One of the queerest fellows in this country, where God did not make them scarce, accosted me, 'Hello! There you are Mr Philosopher; and what are you doing here among this set of lazybones? Are you also losing your fame in wood shifting?'
I: 'No, but when I have nothing better to do I have my fun in looking for one moment at the people who shift it well.'
He: 'In that case it will be but seldom; except for Legal and Philidor, the rest do not understand anything about it.'
I: 'And Mr de Bissy, then?'
He: 'As for him, he is as good a chessplayer as M'lle Clairon is an actress; both of them know all there is to know about their play.'

Legal was M. de Kermur, Sire de Légal, Philidor's teacher and the best player in France until the coming of Philidor. He spanned the entire century, living from 1702 to 1792. When he first met Philidor, who was then very young, he could give him the odds of a Rook, but by 1743, when Philidor was seventeen, he could not afford to give him any odds at all; in 1705 he was decisively beaten by him in a match. Legal seems to have been an excellent combative player, and it was from him that Philidor learned the smothered mate, which is called Philidor's Legacy, although, indeed, it was known long before the eighteenth century. The basic position is as illustrated here (Diagram 24).

White forces smothered mate by 1. Q-B4 ch, K-R1; 2. Kt-B7 ch,K-Kt1; 3. Kt-R6 db.ch,K-R1; 4. Q-Kt8 ch,RxQ; 5. Kt-B7 mate.

Another type of mate, called after Legal, is shown in Diagram 25: Légal's mate runs as follows: 1. KtxP,BxQ; 2. BxP ch,K-K2; 3. Kt-Q5 mate. This is also sometimes known as the Blackburne trap after the famous English grandmaster of the nineteenth century who caught many a simultaneous opponent with it.

Diderot was only one of a number of famous French eighteenth-century writers who were passionately interested in the game. Two others were Voltaire and Rousseau. Voltaire played chess with Frederick the Great and was also a frequenter of the Café de la Régence as, at various times, were Benjamin Franklin, Jakob Grimm (author of Grimm's law and one of the fairy-tale writing brothers), Robespierre and Bonaparte. Voltaire thought chess to be the game which reflected the most honour on human wit, a point he made in 1750, when he wrote the *Philosophy of History*:

The Greeks, before the time of Pythagoras, travelled into India

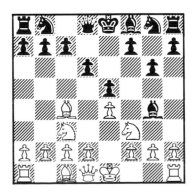

25: *Legal's mate.*

for instruction. The signs of the seven planets, &c, are still almost all over the earth, such as the Indians invented: the Arabians were obliged to adopt their arithmetical characters. Those games which do greatest honour to the human mind, incontestably come from India; as elephants, for which we have substituted towers, in the game of chess, evince. In fine, the people who were the earliest known, the Persians, Phoenicians, Arabians, Egyptians, went from time immemorial to traffic in India, in order to bring home spices, which nature has given to those climates alone; but the Indians never went to ask anything from other nations.

Jean Jacques Rousseau aspired at one time to become a great chessplayer, but his ardour was cooled, as he narrates in his *Confessions,* in the following way:

At Chambéry there was a Genevese named M. Bagueret, who had been employed by Peter the Great at the Russian court; he was one of the greatest rascals and greatest fools that I have ever seen, always full of schemes as mad as himself, who flung millions about like rain and thought nothing of an extra cipher. This man, who had come to Chambéry on account of some law-suit before the Senate, got hold of mamma, as was only to be expected, and in return for the ciphers which he generously lavished upon her, drew her few crowns, one by one out of her purse. I disliked him; he saw it, never a difficult matter in my case—and left no kind of meanness untried, in order to gain my favour. He took it into his head to propose to teach me chess, which he himself played a little. I tried it, almost against my inclination; and, after I had learned the moves indifferently, I made such rapid progress that, before the end of the first sitting, I was able to give him the Rook which at first he had given me. That was enough; I made for chess from that moment. I bought a chess-board and a 'Calabrois' (book by Greco); I shut myself up in my room, and spent days and nights in trying to learn all the openings by heart, in stuffing them into my head by force, and in playing by myself without rest or relaxation. After two or three months of this praiseworthy occupation and these incredible efforts, I went to the cafe, thin, sallow and almost stupid. I tried my hand, I played again with M. Bagueret; he beat me once, twice, twenty times; all the different combinations had become mixed up in my head, and my imagination was so enfeebled, that I saw nothing but a cloud before my eyes. Whenever I wished, with the help of Philidor and Stamma, to practise myself in studying different games, the same thing happened to me; and after exhausting myself with fatigue, I found myself weaker than before. For the rest, whether I gave up chess for a time, or endeavoured to improve myself by constant practice, I never made the slightest progress after the first sitting, and always found myself just where I was when it was over. I might practise for thousands of generations and not be able to do more than give Bagueret the Rook, and nothing else. 'Time well employed!' you will say; and I employed not a little of it this way. I did not finish the first attempt, until I no longer had strength to continue it. When I left my room, I looked like a corpse, and, if I had continued to live in the same manner, I should certainly not have remained long above ground. It will be admitted that it is too difficult, especially in the ardour of youth, for such a disposition to allow the body to enjoy continued good health.

Rousseau, despite this confession of failure (he exaggerated both failures and successes in his *Confessions,* to make them more interesting), remained attached to chess throughout his life. He was apparently a tolerable player—better than Voltaire, for example. All the encyclopédistes (that extraordinary mixture of savants and men of literature who made France predominant in the arts in the eighteenth century) seem to have played chess with varying degrees of skill.

The Stamma, to whom Rousseau refers, was Philip Stamma, of Aleppo in Syria, who had arrived out of the blue in Paris. We know that he came from Aleppo, since he says so himself in his book, *Essai sur le Jeu des Echecs,* which was published in Paris in 1737. But we do not know where and when he was born or when and where he died. The explanation for this mystery is probably that he was born poor and died in poverty. Certainly, for most of his known life he was in what is known delicately as distressed circumstances. In his dedication to the 1737 book he appeals to Lord Harrington, '*Dans la situation où la fortune m'a réduit, la compassion Vous parlera de moi.*' (In the situation to which fortune has reduced me, compassion will speak to you on my behalf.)

Fortune must temporarily have turned its wheel in his favour when he quitted France for England, as someone, possibly Lord Harrington, got him a job as an interpreter of Oriental languages for the government. In 1745, in London, he published a revised and expanded version of his 1737 book, under the title, *The Noble Game of Chess.* Two years later he was disastrously defeated by Philidor in a match of ten games, in which Philidor gave him the considerable odds that a drawn game should count as a win for Stamma. On these conditions, he won only two games, one of which was drawn.

Stamma was not in Philidor's class as a player, but he left his mark on the game's history in his writings, chiefly and curiously, however, by returning to a tradition almost 1,000 years old. The Paris edition of his book consisted entirely of 100 end-games or problems in the old Moslem style. To the work in London he added a large section analysing openings. This included a passage in which he strongly recommended the Queen's Gambit and showed how fatal it was for Black to try to hold on to the Gambit Pawn. Apart from this, his analysis is of no great importance. But what is most interesting and vitally important is that his analysis was not in the descriptive, but in the algebraic notation, presumably as a result of his Arabic upbringing. This reintroduction of the algebraic failed utterly in France, England and Italy, and although most countries have now taken up the algebraic (English-speaking countries and Spain have not) the algebraic then appealed only to German-speaking countries.

Before I come to discuss Philidor and his influence on chess in the eighteenth century, I should mention that Italian interest in the game did not die out with the eclipse of their pre-eminence in chess in Europe. But the Italian centre of play and analysis shifted from Rome and Naples to Modena, where there were three gifted players, Ercole del Rio, Giambatista Lolli and Domenico Ponziani. Ercole del Rio was the first of the three to publish an important work, *Sopra il giuoco degli Scacchi, Osservazioni pratiche d'anonimo Autore*

Modenese (On the game of Chess, practical Observations by an anonymous Modenese Author.) It appeared in 1750, and was significant in that it gave for the first time the Scotch Game: 1. P-K4,P-K4; 2. Kt-KB3,Kt-QB3; 3. P-Q4 and the 3. .,P-QR3 defence to the Ruy Lopez.

In 1763 Lolli published an exhaustive compendium, *Giuoco Di Scacchi* (The Game of Chess), in which he dealt with everything that was known at the time about opening and end-game theory. I have a copy of the first edition and this is a truly magnificent production. On the fly-leaf it states that it is *Osservazioni Teorico-Pratiche sopra il giuoco degli scacchi ossia il giuoco degli scacchi esposito nel suo miglior lume da Giambatista Lolli modenese, Opera Novissima.* (Observations Theoretical-Practical on the game of chess or the game of chess shown in its best light by Giambatista Lolli Modenese, latest work.) All this is contained in 631 large pages with the luxury of a final page of errata.

Finally, in 1769, Ponziani, who was a Professor of Civil Law at the University of Modena, published his *Il giuoco incomparabile degli scacchi* (The incomparable game of chess); he produced a revised and improved version in 1782. Ponziani deals with more openings than Lolli and includes the Allgaier variation of the King's Gambit. It is amusing to see that his contribution to what we now call the Ponziani Opening (1. P-K4,P-K4; 2. Kt-KB3,Kt-QB3; 3. P-B3), was in fact a defence: 3. .,P-B4.

In general, the contributions of the Modena school to European opening theory were greatly handicapped by the fact that the Italians practised a different type of castling (known as free castling) from the rest of Europe. But they also suffered from a fundamental lack of comprehension of what, in fact, Philidor understood better than anyone in his time or for many years afterwards. They totally ignored the importance of a strong pawn centre and, although they realized the need for a speedy development of the pieces, they failed to observe that it was the centre which affected the use of such development.

So, although the theorists of Modena were undoubtedly gifted, they were outside the main stream of European chess; nor do they seem to have made any attempt to join the main course—a great pity, as it would have been extremely interesting to have seen the results of matches between Ercole del Rio or Ponziani and Philidor.

Philidor remained the acknowledged master of chess in the eighteenth century. Again, it must be stressed that the very idea of the world championship had not yet been conceived. That had to wait for the fertile brain of the first (even if self-acknowledged) world champion, Wilhelm Steinitz. Had such a title been in existence, however, Philidor would undoubtedly have been its holder from about 1747 to his death, a span of nearly fifty years.

François André Danican Philidor was born near Paris in 1726. He was already a fine player at the age of fourteen, the first of a famous band of boy prodigies which was eventually to include such names as Reshevsky, Capablanca and Bobby Fischer. But he was exceptional in his precocity in that he also had a great gift for musical composition. By eleven, he had had a motet of his own composition performed at the Chapel Royal in Versailles, where he was a choir boy. He came from a long line of musicians who had been attached to the Palais Royal in one capacity or another. The family name had, in fact, been Danican, and the first to append Philidor was an hautboy player whose performances had been praised by Louis XIII. The king had compared him with a man called Filidori, a predecessor of Danican's in the orchestra's wood-wind section.

Our Philidor, too, had been destined both by birth and by nature to be a musician, and he became a famous one. His musical powers, however, are no concern of this work, except in so far as they impinged upon and affected his chess career. But they must be considered, even if briefly, since they did indeed influence the course of events. He was the greatest of chessmasters among composers, just as he was the greatest of composers among chessmasters. At one time he was acknowledged to be the leading operatic composer in France, but his work did not look forward enough, and he was displaced by André Grétry, who became known as 'the Molière of music'. I have listened to some of Philidor's music and found it pleasant, melodious and competent. But it lacks the stamp of originality which characterizes great composing.

He himself always regarded musical composition as his genuine profession, and there exists an announcement in a newspaper in which he declared that this, and not playing chess, was his true work. But, as his operas began to be outmoded, he turned more and more to chess for a livelihood. We have seen how he defeated Stamma overwhelmingly, even after giving the weaker player the peculiar odds of having a draw count as a win.

He spent a great deal of his chess career in London, where this match took place, for although his fame was wide in France, it was in England that he could earn the most from playing the game. He was, in fact, in London during the French Revolution, on the proscribed list of emigrés, and was unable to return because someone had informed against him. He died in the English capital on 31 August, 1795, and was buried in St James's, Piccadilly. More than

An engraved portrait of Philidor.

The acknowledged master of eighteenth-century chess— Philidor playing blindfold at Parsloe's in London in the presence of the Turkish Ambassador on 23 February 1784.

130 years later, when it was reported that his grave and tombstone were hardly distinguishable, a fresh headstone with a suitable inscription was erected.

We have, alas, little evidence of his real worth as a player. It was the pernicious practice at the time for the best players to give odds to weaker ones, no doubt as an inducement to them to play for wagers. The games that have survived then are almost entirely of this character and consequently lack that harmonious and purposeful flow of strategy which one might have expected from Philidor. It is, on the other hand, certain that where he excelled was in his understanding of the game. A contemporary, discussing leading players, spoke of the 'enterprise and spirit of Cunningham (Alexander Cunningham, a fine Scots player who established himself at the Hague), the brilliant promptness at resource of Salvio and the comprehension and foresight of Philidor.'

One gift he had which astonished and delighted the world was the art of blindfold play. This apparently had not been done before, in Europe at any rate, and Parisians marvelled when in 1744, at the age of eighteen, he played two opponents simultaneously while he himself was blindfold. He was to do this regularly throughout his life, and a letter exists from Diderot, written in 1782, in which he advises him to desist from such dangerous pursuits:

> I should more readily excuse you for these dangerous experiments if you had wagered enough to win five or six hundred guineas. But to risk your talent and your reason for nothing is simply inconceivable. Besides, I have talked about this to M. Legal, and this is his answer: 'When I was young, I decided to play a single game of chess without seeing the board, and at the end of that game I found myself so fatigued mentally that it was the first and last time of my life. It is foolish to run the risk of going mad for vanity's sake.' Now, when you shall have lost your ability, will the English come forward to rescue your family? Do not believe, Sir, that what has not yet happened to you will not happen. Take my advice, write more fine music for us, write it for many years yet, and do not expose yourself further to the possibility of being an object of scorn, a state in which so many are born. At most they will say of you, 'There is that Philidor creature, he is nothing any more, he lost all the sense he had by pushing little pieces of wood across a chessboard.'

Philidor ignored this advice, probably through the necessity of earning a living, and lived for thirteen years more. During this last period, he wrote the final version of his *Analyze du Jeu des Echecs* (Analysis of Chess), which was first published in Paris in 1749, when he was only twenty-three. It is amazing that one so young should have produced the first genuine book of instruction which gave a reasoned and lucid explanation of the modern game. In his writing, as well as in his play, he showed that tremendous capacity for comprehension to which I have already referred. His plan was to show the reader how the game appeared to a master and by what means the master achieved his ends. He had indeed, by twenty-three or even earlier, already worked out for himself his theory of the use of pawns, as exemplified in his famous epigram, 'Pawns are the soul of chess.' Consider this passage from his preface to the first edition:

My chief intention is to recommend myself to the Public, by a novelty no one has thought of, or perhaps ever understood well; I mean how to play the pawns: they are the very life of this game. They alone form the Attack and the Defence; on their good or bad situation) depends the gain or loss of the game. A player who, when he has played a pawn well, can give no reason for his moving it to such a square, may be compared to a General, who with much practice has little or no theory.

Many and various perceptive observations throughout the analysis support and underline his theory of pawn-play. For example, this on pawn captures:

When you have two bodies of pawns, and an opportunity of transferring a pawn from one body to another, the pawn should pass to the larger division, to concentrate them.

Unlike the Modenese theorists, he lays continual emphasis on the value of the centre:

None of the attacks of the adversary are dangerous because they do not break your centre.

This is a notion which present-day players can also bear in mind.

And then there is his comment on exchanging towards the centre rather than away from it:

It is policy to decline changing your king's pawn for the adverse king's bishop's, or your queen's pawn for the queen's bishop's; on account of the greater utility of the royal pawns (the Q and KPs) occupying the centre, they preclude the adversary from the most advantageous posts.

This is pretty obvious to us nowadays, but it was Philidor who first formulated the idea in all its clarity.

His openings analysis is superior to that of his predecessors and he makes an interesting remark about the King's Gambit—that he thinks it should lead to a draw, an extremely iconoclastic way of looking at things in those days. It was eventually to be supported by Spielmann—about 180 years later! The book is also much richer in genuine end-game analysis than were its predecessors. In the first edition we find the celebrated analysis of the ending of Rook and Bishop against Rook. But we get much more about the endings in the later editions. There is the mate with Bishop and Knight; a study of the Rook and pawn versus Bishop, showing when it is a win and when it is drawn; an analysis of the Queen versus Rook and pawn, and of the Queen versus Rook endings; sections on Rook and pawn against Rook, Queen and pawn against Queen and—a famous analysis this—Queen against the advanced passed pawn on the seventh rank. The last section deals with Knight against Pawn, two pawns against one pawn and two isolated pawns versus two united pawns.

No one had written in this style before, and the pattern was definitively set for all books of instruction on the game. Probably Philidor's fame, in its lasting quality at any rate, derives chiefly from his *Analysis of Chess*. Other great players later on were content to (and able to) allow their games to speak for themselves. It seems, however, that it was not the practice in Philidor's day to record one's moves. What would one not give for the games of the match Philidor–Stamma? But Philidor's reputation, resting securely on the basis of what was really one single work, was something to conjure with as late as the 1860s, as evidenced by a remark made in one of Anthony Trollope's novels about an unfortunate and oppressed cleric, who had to deal with the strong-willed Mrs Proudie: 'What could he do against Mrs Proudie—it was like Philidor against a board player.'

The eighteenth century was a great age for chess-sets of a ceremonial and resplendent type. Until then, with rare exceptions, they had been workmanlike rather than decorative. Consider James Rowbothum's description, 1562, of an English set in his translation of Damiano, in which he compares home with foreign manufacture:

> Our Englishe Cheastmen are commonly made nothing like unto these foresayde fashions: to wit, the King is made the highest or longest; the Queene is longest nexte unto him: the Bishoppe is made with a sharpe toppe and cloven in the middest not muche unlyke to a bishops Myter: the knight has his top cut asloope, as thoughe beynge dubbed knight: the Rooke is made lykest to the Kinge, and the Queene, but that he is not so long: the Paunes be made smalest & least of all, & thereby they may best be knowen.

The sets must have been very humdrum, and this is perhaps a good explanation as to why so little has come down to us from this period. Nor was the English school at all imaginative until the nineteenth century, except for some beautiful ceramic chess-pieces, made by Wedgwood and Rockingham.

But it was a different story with the French in the eighteenth century. Using African ivory and bone in particular, they produced some sets which were charming in their neatness and others which were superbly striking. Especially notable in this respect was a school of craftsmen who worked in Dieppe and specialized in sets made of bone. The eighteenth century too saw the import from the East—from China and from India—of many beautiful sets, mostly made expressly for the European market. They are distinguished for the intricacy of their workmanship; the normal colouring is white (or rather cream) and red.

It was also in this century that von Kempelen's Automaton appeared. This was the life-sized figure of what was supposed to be a Turk, seated at a chess-board. He took on all comers and usually beat them. Looked at from the outside—and even if some of the internal machinery was inspected—it seemed to be entirely automatic, and it performed its movements in a jerky, mechanical fashion. In reality there was sufficient room for a small man to hide inside and set the works in motion. The operation of moving the pieces was apparently effected by magnetism. The machine was first shown at Vienna in 1770 and it visited many other cities, including Dresden, Leipzig, Paris and London.

The Turk outlived, if that is the right word, its inventor and on his death it was sold to Maelzel, who took it to the palace of Schön-

A beautiful ceramic chess board and pieces made at Meissen in the mid-eighteenth century. One side of the board has a green lattice design, the other is chequered in purple. In addition, both have a design in gold.

brunn outside Vienna in 1809, where it met and defeated no less a person than Napoleon Bonaparte. Hidden inside at that time was the German master, Johann Allgaier. A number of famous masters inhabited the figure after him, among them William Lewis of England and the Frenchman, Jean-François Mouret, who was practically a dwarf. Some games with the Automaton, purporting to stem from 1820, are to be found in George Walker's *Chess Studies*, which was published in 1844. In my copy there are fifty such games in all of which Mouret gives the odds of pawn and a move and is triumphant even against a player as strong as John Cochrane. But the games are of poor quality and no doubt the players were over-impressed by their mechanical foe.

The Automaton Chess Player, invented in 1769 by Wolfgang von Kempelen. The works were actually operated by a small man hiding inside.

chapter **10**

The early nineteenth century
France, England and Germany

With the nineteenth century the middle classes really began to take a hand. The Industrial Revolution was well under way, and the wider dispersal of powers and profit which accompanied it meant also a wider dispersal of leisure time for such gentlemanly pastimes as chess. Once again the game's progress and its popularization go hand in hand with the social progress. The signs were of course already there in the later part of the eighteenth century. Benjamin Franklin, in Paris to represent the United States (a country which was eventually to produce a player, Paul Morphy, whom many rank as the greatest player in the game's history) pointed the way in his piece on the *Morals of Chess*. He wrote it in 1779, but, remarkably, it reads as though it were written in Victorian England:

> Playing at chess is the most ancient and most universal game known among men; for its original is beyond the memory of history, and it has, for numberless ages, been the amusement of all the civilized nations of Asia, the Persians, the Indians, and the Chinese. Europe has had it above a thousand years; the Spaniards have spread it over their part of America, and it begins lately to make its appearance in these states. It is so interesting in itself, as not to need the view of gain to induce engaging in it, and thence it is never played for money. Those, therefore, who have leisure for such diversions, cannot find one that is more innocent; and the following piece, written with a view to correct (among a few young friends) some little improprieties in the practice of it, shows, at the same time, that it may, in its effects on the mind, be not merely innocent, but advantageous to the vanquished as well as the victor.
>
> The Game of Chess is not merely an idle amusement; several very valuable qualities of the mind, useful in the course of human life, are to be acquired and strengthened by it, so as to become habits ready on all occasions; for life is a kind of Chess, in which we have points to gain, and competitors or adversaries to content with, and in which there is a vast variety of good and ill events, that are, in some degree, the effects of prudence, or the want of it. By playing at chess then we may learn: 1st Foresight . . . 2nd Circumspection . . . 3rd Caution.

Note the reference to leisure—if ever there was a sign of the shape of things to come! He goes on to give rules as to how to behave over the board, which, while perfectly in order for a well-conducted world, are, alas, too near the ideal ever to be followed in real life.

By the turn of the century, France was still the leading chess country, but there were signs that other countries, notably England and Germany, were pulling up fast. However, Philidor's influence and his successes against foreign opposition were too recent for the French as yet to abandon their hold on the leadership. Their first great player following Philidor was an extraordinary man, Alexandre Louis Honoré Lebreton Deschapelles (1780–1847), who was brilliant in many spheres—as accomplished, for example, in the art of lying as he was in whist, at which he was reputed to make between 30,000 and 40,000 francs a year. As evidence of his brilliance at whist there is still the Deschapelles coup; and as for lies—he claimed to have learned chess and reached the peak of his powers all within the space of two days! How great a player he was is very difficult to say, since he was so confident of his superiority that he insisted on playing everyone at odds. When in 1821, however, he felt himself unable to give his pupil, Louis Charles Mahé De la Bourdonnais, the odds of pawn and two moves, he promptly retired from chess and concentrated on whist.

Cruikshank's depiction of a game of chess in 1835.

Pub.^d by Thos McLean, 26 Haymarket. Augt 1.st 1835.   G Cruik.^s

GAME of CHESS.

*Chess-players depicted by
van Leyden, 1494–1533.*

His successor as France's leading player was De la Bourdonnais,
who was involved in a famous series of matches with the Irishman,
Alexander McDonnell, in 1834. How many games they played is a
matter of doubt, but the figure of eighty-five is usually mentioned.
The series aroused great enthusiasm on both sides of the Channel,
for McDonnell was regarded as the best British player and De la
Bourdonnais was certainly the best French. De la Bourdonnais won
the match by forty-four wins, twenty-eight losses and thirteen
draws, and a French poet, F. J. P. A. Méry, used the thirty-ninth
game his compatriot won as the subject for a poem entitled *Une
revanche de Waterloo.*

The brilliance of the games was lauded in both countries, and they
have had a good press ever since. How many of those who have so
highly praised them, however, have in fact played through all the
games is a matter for speculation, especially if you've done so yourself. I did this some years ago with the notion of analysing them and
presenting them as a study of the methods of the best players of the
early nineteenth century, and I was appalled by the low quality of the
play in general. True, there were flashes of brilliance, usually on the
loser's side. But the standard of technique, in particular that con-
nected with the endings, was very low. Poor McDonnell even came
down to an ending with Rook and two pawns against Rook, which
he obviously had not the faintest idea how to win. He wandered on
in a fog until he himself contrived to lose his Rook—and the game—
through a gross blunder. De la Bourdonnais was not quite so bad in
the endings as McDonnell, but he had little idea as to how the openings should be played. The worst facet of the games to me, however,
was the lack of any reasoned, cohesive strategy. Decriers of present-
day chess, with its tendencies towards many draws, have pointed out
how few draws there were in this match. But the answer to that is
simply that both men, McDonnell in particular, played the defence
so inaccurately that many draws just fell by the wayside.

The most brilliant game of the match is the famous fiftieth, in
which there are indeed some nice moves by McDonnell. But even
here White missed a very good chance of drawing on his fiftieth
move. There has been some controversy on this point, Saint Amant
thinking that the return of the Queen would have given equality,
and Sir George Thomas (1881–1972, British Champion 1923 and
1934) believing that Black would still have had a clear advantage.
On consideration, I have to agree with Saint Amant. Here is the
game in question:

White: De la Bourdonnais. Black: McDonnell. Queen's Gambit
Accepted.

1. P-Q4,P-Q4; 2. P-QB4,PxP; 3. P-K4,P-K4; 4. P-Q5,P-KB4;
5. Kt-QB3,Kt-KB3; 6. BxP,B-B4; 7. Kt-B3,Q-K2;
8. B-KKt5,BxP ch; 9. K-B1,B-Kt3; 10. Q-K2,P-B5;
11. R-Q1,B-Kt5; 12. P-Q6,PxP; 13. Kt-Q5,KtxKt;
14. BxQ,Kt-K6 ch; 15. K-K1,KxB; 16. Q-Q3,R-Q1;
17. R-Q2,Kt-B3; 18. P-QKt3,B-QR4; 19. P-QR3,QR-B1;
20. R-Kt1,P-QKt4; 21. BxP,BxKt; 22. PxB,Kt-Q5;
23. B-B4,KtxBP ch; 24. K-B2,KtxQR; 25. RxP ch,K-B3;
26. R-B7 ch,K-Kt3; 27.R-QKt7,Kt(Q7)xB; 28. PxKt,RxP;
29. Q-Kt1,B-Kt3; 30. K-B3,R-B6; 31. Q-R2,Kt-B5 ch;
32. K-Kt4,R-KKt1; 33. RxB,PxR; 34. K-R4,K-B3;
35. Q-K2,R-Kt3; 36. Q-R5,Kt-K6 and wins (Diagram 26).

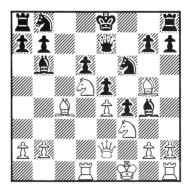

*26: Position after White's 13th
move.*

*Chess set by Christoph Augermair,
early seventeenth century.
Pomeranian work in ebony, silver
and ivory.*

Neither player survived the match long. It had been intended to resume play as soon as De la Bourdonnais could return to England, but McDonnell fell ill with Bright's Disease and died in 1835 at the early age of thirty-seven. De la Bourdonnais too fell ill—with dropsy—and he could earn nothing, since he was unable to get to the Café de la Régence to play his opponents for money. He was on the brink of starvation when he was invited to London to act as the professional in a new and popular salon of chess, The Divan. This he accepted, at a salary of two guineas a week, in those days a handsome income. But he too died in 1840, before he could play a single game. He was buried in Kensal Green Cemetery; it is a curious coincidence that the graves of France's two best players, Philidor and De la Bourdonnais, are both in London.

The rivalry between France and England continued, but, as we shall see, it was turning in England's favour. Meanwhile, however, Germany was coming to the fore. Berlin, as was only to be expected, was the centre of the upsurge in chess there. And at the centre of the centre were the so-called Pleiades, or seven stars of Berlin chess. The seven contained some players who were to become celebrated, as well as some chess-writers and end-game and opening theorists. Perhaps the most important were Paul Rudolph von Bilguer and Baron Tassilo von Heydebrand und der Lasa, who was usually known simply as von der Lasa. Bernhard Horwitz too later became well known as an endings expert and composed many fine studies in collaboration with Joseph Kling. Bilguer was responsible for the great *Handbuch,* a triumph of German method and research. He did not live to finish it, but von der Lasa took over and published it in 1843. It had a life of 100 years and is still consulted for some variations that have been forgotten or mislaid.

A little later than the Pleiades, three players emerged who were to make German chess the strongest in Europe: Max Lange, to whom we owe a celebrated version of the Two Knights' Defence; D. Harrwitz, who was to give Morphy more trouble than any other opponent during that genius's visit to Europe, and above all, the great Adolf Anderssen, a genius of combination and one of the finest 'chess gentlemen' who ever lived.

During the 1840s, however, the leading chess cities in Europe remained Paris and London. In Paris a new and very strong player appeared, Pierre Charles Fournié de Saint Amant (1800–1872). He had been a pupil of Deschapelles and played De la Bourdonnais at the Café de la Régence; but he does not seem to have started genuine competitive play until he went into the wholesale wine trade, in 1823. He visited England in 1836, shortly after the death of McDonnell, and he encountered little real opposition, meeting and beating players who were by no means the best in England (James Cunningham Fraser, George Perigal, W. W. Popert and George Walker). But on a later visit he faced formidable competition when he played Howard Staunton, against whom he won three games, lost two and drew one. The nature of this contest created some controversy. Saint Amant claimed that it was a match, but Staunton, to whom argument was the very breath of life, stated in no uncertain terms that what they had played was merely a set of off-hand games. The matter was settled by a formal match of twenty-one games played for a stake of £100 a side in Paris in 1843. This time Staunton had a convincing victory—eleven wins, six losses and four

*Howard Staunton, the first
English player to be regarded as
Europe's best.*

draws. Now at last an English player was the first in Europe, and for the first time so far, England had a player who was regarded as the world's best. Had that non-existent title been invented then, he would have been called world champion.

An examination of the games shows them to be of much superior quality to those of the De la Bourdonnais-McDonnell match. Blunders were much rarer and there was no shortage of strategic conceptions. Murray has rightly said that the games were regarded as classical specimens of play, and it is also interesting to observe how much better the openings were handled than in the De la Bourdonnais–McDonnell encounter.

I give the fourth game of the match as a good example:
White: Staunton. Black: Saint Amant. Queen's Pawn, Benoni Defence.

1. P-Q4,P-QB4; 2. P-Q5,P-B4; 3. Kt-QB3,P-Q3; 4. P-K4,PxP;
5. KtxP,P-K4; 6. B-Kt5,Q-R4 ch; 7. P-B3,B-B4;
8. Kt-Kt3,B-Kt3; 9. B-Q3,BxB; 10. QxB,P-KKt3;
11. KKt-K2,B-K2; 12. Kt-K4,Q-Kt3; 13. 0-0,Kt-Q2;
14. BxB,KtxB; 15. Kt-Kt5,P-KR3; 16. Kt-K6,Kt-KB1;
17. KtxKt,RxKt; 18. P-QKt4,PxP; 19. PxP,K-B2;
20. K-R1,K-Kt2; 21. P-KB4,QR-Q1; 22. QR-Q1,P-KR4;
23. Q-QB3,Q-Kt4; 24. Q-Q2,R-B4; 25. Kt-Kt3,R-B3;
26. PxP,RxR ch; 27. RxR,PxP; 28. Q-Kt5,R-Q2;
29. QxKP ch,K-R3; and White announced mate in four moves
by 30. Q-R8 ch,K-Kt4; 31. Kt-K4 ch,K-Kt5;
32. P-R3 ch,K-R5; 33. R-B4.

Howard Staunton's origins are obscure, and some legends have grown up which seem to have no foundation in fact. He is supposed to have been the illegitimate son of Frederick Howard, fifth Earl of Carlisle, and to have squandered a few thousand pounds he allegedly inherited under his supposed father's will. No such bequest, however, appears in the will, so all that one can say about the story is *si non è vero è ben trovato*. It might have been invented by one of Staunton's numerous enemies; he was adept at creating them. Or he might have invented it himself in order to cut a dash. He claimed to have been an actor in his early years, and to have played the part of Lorenzo, supporting Edmund Kean's Shylock. There is no proof of this, but if it is true then it was possibly from this that he derived his lifelong interest in Shakespeare, in which he eventually became a noted scholar, editing an edition of Shakespeare, which is occasionally quoted in variorum editions, but with little respect.

He learned chess at the comparatively late age of nineteen, and was slow to mature as a player. He first came to prominence by beating Popert in a match by eight wins, three losses and two draws. Then, in a series of games played in 1841–2 he defeated John Cochrane by fourteen wins, four losses and no draws. The results of his two encounters with Saint Amant, I have already given; and he reinforced his claim to be Europe's leading player by two good victories in 1846—against Horwitz, whom he beat by fourteen wins, seven losses and three draws, and against Harrwitz, by seven wins, no losses and no draws. Meanwhile he had, in 1841, already revealed his literary quality and aspirations by founding the first English chess magazine, the *Chess Player's Chronicle*. He continued to edit it until 1852 with a vigour which left the reader no alternative but to become either friend or foe of the editor.

In 1847, his first and most important work on chess appeared, *The Chess Player's Handbook*. It was an enormous success and became a model of what a handbook should be. Writers have been imitating its plan and arrangement ever since. Curiously enough, it was not exactly original, and in the preface Staunton acknowledged a great debt to the *Handbuch* of Bilguer and von der Lasa. But he did add many of his own analyses, and both the plan and the writing can hardly be faulted in their lucid directness.

Staunton now conceived a startling idea—to stage an international chess tournament which should include all the best players in Europe. It was decided to have it coincide with the Great Exhibition to be held in London in 1851, and Staunton worked with the utmost energy to raise money for the event. It was eventually endowed with a prize-fund of over £500, a very big sum for that time. A peculiar and not particularly fair system of pairing the players was devised (possibly this was a vague echo of the 1574 event in Madrid). The sixteen players were drawn against each other by lot to play a series of knock-out matches. Since some of the best players met early, the finals were not contested by the best, though there is no doubt that the single best player, the German, Anderssen, won in the end.

There were indeed some hitches even before the tournament started. The powerful London Club, which was hostile to the project because it was Staunton's idea, refused to have anything to do with it; this meant that Harrwitz, who was a member of the club, was absent. Then the Russian, Jaenisch, arrived too late to compete, as did the formidable N. T. Buckle, a player who by now was second only to Staunton in England. (Buckle incidentally was a famous historian whose *History of Civilization* was to break new ground in the field.) Thus, when the competitors assembled in May of 1851,

The match between Staunton and Saint-Amant, Paris 1843, played for a stake of £100 a side.

two places had to be given to weaker players to make up the sixteen; and the chance of the draw brought two of the strongest players together, Anderssen opposing Kieseritsky and beating him by $2\frac{1}{2}-\frac{1}{2}$. The rules laid down that draws did not count, and that the first player to win two games in Round One won his match, whereas in the remaining rounds it was necessary to win four games.

The rounds went as follows:

Round 1

Anderssen $2\frac{1}{2}$, Kieseritsky $\frac{1}{2}$. Staunton 2, Brodie 0. Wyvil 2, Lowe 0. Szen 2, Newham 0. Capt. Kennedy 2, Mayet 0. Horwitz $2\frac{1}{2}$, Bird $1\frac{1}{2}$. Williams 2, Löwenthal 0. Mucklow 2, E. Kennedy 0.

Round 2

Anderssen 4, Szen 2. Staunton $4\frac{1}{2}$, Horwitz $2\frac{1}{2}$. Wyvil $4\frac{1}{2}$, Capt. Kennedy $3\frac{1}{2}$. Williams 4, Mucklow 0.

Round 3

Anderssen 4, Staunton 1. Szen 4, Horwitz 0. Wyvill 4, Williams 3. Capt. Kennedy 4, Mucklow 0.

Round 4

Anderssen $4\frac{1}{2}$, Wyvil $2\frac{1}{2}$. Williams $4\frac{1}{2}$, Staunton $3\frac{1}{2}$. Szen $4\frac{1}{2}$, Capt. Kennedy $\frac{1}{2}$. Horwitz won against Mucklow by default.

So the prize list was as follows: 1. Anderssen 15, 2. Wyvill 13, 3. Williams $13\frac{1}{2}$, 4. Staunton 11, 5. Szen $12\frac{1}{2}$, 6. Capt. Kennedy 10, 7. Horwitz 5 and 8. Mucklow 2.

Staunton was not content. Not only had he lost to Anderssen in the third round, but he had lost to Williams in the final round—and he was accustomed to beating Williams while giving him odds. He accused him of deliberate slowness, and indeed Williams had a good claim to be considered the slowest player of all time. There were no chess clocks then, to time the contestants, and Williams took advantage of this. In those days, too, there was a special scorer for each game and the players did not take down the moves themselves. It was averred that when one score was handed in, that of a game in which Williams was one of the competitors, the scorer had noted in the margin 'both players now asleep'.

But, as an examination of the following game from the Anderssen–Staunton match in Round Three shows, Anderssen was the deserved victor.

White: Anderssen. Black: Staunton. French Defence.

1. P-K4,P-K3; 2. P-Q4,P-KKt3; 3. B-Q3,B-Kt2; 4. B-K3,P-QB4;
5. P-QB3,PxP; 6. PxP,Q-Kt3; 7. Kt-K2,QxKtP;
8. QKt-B3,Q-Kt3; 9. R-QB1,Kt-QR3; 10. Kt-Kt5,B-B1;
11. 0-0,P-Q3; 12. P-Q5,Q-R4; 13. B-Q4,P-K4; 14. B-B3,Q-Q1;
15. P-B4,P-B3; 16. PxP,BPxP; 17. Q-R4,B-Q2;
18. B-Kt4,Kt-R3; 19. K-R1,Kt-KB2; 20. Q-R3,Kt-B4;
21. KtxP ch,BxKt; 22. BxKt,BxB; 23. QxB,Q-K2;
24. Q-B7,Kt-Q3; 25. Q-R5,P-R4; 26. R-B7,R-QB1;
27. KR-B1,P-R3; 28. Kt-Q4,R-B1; 29. Kt-K6,RxR;
30. RxR,R-B2; 31. Q-Kt6,R-B3; 32. P-KR3,P-Kt4;
33. Q-Kt2,Kt-Kt4; 34. BxKt,PxB; 35. QxKP,P-R5;
36. RxP,R-B8 ch; 37. K-R2,Q-B3; 38. R-Kt8 ch,K-K2;
39. P-Q6 ch,K-B2; 40. R-B8 ch,K-Kt3; 41. RxQ ch,RxR;
42. QxP ch,K-B2; 43. Q-Kt7 ch,KxKt; 44. Q-K7 mate (Diagram 27).

But Anderssen's best and most famous game was not played in the

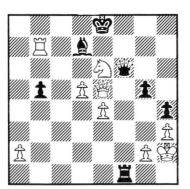

27: Position after Black's 37th move.

London tournament, but during another session at The Divan against Kieseritsky. It became known as 'the immortal game':

White: Anderssen. Black: Kieseritsky. King's Bishop's Gambit.

1. P-K4,P-K4; 2. P-KB4,PxP; 3. B-B4,P-QKt4; 4. BxP,Q-R5 ch;
5. K-B1,Kt-KB3; 6. Kt-KB3,Q-R3; 7. P-Q3,Kt-R4;
8. Kt-R4,P-QB3; 9. Kt-B5,Q-Kt4; 10. P-KKt4,Kt-B3;
11. R-Kt1,PxB; 12. P-KR4,Q-Kt3; 13. P-R5,Q-Kt4;
14. Q-B3,Kt-Kt1; 15. BxP,Q-B3; 16. Kt-B3,B-B4;
17. Kt-Q5,QxP; 18. B-Q6,QxR ch; 19. K-K2,BxR;
20. P-K5,Kt-QR3; 21. KtxP ch,K-Q1; 22. Q-B6 ch,KtxQ;
23. B-K7 mate (Diagram 28).

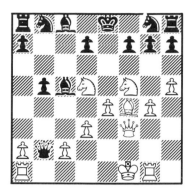

28: Position after Black's 17th move.

With this event, the supremacy of the German school was confirmed, and Anderssen himself was to show in many another tournament thereafter that he could be justifiably regarded as Europe's best player.

From now on Staunton declined as a player, and he busied himself more and more with writing. He probably felt that to attempt to make a comeback would be hopeless and that he might meet with humiliating defeats. In addition, he had been severely ill with pneumonia, which had left his heart weak, and undue strain would have been unwise. What happened to him later, however, is relevant to our further story, so I keep the account for its proper place in time, in the next chapter.

But he had, before the 1851 tournament, already made one more lasting contribution to chess. The firm of Jacques, which subsequently became famous for the chess-sets it produced, was sent a pattern for a new type of chessman by Nathaniel Cook, a friend of Staunton's. The design was neat and elegant, and yet it carried an air of solid worth which made it a pleasure to play with. Jacques, realizing that Staunton's name, after his defeat of Saint Amant, was a household word in the chess world, and even more so after his successful publication of the *Handbook,* asked his permission to call it the Staunton pattern. He also suggested that a replica of his autograph should appear on the box containing the men. Staunton approved, and to this day a Staunton set is one of the finest in the world.

chapter *11*

The advent of Paul Morphy

Paul Morphy, the great American player.

So far, in the history of modern chess at any rate, I have been considering the Old World only, and, more specifically, western Europe, since that was where progress in the game was most notable. It should be remarked, incidentally, that eastern Europe, particularly wherever the Slavs were to be found, also witnessed considerable development. As was seen in earlier chapters, Russia was one of the first countries into which chess percolated, and there was constant activity there, from the Middle Ages on into the eighteenth and nineteenth centuries to which my account has now brought me. Such important figures as Petroff and Jaenisch were known to the world outside Russia as strong masters who were also original thinkers on the game and its theory. Russia was not, however, for some time to produce a player who would have a profound effect on the course of chess theory; that falls into the next chapter.

In the 1850s, the new important influence came from the New World, from the Americas. Not indeed from South America, which, for the most part under the stultifying rule of Spain, was backward in the arts and pursuits of civilization, but from North America, and in particular from the USA.

We have already seen that in the eighteenth century the United States had a powerful advocate for the game in Benjamin Franklin, than whom no one could have been better fitted to carry and replenish the torch of civilisation. But the real upsurge in American civilisation did not come till the third quarter of the next century. As always, with the advance of civilisation there came an advance in chess. The year 1857 was a most significant point in this advance, for it was marked by a semi-international tournament that took place in New York, and in which the first prize was won by a twenty-year-old player from New Orleans named Paul Morphy. I call the event 'semi-international', since in it there participated another player who, though only a few years older than Morphy, had already achieved a reputation as a very fine player. He was the talented German master, Louis Paulsen, then twenty-four years old.

The event, organized on the same lines as that of London 1851, was a knock-out tourney with sixteen players. Draws did not count and the first person to win three games won his match, until the final, when the win of five games was required. Play started on 6 October, 1857, and both Morphy and Paulsen reached the semi-final round without dropping even half a point, or, to put it more accurately, winning every game. Opposition then became a little stronger, since each drew one game.

In the final, Morphy gave evidence of his superiority by winning five games, drawing two and losing one. Despite the overwhelming nature of his win in figures, which in modern terms would have been 6–2, Morphy did not by any means have it all his own way. Most of the games were most strenuously contested and quite even. Morphy was clearly the better of the two, but Paulsen was also a player of some genius. He had not yet perfected his system of playing the defence in the Sicilian, which, as will be seen later, was to prove his greatest contribution to chess theory (it is commemorated in the title of one of the chief variations of the Sicilian Defence). But at that time his thinking on the subject was still in the embryonic stage, and all that he gained from his four Sicilians in this match was one draw and three losses. He did, however, win a game, as follows:

White: L. Paulsen. Black: P. Morphy. 4th match game, 2 Nov., 1857. Three Knights' Defence.

 1. P-K4,P-K4; 2. Kt-KB3,Kt-QB3; 3. Kt-B3,B-B4;
 4. B-Kt5,P-Q3; 5. P-Q4,PxP; 6. KtxP,B-Q2; 7. KtxKt,PxKt;
 8. B-R4,Q-R5; 9. o-o,Kt-B3; 10. Q-B3,Kt-Kt5; 11. B-B4,Kt-K4;
 12. Q-Kt3,Q-B3; 13. QR-Q1,P-KR3; 14. K-R1,P-Kt4;
 15. BxKt,PxB; 16. P-Kt4,B-Q3; 17. R-Q3,P-KR4;
 18. KR-Q1,P-R3; 19. Kt-K2,R-Q1; 20. P-QR3,P-Kt5;
 21. P-QB4,Q-R3; 22. P-B5,P-R5; 23. Q-K3,B-K2;
 24. P-B4,KPxP; 25. QxP,QxQ; 26. KtxQ,R-R3;
 27. Kt-K2,P-B4; 28. P-K5,R-K3; 29. Kt-B4,RxP;
 30. RxB,RxR; 31. BxP,B-Q3; 32. PxB,PxP;
 33. K-Kt1,K-Q1; 34. BxR and wins.

Had one not known otherwise one would have assumed that it was Morphy who had the White pieces and said that White's thirteenth, sixteenth and twenty-ninth moves were pure Morphy. Perhaps something rubbed off on his opponent, or perhaps it may have been the other way round!

Another noteworthy point was that the game took eleven hours. Both players were slow to move (it was still in the days before chess clocks) and indeed another game of the match, in which fifty-six moves were played, took some fifteen hours. They moved twice as slowly as we do nowadays!

The result of the tournament caused a great sensation. The Hungarian master, J. J. Löwenthal, commented, 'The grey-beards were fairly pushed from their pedestals. Youth and genius proved far more than a match for age and experience. All went down, almost without a struggle, before the conqueror of New Orleans, and second in the contest stood Paulsen, who was only a few years older than Paul Morphy'. At the prize-giving ceremony on 11 November in the Descombes Rooms in New York, Morphy made a speech in which he glowingly praised Paulsen's wonderful powers of blindfold chess (Paulsen was later to establish a record for the time of ten simultaneous blindfold games). Morphy himself was a fine blindfold display player, as will be seen, but he did not concentrate on it to anything like the extent that Paulsen did.

The round-by-round details of the tournament were as follows:

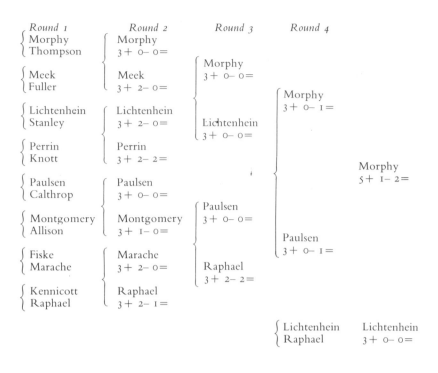

The brackets indicate the pairings, and + means won games, – means lost games and = means drawn games.

It is interesting to look at the way Morphy handled the openings. Against the Sicilian Defence he played what is now regarded as normal with 2. Kt-KB3 and 3. P-Q4. Against the Ruy Lopez he did not play what is now called the Morphy Defence (that was to come later in his career, in his match with Anderssen); instead, he played 3. .,Kt-B3. He always replied to 1. P-K4 with P-K4 as Black. Against the Queen's Pawn he used the Dutch Defence, 1. .,P-KB4. One astonishingly modern line that he employed with Black against Lichtenhein was a remarkable anticipation of the Semi-Tarrasch, which has only come into the fore this century.

In the middle-game he was most competent, polishing off the lesser lights with appropriate promptness and neatness. He was brilliant where brilliance was required, as is illustrated by his famous game versus Paulsen in the final round:

White: Paulsen . Black: Morphy. 8 Nov., 1857. Four Knights' Game.

1. P-K4,P-K4; 2. Kt-KB3,Kt-QB3; 3. Kt-B3,Kt-B3;
4. B-Kt5,B-B4; 5. O-O,O-O; 6. KtxP,R-K1; 7. KtxKt,QPxKt;
8. B-B4,P-QKt4; 9. B-K2,KtxP; 10. KtxKt,RxKt;
11. B-B3,R-K3; 12. P-QB3,Q-Q6; 13. P-QKt4,B-Kt3;
14. P-QR4,PxP; 15. QxP,B-Q2; 16. R-R2,QR-K1;
17. Q-R6,QxB; 18. PxQ,R-Kt3 ch; 19. K-R1,B-R6;
20. R-Q1,B-Kt7 ch; 21. K-Kt1,BxP dis ch;
22. K-B1,B-Kt7 ch; 23. K-Kt1,B-R6 dis ch; 24. K-R1,BxP;
25. Q-B1,BxQ; 26. RxB,R-K7; 27. R-R1,R-R3;
28. P-Q4,B-K6; White resigns (Diagram 29).

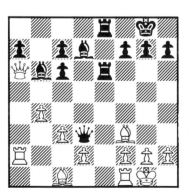

29: Position after White's 17th move.

This game has been submitted to frequent and microscopic analysis and, by dint of great application, better moves have been found

Paul Morphy plays blindfold in the Café de la Régence in Paris.

for both sides. But it remains a game of great beauty with a dazzling stroke by Black on his seventeenth move.

This was the only tournament in which Morphy ever played, for such events were rare during the meteoric but, alas, short chess career he was to enjoy. It is a great pity, since the Morphy style was eminently adapted to winning beautiful games against varied opposition. Had there been the profusion of tournaments that there are now, we would have had an equal profusion of wonderful games from him. True, he was very successful in match-play, but the qualities necessary for match-play are greyer and less colourful.

Before I continue with his story, I must retrace my steps slightly to show how he emerged as the star of American chess. He was born on 22 June, 1837 (also the year of Queen Victoria's ascension) and was the son of Judge Alonzo Morphy of the High Court of Louisiana. The family were of Spanish origin, went to the United States from Madrid at the end of the eighteenth century, and lived in New Orleans. It would seem that the Morphys were a chess-playing family. Paul's father played a great deal without being at all a strong player, but his brother (Paul's uncle), Ernest Morphy, was both keen and good. Löwenthal wrote that he was 'generally considered the chess king of New Orleans'.

Paul Morphy was a precocious child and in many respects his early boyhood resembled that of Capablanca. As with him, it was from watching his family play chess that he picked the game up; another curiously close parallel is that both were already formidable chessplayers by the age of twelve. Ernest Morphy apparently guided the boy's progress at the game and fostered it with intelligent care. He described him as a player in a letter he sent on 31 October, 1849 to Lionel Kieseritsky, who was then the editor of a chess magazine called *La Régence*:

> I send you herewith a game of chess played on the 28th instant between M.R----- and the young Paul Morphy, my nephew, who is only twelve. This child has never opened a work on chess; he has learnt the game himself by following the parties played between members of his family. In the openings he makes the right moves as if by inspiration; and it is astonishing to note the precision of his calculations in the middle and end game. When seated before the chess-board, his face betrays no agitation even in the most critical positions; in such cases he generally whistles an air through his teeth and patiently seeks for the combination to get him out of trouble. Further, he plays three or four severe enough games every Sunday (the only day on which his father allows him to play) without showing the least fatigue.

I have quoted this letter in full for two reasons. Firstly, it is always fascinating to read about the behaviour of a genius in his youth. Secondly, the description of his play really sums up Morphy's supreme excellence as a player in a way that is all the better for being without the usual attempts to bring some high philosophical concept to bear on what is in fact explicable in quite ordinary human and common-sense terms.

What is indeed astonishing is that such a chess genius should have arisen and prospered almost by itself, without the opposition of really strong players. The level of play among his regular opponents can be judged by the fact that one of the most frequent was Charles Amédée Maurian to whom he could successfully give the odds of a Knight—and Maurian was one of the strongest of those with whom he played casual games.

The R. mentioned in the letter was Eugene Rousseau, a fairly strong amateur player who was born in France but lived in New Orleans, where he played a number of off-hand games with the young Morphy, with distinct lack of success. Alexander Cockburn refers to him as 'a strong international grandmaster', but this is a myth betraying complete ignorance of the subject. It is, however, worth dispelling, since otherwise it could gain credence. Rousseau was not a grandmaster, not even a master, and the extent to which he was 'international' lies in the solitary fact that he played in—and came bottom in—the Paris tournament of 1867.

Nevertheless, it was still a feat for the twelve-year-old boy to dispose of mature opposition so efficiently. I give the game in evidence of his strength and also of Rousseau's amateurish weakness: White: P. Morphy. Black: E. Rousseau. Irregular (Rousseau?) Defence.

1. P-K4,P-K4; 2. Kt-KB3,Kt-QB3; 3. B-B4,P-B4;
4. P-Q3,Kt-B3; 5. 0-0,P-Q3; 6. Kt-Kt5,P-Q4; 7. PxQP,KtxP;
8. Kt-QB3,QKt-K2; 9. Q-B3,P-B3; 10. QKt-K4,PxKt;
11. Q-B7 ch,K-Q2; 12. Q-K6 ch,K-B2;
13. QxKP ch,Q-Q3; 14. QxQ ch,KxQ; 15. Kt-B7 ch,K-K3;
16. KtxR,PxP; 17. PxP,K-B3; 18. P-QKt4,B-K3;

19. R–K1,B–Kt1; 20. B–Kt2 ch,K–Kt4; 21. R–K5 ch,K–R3;
22. B–B1 ch,P–Kt4; 23. RxP, and wins (Diagram 30).

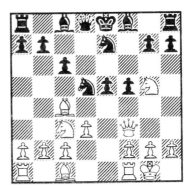

30: Position after Black's 9th move.

The combination on White's tenth move is pleasing, but the cynic might remark, on playing over this game that, while White plays like a mature master, Black plays like a child of ten.

More impressive, from the point of view of the opposition involved, were the results of two games which J. J. Lowenthal played with the boy during a visit to New Orleans that same year. Admittedly, Löwenthal was not of the strength that he was to possess some ten years later; but he was a genuine masterplayer, and the fact that Morphy won one game from him and drew the other is convincing proof of his precocious genius.

His progress was rapid, and it was also aided by a fresh addition of chess knowledge through study. It was his habit, however, to look at books on chess, absorb their content and then give them away to his friends, for he had a remarkable memory and had no need to retain books for consultation. When he was fifteen, he thus absorbed and then gave away the book Staunton wrote about the London 1851 tournament. To the heading on the title-page, 'By H. Staunton, Esq., author of the "Handbook of Chess", "Chess-player's Companion" etc.', Morphy added '(and some devilish bad games)'. This is a little unfair, but reassuringly childish and amusing.

Meanwhile his education, first at the Jefferson Academy in New Orleans and then at the Jesuit St. Joseph's College at Spring Hill, near Mobile, Alabama, had been proceeding apace. He was an excellent student and went on to the University of Louisiana where he decided to become a lawyer and was admitted to the Bar when he was not quite twenty in April, 1857.

This brings us to the time when he played in the 1857 tournament. As a result of his success there, and also because he had won a number of games in New York, mostly giving various odds, it became manifest that he was America's strongest player. In 1858 the New Orleans Chess Club wrote to Staunton inviting him to come to New Orleans to play a match with Morphy, the stakes being $5,000, of which $1,000 was to go to Staunton whether he won or lost. Staunton politely refused, saying that the journey and his own work were too arduous. He was then chess editor of the *Illustrated London News* and he mentioned the invitation in that journal, writing that he was unable to go to the States but stating, injudiciously as it turned out, that 'If Mr. Morphy—for whose skill we entertain the liveliest admiration—be desirous to win his spurs among the chess chivalry of Europe, he must take advantage of his purposed visit next year; he will then meet in this country, in France and in Germany, and in Russia, many champions whose names must be as household words to him, ready to test and do honour to his prowess.'

This statement allowed Morphy to entertain the hope that if he came to England he would have the opportunity of playing his desired match against Staunton. To do Staunton justice, he did not definitely write that this specific opportunity would exist; with hindsight, one can see that if he had wished to avoid all mal-entendus, he should have said that he himself was retiring from competitive chess and would not be available.

Why did he not do this? I suggest that at the back of his mind, as there is at the back of the mind of every defeated champion (remember that European supremacy had passed from him to Anderssen with the German's victory in London in 1851), was the thought, 'All right, I am retiring from the fray, but who knows, I might make a comeback and play this young genius and show the world I am still the old great Staunton.'

Morphy and his supporters, however, believed that Staunton was ready to play the match, and the young man set sail for England, arriving in Liverpool on 21 June 1858, just one day before his twenty-first birthday. Negotiations were soon under way for the proposed contest, and although Staunton put the date off from time to time under the justifiable plea that he was projecting a great literary work (a new edition of Shakespeare), he did indeed agree to play the match eventually.

Meanwhile, there was the possibility that either or both would compete in the international tournament to be held in Birmingham in August of that year. Morphy had provisionally entered, but Staunton had not as yet made up his mind. In the interval Morphy played and won two matches against Löwenthal, who was by now much advanced in public estimation both as a player and a chess journalist; Morphy won by nine to three and two draws. Against the Reverend Owen, one of England's strongest amateurs, he won five, lost none and drew two. Perhaps it should be mentioned, inter alia, and without meaning any disrespect to the cloth, that this century witnessed a sort of rash of reverends in English chess, some of whom were very strong players, but some of whom were also more bitterly polemical than the laity.

In the end, Morphy did not play at Birmingham, while Staunton unwisely did. The tournament, another knock-out affair like that in London in 1851, included some of Staunton's old rivals, notably Saint Amant, as well as a number of the stars of the future: Bird,

Some chess celebrities of the mid-nineteenth century. Left to right: Löwenthal, de Rivière, Wyvill, Falkbeer, Staunton, Lord Lyttelton, Captain Kennedy.

Falkbeer, the Reverend Owen and Löwenthal, who won first prize. Staunton was knocked out in the second round by Löwenthal—two to nothing. I believe that, after this bitter pill, he had decided to abandon competitive chess, but he still gave Morphy to understand that he was only postponing their match.

Morphy then went to Paris, to play against Harrwitz and Anderssen who, with Staunton more or less out of action, could be considered the two leading European players. Morphy's matches against these two constituted the high point of his career. Never before or after did he meet with such worthy and distinguished opposition, and the results confirmed his position as beyond all question the world's leading player. Some contend that they proved him to be possibly the best chessplayer the world has ever seen, although this was disputed when more than 100 years later, another American genius, Bobby Fischer, made his extraordinary mark on the chess scene.

In September, 1858, Morphy met Daniel Harrwitz, the German master who had settled in Paris, succeeded Kieseritzky as the professional at the Café de la Régence and become known as the 'King of the Régence'. The match was to be won by the first player to take seven games, but Harrwitz, obviously finding the case hopeless, retired in October when the score stood at Morphy five wins, Harrwitz two wins and one draw. Harrwitz pleaded illness as his reason for giving up, but there is evidence to show that it was Morphy rather than he who was genuinely indisposed during the course of the match.

Nevertheless, Harrwitz had put up the strongest resistance that Morphy ever encountered, and it was his style of play to which Morphy found it most difficult to reconcile his own method of conducting the game. For one thing Harrwitz was a Queen's Pawn player (in the match he invariably commenced with 1. P-Q4), while Morphy was eminently a King's Pawn player. On the whole, too, Harrwitz preferred to keep the position closed, and Morphy had been accustomed in all his games hitherto to open and direct manoeuvring. It says much for his genius that, after a most indifferent start (he lost the first two games), he was able to readjust his methods to meet the novel threats contained in his opponent's methods.

Once he had become adjusted to the style of play of the 'King of the Régence', Morphy allowed his opponent no chance of recovery. It is interesting to compare two games in which the opening variation was the same. First, the second game of the match:
White: Morphy. Black: Harrwitz. Philidor Defence.

1. P-K4,P-K4; 2. Kt-KB3,P-Q3; 3. P-Q4,PxP; 4. QxP,Kt-QB3;
5. B-QKt5,B-Q2; 6. BxKt,BxB; 7. B-Kt5,Kt-B3;
8. Kt-B3,B-K2; 9. 0-0-0; 10. KR-K1,P-KR3;
11. B-R4,Kt-K1; 12. BxB,QxB; 13. P-K5,BxKt;
14. PxB,Q-Kt4 ch; 15. K-Kt1,PxP; 16. RxP,Q-Kt7;
17. Kt-Q5,QxRP; 18. KR-K1,Q-Q3; 19. R-Kt1,K-R2;
20. Q-K3,P-KB4; 21. Kt-B4,Q-QKt3; 22. Q-K2,R-B2;
23. Q-B4,Q-KB3; 24. Kt-R5,Q-K2; 25. QR-K1,Q-Q2;
26. P-R3,Kt-Q3; 27. Q-Q4,R-KKt1; 28. R-Kt2,Kt-K1;
29. Q-B3,P-B5; 30. R-R1,P-KKt3; 31. QR-Kt1,Q-Q4;
32. Q-K1,QxKt; 33. R-Kt5,QxP; 34. Q-K6,R-B3;
35. Q-K7 ch,R-Kt2; 36. QxKt,PxR; 37. Q-K1,Q-B3 and
Black won.

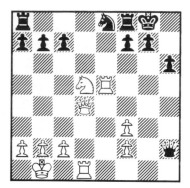

31: Position after Black's 17th move.

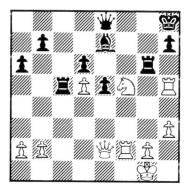

32: Position after Black's 30th move.

Morphy's play is curiously uncertain in this game and certainly better than his 18. KR-K1, was 18. P-KB4, cutting off the Black Queen (Diagram 31).

And now the fourth game of the match, in which Morphy's superiority as a player and his magnificent powers of sweeping aside all opposition are beautifully illustrated:

White: Morphy. Black: Harrwitz. Philidor Defence.

1. P-K4,P-K4; 2. Kt-KB3,P-Q3; 3. P-Q4,PxP;
4. QxP,Kt-QB3; 5. B-QKt5,B-Q2; 6. BxKt,BxB;
7. B-Kt5,P-B3; 8. B-R4,Kt-R3; 9. Kt-B3,Q-Q2; 10. 0-0,B-K2;
11. QR-Q1,0-0; 12. Q-B4 ch,R-B2; 13. Kt-Q4,Kt-Kt5;
14. P-KR3,Kt-K4; 15. Q-K2,P-KKt4; 16. B-Kt3,R-Kt2;
17. Kt-B5,R-Kt3; 18. P-B4,PxP; 19. KRxP,K-R1;
20. R-R4,B-B1; 21. BxKt,BPxB; 22. R-KB1,Q-K3;
23. Kt-Kt5,Q-Kt1; 24. R-B2,P-QR3; 25. KtxBP,R-B1;
26. Kt-Q5,BxKt; 27. PxB,R-B2; 28. P-B4,B-K2;
29. R-R5,Q-K1; 30. P-B5,RxP; 31. RxP ch,KxR;
32. Q-R5 ch,K-Kt1; 33. KtxB ch,K-Kt2; 34. Kt-B5 ch,K-Kt1;
35. KtxP, resigns (Diagram 32).

Compare this game and the attack on the King-side with the sixth game of the World Championship match between Bobby Fischer and Boris Spassky in 1972 (p. 225). In essence the attack is the same and, save for the difference in the minor pieces, the set-up of the major pieces is astonishingly similar, right down to the Black Queen being on K1 in both cases—plus ça change . . .!

Morphy had intended returning to England after this match, in order to play against Staunton, but an interchange of letters, culminating with one on 9 October in which Staunton definitely cried off owing to his absorption in literary work, made it clear that the matter was hopeless. He therefore abandoned all intentions of playing Staunton and prepared to meet Adolf Anderssen in December.

Meanwhile, he was feted throughout Paris as the greatest player ever to visit that city and he competed in a number of off-hand games with noted personalities, both from the chess-world and from other spheres. It was during this period that he played what was perhaps the most celebrated Queen sacrifice in the history of the game. This was in a consultation match against Count Isouard de Vauvenargue and the Duke of Brunswick, in a box at the Paris Opera during a performance of 'The Barber of Seville'. There has been some dispute over whether it was this opera of Rossini's or another, 'La Cenerentola', but at the moment of writing, the 'Barber' has it. There is also the piquant point that this particular Duke of Brunswick (perhaps ex-Duke is more correct, since he had been deposed) was a descendant of Augustus, Duke of Brunswick, who, under the pseudonym of Gustavus Selenus, wrote a celebrated work on chess entitled *Das Schach oder König Spiel* which was published in Leipzig in 1616.

The game itself, if no very deep matter, has a classic purity that is eternally refreshing:

White: Morphy. Black: Duke of Brunswick and Count Isouard de Vauvenargue.

1. P-K4,P-K4; 2. Kt-KB3,P-Q3; 3. P-Q4,B-Kt5; 4. PxP,BxKt;
5. QxB,PxP; 6. B-QB4,Kt-KB3; 7. Q-QKt3,Q-K2;
8. Kt-B3,P-B3; 9. B-KKt5,P-Kt4; 10. KtxP,PxKt;

11. BxKtP ch,QKt-Q2; 12. 0-0-0,R-Q1; 13. RxKt,RxR;
14. R-Q1,Q-K3; 15. BxR ch,KtxB; 16. Q-Kt8 ch,KtxQ;
17. R-Q8 mate (Diagram 33).

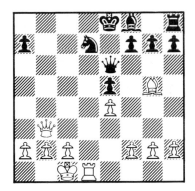

33: Position after Black's 15th move.

Finally, in December 1858, there came the highest point in Morphy's chess career when the great Adolf Anderssen came from Breslau to Paris to play a match on exactly the same terms as those in the Harrwitz encounter: the match would be won by the first player to win seven games. But there was little or no resemblance between the two Germans, either as players or as persons. Anderssen was chivalrous, cultivated and generous in his praise and appreciation of his young opponent. It was he who had come from Breslau to play Morphy, although the American was the challenger. In addition, Anderssen, a professor of mathematics at the Friedrich Gymnasium in Breslau, had to devote his vacation to the match, which was played in a surprisingly brief period of time from 20 to 28 December.

Morphy, who had begun to feel unwell during the Harrwitz match, had in fact intended to go back to New Orleans before Christmas, but his doctor advised against his making the trip until he had fully recovered. When Anderssen arrived, he found Morphy confined to his bed, and refused to start playing the match until he seemed better. Anderssen himself, aside from a small knock-out tournament in which he had done rather badly at Manchester in 1857, had had no real practice since he won the London Tournament of 1851. It was no doubt this that he meant when, at the end of the match, he said that he had been wrong to suppose that he could bottle up his chess and put it in a glass case.

The match started well for him, however; he won the first and drew the second game. Then came a quick win in twenty moves for Morphy, who also won the fourth game, although it was much longer. The real crunch came in the next three games, all of which went to Morphy, leaving Anderssen in a hopeless plight. In the end Morphy won the match by seven wins, two losses and two draws. Anderssen made no excuses and admitted his opponent's superiority. To the remark by an admirer that he was not playing as well as he had done against the Berlin player, Jean Dufresne, he replied, 'No, Morphy won't let me!'

Treatment of the openings by both sides was much superior to that of previous matches and made, for instance, the players in the De la Bourdonnais–McDonnell match look like tyros by comparison. Two types of Ruy Lopez were played, a slow one by Anderssen (1. P-K4,P-K4; 2. Kt-KB3,Kt-QB3; 3. B-Kt5,P-QR3; 4. B-R4,Kt-B3; 5. P-Q3), and one at a quicker, faster tempo by Morphy (1. P-K4,P-K4; 2. Kt-KB3,Kt-QB3; 3. B-Kt5,Kt-B3; 4. P-Q4).

As White, too, Anderssen often played the opening named after him, 1. P-QR3, which usually transposed into a kind of English Opening or Sicilian Defence with a move in hand. As Black, with the exception of the one Ruy Lopez already mentioned and an Evans Gambit in the first game (1. P-K4,P-K4; 2. Kt-KB3,Kt-QB3; 3. B-B4,B-B4; 4. P-QKt4,BxP; 5. P-B3,B-R4), Anderssen played half-open defences with singular lack of success. He lost two Centre Counters (1. P-K4,P-Q4), a Sicilian Defence and a dubious form of the French Defence.

Perhaps the neatest win of the match was the seventh game:

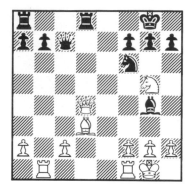

34: Position after Black's 16th move.

White: Morphy. Black: Anderssen. Centre Counter Defence.
1. P-K4,P-Q4; 2. PxP,QxP; 3. Kt-QB3,Q-QR4;
4. P-Q4,P-K4; 5. PxP,QxP ch; 6. B-K2,B-QKt5;
7. Kt-B3,BxKt ch; 8. PxB,QxP ch; 9. B-Q2,Q-B4;
10. R-QKt1,Kt-QB3; 11. 0-0,Kt-B3; 12. B-KB4,0-0;
13. BxP,Kt-Q5; 14. QxKt,QxB; 15. B-Q3,B-Kt5;
16. Kt-Kt5,KR-Q1; 17. Q-Kt4,B-B1; 18. KR-K1,P-QR4;
19. Q-K7,QxQ; 20. RxQ,Kt-Q4; 21. BxP ch,K-R1;
22. RxBP,Kt-B6; 23. R-K1,KtxP; 24. R-B4,R-R3; 25. B-Q3,
resigns (Diagram 34).

The difference in style between the two players—between the old established, albeit highly romantic, ways of Anderssen and the new classically logical, yet equally brilliant style of Morphy—was most marked in this match. Although Anderssen's career, despite this disastrous defeat, was to go on much longer than Morphy's, and with great success, it was the American's method of play which was to have the larger future influence.

Yet then, there were indications that Morphy was losing interest in the game. He returned home to a hero's welcome, and tried to settle down to a law career, but he was hampered by people who obstinately insisted that he was a chess genius, and must play chess. All too soon he began to evince a distaste for the game—in its international or more official forms, at any rate. Two not particularly well-authenticated stories are told in illustration of a rather bizarre combination of his disinterest and his incredible memory. The first relates to a visit to New Orleans by Johannes Zukertort in 1882, when he was supposed to have met Morphy in Canal Street and handed him his card. Morphy put it in his pocket without looking at it, but nevertheless addressed him by his name and spoke to him in French. Zukertort, very surprised, asked him how he knew who he was or indeed that he could speak French. Morphy replied, 'I met you in Paris in 1867 and you spoke French then.' (Morphy had made two more visits to Europe).

The other story, though apt, has the air of a *ben trovato* incident invented by one of Steinitz's many enemies. According to C. A. Buck, in his book, *Paul Morphy: His Later Life* (published in 1902), when Wilhelm Steinitz visited New Orleans in 1883, he wanted very much to meet Morphy. A friend, trying to arrange this, told Morphy that Steinitz was in town. 'I know it,' he replied, 'his gambit is not good.'

By this time, alas, it was clear that Morphy was in the grip of a persecution mania. Although this was not serious enough to render him certifiably insane, there is no doubt that he spent the last twenty years of his life in increasing seclusion and melancholia, living quietly with his sister Helena and his mother. He died on 10 July, 1884 after having gone for a walk and returned to take a bath. His mother became alarmed when he failed to reappear, went up to the bathroom and found him dead in the tub. The cause of death was congestion of the brain. Helena wrote to Max Lange in January, 1885, 'For many years preceding his death he was averse to any social intercourse and confined himself to a gloomy retirement apart from his former friends.'

It is sad to think of all the fine chess that could have been produced during his long years of retirement. Well may Fiske have called him 'the pride and the sorrow of chess'.

Chessmen and inlaid gaming board said to have been given to Samuel Pepys by King James II.

Blue and white jasper chess pieces, modelled by John Flaxman in 1784, and produced by the firm of Wedgwood in 1790.

And yet, in the brief space of two years he caused a revolution in the way of thinking about chess—above all in the openings that had not been dreamed of by other minds in some three hundred years. He conceived the notion of *positional development*. This is everyday practice with our masters nowadays, but when Morphy first came on the scene it was as startling an idea as the first concept of perspective must have been to the world of pictorial art. Every player of any merit knew that it was vital to get the pieces out in order to get on with the game, but the placing of them in their right true positions—above all, their situation apropos and in the centre—this we owe to Morphy. It is no accident that, despite the normally weak nature of his opposition, he should have produced so many aesthetically pleasing games. Beauty, both of idea and execution, is bound up in his supremely logical method of play. That he was also highly gifted in such matters as calculation and combination, in what one might term the weapons and armoury of the middle-game and of the ending, was a happy coincidence of talents. Or perhaps the one necessarily flowed from the other. Morphy together with Capablanca were the most gifted players of natural genius that we have so far seen.

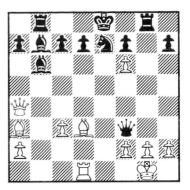

35: *Position after Black's 20th move.*

With Morphy's disappearance from the international scene, Anderssen once again became acknowledged as the leading player in Europe and in the world. He had also risen in his profession of teaching (he achieved professorial rank in 1865) and seemed able to afford much more time for playing chess.

But there is one reference I have to pick up as regards his earlier chess-playing activities because it describes a famous game with a combination of rare beauty which he played against Dufresne in 1853. Anderssen won, and the game has borne the title ever since of the 'Evergreen'.

White: Anderssen. Black: Dufresne. Evans Gambit.

1. P-K4,P-K4; 2. Kt-KB3,Kt-QB3; 3. B-B4,B-B4;
4. P-QKt4,BxP; 5. P-B3,B-R4; 6. P-Q4,PxP; 7. o-o,P-Q6;
8. Q-Kt3,Q-B3; 9. P-K5,Q-Kt3; 10. R-K1,KKt-K2;
11. B-R3,P-Kt4; 12. QxP,R-QKt1; 13. Q-R4,B-Kt3;
14. QKt-Q2,B-Kt2; 15. Kt-K4,Q-B4; 16. BxP,Q-R4;
17. Kt-B6 ch,PxKt; 18. PxP,R-Kt1; 19. QR-Q1,QxKt;
20. RxKt ch,KtxR; 21. QxP ch,KxQ; 22. B-B5 db.ch,K-K1;
23. B-Q7 ch,K-Q1; 24. BxKt mate.

The combination must have been conceived well before the seventeenth move and the latter part of the game reminds one of the richly ornate architecture of a baroque church (Diagram 35).

In 1861, Anderssen won a match by the narrow margin of one point over Ignatz Kolisch, a strong Hungarian master, who drew a match with Louis Paulsen that same year and whose subsequent romantic career will be given in the next chapter. This match was the first to be timed in the modern way with a set number of moves for a predetermined period. Up to then the players were allowed so much time per move.

Then came a new landmark in the history of tournaments, the London Tournament of 1862, organized by the British Chess Association. This was the first in which players all played each other. Although this all-play-all system was inaugurated in London, it subsequently became known as the American system, presumably because the United States imitated it. Another important innovation was the introduction of a time limit, a fairly fast one of twenty moves in two hours. Draws were still not counted.

Anderssen scored an overwhelming success, coming first with 11 points. Second was L. Paulsen with 9, followed by the Reverend Owen and the Reverend MacDonnell with 7 each, Barnes, Dubois and Steinitz, 6, Hannah, 4, Blackburne and Löwenthal, 3, Deacon, Mongredien, Dean and Robey, 2.

Staunton's name, it will be noted, had disappeared from the list of competitors; by now he was so immersed in literary work (notably editions of Shakespeare) that he had no time for playing chess. He did, however, continue to write about chess and chess-players and so to make enemies. He died at the age of sixty-four on 22 June, 1874, taking with him the secret of his birth.

But the tournament contained many other new and important figures. Louis Paulsen (1833–1891), whom we have already seen competing in New York in 1857, was a player whose importance has been continually underestimated. A great blindfold player, he also introduced some most important opening lines which have remained valid to this day; defences such as the Paulsen system in the Sicilian and attacks such as the Goring gambit.

The most memorable newcomer, however, was Wilhelm Steinitz, a Jew from Vienna who had settled in England and was soon to rival Anderssen. Another man also to become his rival was the Mancunian, Joseph Henry Blackburne (1841–1924), who eventually developed into England's strongest player.

In the same year as this tournament Anderssen drew matches against Paulsen and Berthold Suhle (1837–1904), a strong Berlin master. Meanwhile Steinitz had been improving rapidly, and in 1866 he beat Anderssen in a match.

chapter 12

Steinitz, the founder of modern chess

Wilhelm Steinitz, from whom stem most of the ideas which go to form modern chess, was born in Prague of Jewish parentage (an extraordinary proportion of the leading players of the nineteenth and twentieth centuries were Jews) on 17 May, 1836. We will see him in better historical perspective if we realize that this was about a year before Paul Morphy was born. The point is worth emphasizing, for there has been a tendency towards harshness in contrasting and differentiating his theories of play from those implicit in the game of Morphy. It is as though Steinitz's denigrators (there were many, since his sharp pen and wit incurred fierce enmity) wished to portray a picture of him as a man who broke the bright image of the crusader, Paul Morphy. The implication is that, for sordid gain, he produced an ugly, cramped style of play which tarnished instead of enhancing chess. The supposed anecdote I gave in the preceding chapter, if devised, was devised for this purpose. As evidence of a circumstantial kind, there is a variant of Buck's story which relates that Steinitz actually called on Paul Morphy at his home and sent in his card. Morphy looked at the card and said to his servant, 'Tell him his gambit's no good.'

It should be observed that those who approved of Steinitz's theories also tended to consider them as contrasting with and cancelling out Morphy's. Richard Réti, for example, in his *Modern Ideas in Chess,* published in successive editions in the 1920s, divides the theorists into chronological schools, calling one romantic and the other classical, etc. Despite the convenience of this approach for the historian, it has its drawbacks and fallacies, as I shall endeavour to explain at the end of this chapter, after the progress of chess in the nineteenth century has been described. Specifically, the danger here is that, if the contrast is accepted as all-embracing, one must think of Steinitz's theories as annulling those of Morphy. Such a thesis is in any case difficult either to disprove or to prove, because, while Steinitz himself committed his theories to paper in most articulate form, Morphy retired from the game before he could do so, as he had at one time intended.

To revert to Steinitz's early life: like most of the intellectually-disposed citizens of the Austro–Hungarian Empire, he went to study in the imperial city of Vienna. Ostensibly it was mathematics that

Steinitz, photographed during the Hastings Tournament in 1895.

he went to learn; but, if Oxford is the city of lost dreams, then Vienna must be called the city of lost mathematicians. The number of those who entered Vienna's university as mathematic students and emerged as chessmasters must run into several hundreds. Soon Steinitz, like Breyer, Réti, and many others later on, was doing nothing but playing chess and eking out a very bare living with journalism.

As I said in the last chapter, his first appearance on the international scene was in London in 1862, where he obtained a creditable, if not particularly impressive, result by coming equal fifth with Dubois, who was then and for a long time Italy's leading player. That he was better than Dubois he proved by defeating him in another match that year by 5+ 3− 1=.

Steinitz had come to England with the reputation of being a brilliant but unsteady and untried combinational player, eminently suitable for the classification of 'romantic'. Oddly enough, he had acquired the nickname of '*Der Österreichische Morphy*' (the Austrian Morphy) chiefly on the grounds that most people thought of Morphy as a genius supremely brilliant in chess rather than a chess genius pure and simple, thereby unconsciously belittling their hero.

In 1862 however, in the realms of romantic chess he was not of the stature of the great romantic, Adolf Anderssen; in a game full of tactical strokes, traps, pitfalls and stabs both in front and back, Anderssen destroyed him. In a short while, however, Steinitz was to reveal his great gifts in this line (the positional ones and in particular, the theories stemming from them and explaining them were to come much later) and it is characteristic of Anderssen's generous nature that it was he who seems first to have called his thrusting young rival 'the Austrian Morphy'.

An example of his early brilliance is the following game played at the 1862 London tournament:

White: Steinitz. Black: Mongredien. Centre Counter Defence.

1. P-K4,P-Q4; 2. PxP,QxP; 3. Kt-QB3,Q-Q1; 4. P-Q4,P-K3;
5. Kt-B3,Kt-KB3; 6. B-Q3,B-K2; 7. o-o,o-o; 8. B-K3,P-QKt3;
9. Kt-K5,B-Kt2; 10. P-B4,QKt-Q2; 11. Q-K2,Kt-Q4;
12. QKtxKt,PxKt; 13. R-B3,P-KB4; 14. R-R3,P-Kt3;
15. P-KKt4,PxP; 16. RxP,KtxKt; 17. BPxKt,KxR;
18. QxP,R-KKt1; 19. Q-R5 ch,K-Kt2; 20. Q-R6 ch,K-B2;
21. Q-R7 ch,K-K3; 22. Q-R3 ch,K-B2; 23. R-B1 ch,K-K1;
24. Q-K6,R-Kt2; 25. B-Kt5,Q-Q2; 26. BxP ch,RxB;
27. QxR ch,K-Q1; 28. R-B8 ch,Q-K1; 29. QxQ mate
(Diagram 36).

Though conventional in its set-up this attack has many pleasing points and is conducted with enormous élan.

Sensing that England was a land of opportunity as far as chess was concerned, Steinitz decided to remain after the London tournament. It was remarkable with what speed he not only learned to speak English, but to write it fluently. He soon poured out voluminous writings on chess, and their expressive force and nervous energy still make them a pleasure to read. This same nervous energy was also very evident in his everyday relationships, and in his behaviour towards other chessmasters or organizers. In consequence he made as many enemies as Staunton did, and his bitter remark when he left England in 1882—that he had been a 'foreigner' for twenty years—was in some ways no exaggeration.

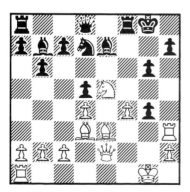

36: Position after Black's 15th move.

There is no doubt that Steinitz was a prickly character. He was also just as independent and single-minded in his pursuit of world supremacy as Bobby Fischer was to be a hundred years later. An example of this independence of mind appears in a story concerning his early days as a professional player in Vienna. He was playing against a celebrated banker named Epstein, and at one point the game looked difficult. Steinitz spent a long time considering his move and the banker, growing impatient, tried to hurry him on with the interjection, 'Na!' Steinitz did not reply, but started to play quickly. Then it was his opponent's turn to become deeply immersed in thought and Steinitz took his revenge with a sarcastic, 'Na?' The banker lost his temper and explained, 'Young man, do you know who I am?' Back came the calm reply, 'Oh yes, you are the banker Epstein—on the Stock Exchange. Here, however—I am Epstein.'

His progress in chess was as rapid as his progress in English. At the turn of the year he disposed of Blackburne with great ease in a match by 7+ 1− 2= and, although Blackburne was not yet at the peak of his powers and in any case was known to be a poor match-player, this was a result that could not be ignored. Steinitz also won matches against lesser lights over the next few years—against Mongredien, Owen and Deacon. In 1865, he won a tournament in Dublin that was smaller than the one in London in 1851, but played on the same lines; in Dublin however, there was a time limit, and the passing minutes were measured by a sand-glass. There he played a famous game against the Reverend MacDonnell, which was later held up by Réti as a perfect illustration of his modern way of playing and thinking:

White: Steinitz. Black: Reverend G. A. MacDonnell. Philidor Defence.

1. P-K4,P-K4; 2. Kt-KB3,P-Q3; 3. B-B4,B-K2; 4. P-B3,Kt-KB3;
5. P-Q3,0-0; 6. 0-0,B-Kt5; 7. P-KR3,BxKt; 8. QxB,P-B3;
9. B-Kt3,Kt-Q2; 10. Q-K2,Kt-B4; 11. B-B2,Kt-K3;
12. P-KKt3,Q-B2; 13. P-KB4,KR-K1; 14. Kt-Q2,QR-Q1;
15. Kt-B3,K-R1; 16. P-B5,Kt-B1; 17. P-KKt4,P-KR3;
18. P-Kt5,PxP; 19. KtxKtP,K-Kt1; 20. K-R1,Kt(B3)-R2;
21. Kt-B3,R-Q2; 22. R-KKt1,B-Q1; 23. B-R6,P-B3;
24. R-Kt2,P-Q4; 25. QR-KKt1,R(K1)-K2; 26. PxP,PxP;
27. B-R4,R-Q3; 28. RxP ch,RxR; 29. RxR ch,QxR;
30. BxQ,KxB; 31. Q-Kt2 ch,K-R1; 32. Kt-Q2,B-Kt3;
33. B-K8 and White won (Diagram 37).

Réti points out the typical scheme of opening play by which Steinitz keeps the centre closed with his moves three to five, and also how Steinitz avoids exchanges on his twenty-first move so as not to relieve his opponent in his cramped position. How much of this was part of a conscious system by Steinitz it is difficult to say. But later on, at any rate, he was to work out his system on paper, and it would naturally be based on his own experience and practice as a player. This victory must have been particularly sweet to him, since in 1862 the Reverend MacDonnell had come ahead of him in the London tournament.

The next year, 1866, was to prove a vital turning point in Steinitz's career. He won first prize in a tournament held in London by the British Chess Association from 19 June to 12 July. This was held on the knock-out model of 1851, and Steinitz defeated the next strongest player, Cecil de Vere, in the very first round. Six days

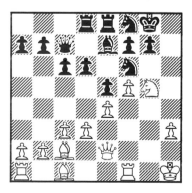

37: Position after White's 20th move.

after the end of the tournament, he faced the world's acknowledged leading player, Adolf Anderssen, in a match which ended in a victory for him by 8+ 6–. There were no draws and the advantage oscillated to and fro many times; but on 10 August, 1866 Steinitz had won the necessary eight games and with them the right to regard himself as the world's leading player.

It is not clear how soon after this he claimed to be the world champion, but it is certain that it was he who invented the idea of a world championship, and that he was soon talking of his matches as being contests for the title. The very introduction of this concept was of tremendous importance to the unification of world chess. At one sweep a link was forged among chessplayers wherever they existed.

When Steinitz conceived the notion, there was already at least a partial link between Europe and the Americas, in the sense that there was constant communication between them.

There was no official recognition of Paul Morphy as world champion, but he was so *de facto* if not *de jure*. But the connection between the two continents was greatly strengthened and more and more examples occurred of the interchange of great players between them. Very much later on, well into the twentieth century, as communications improved through the introduction of air travel and as civilisation reached out still further into the other continents, this world championship nexus extended to Africa, Asia and Australasia.

The idea spread too, not only in terms of space but in terms of sex and age. When Steinitz instilled the idea of a world championship into the minds of chess-players, he also did much for the popularization of chess amongst women. Their motivation for playing chess received a great impetus once it became known that a world championship title existed for them too at the end of the rainbow. This also applied to the young of both sexes when, in the course of time, world championship titles were instituted for various junior ages.

Naturally, Steinitz had nothing like this in mind when he first made his claim to be world champion and no doubt the intention was purely selfish or, to put it more mildly, self-interested. But, whether he intended it or no, whether he caught even half a glimpse of what he was initiating with his claim to be world champion, all this does not matter at all. The effect was great and enduring, no matter what was the intention or the foresight.

Nevertheless, his claim to be world champion was not enough by itself, nor could it be based on one match only against an ageing Anderssen. Remember that when the 1866 match was played Anderssen was 48 and Steinitz 30. Naturally, Steinitz himself knew he was the best player in the world but that world needed convincing. This, to do him justice, he set about doing with great energy, taking part in many tournaments and playing many matches.

It is interesting to note that he was more successful in his matches than in tournament play. For nearly thirty years, from the time he assumed the title in 1866, to when he lost it in 1894, he never lost a match. But his tournament record was far less impressive. His wins of first prize in important tournaments during this period were confined to Vienna in 1873, and to an equal first in Vienna in 1882; there were also two seconds of great value—at Baden-Baden in 1870 and London in 1883. The fact, however, that they were seconds undermined his position vis-à-vis those who came first—Anderssen in Baden-Baden, and Zukertort in London.

There was a simple reason for this disparity which did honour to Steinitz's sincerity as a theorist. Not all his ideas were sound, and where he erred was in a tendency to artificial manoeuvres or systems. The idea, for example, that the King should be used not only in the ending, but also in the middle-game and even in the opening, was doomed to failure. However, he felt in honour bound to use them on every occasion. In match play, the validity or otherwise of one's ideas is not so important as the power to dominate one's opponent's personality, and to lead the game into realms where he feels uneasy. Thus, Steinitz could conquer in matches, but not in tournaments.

The year after he won his match against Anderssen, he played in two important tournaments, a large one in Paris, and a smaller one, at Dundee in Scotland. In Scotland, he came second to the talented German master, Neumann. The event was notable for two firsts. It was the first time in a tournament that a draw was counted for half a point. It was also the first time that Steinitz used his celebrated gambit, which involved moving the King early in the game. This was the only defeat suffered by Neumann. Steinitz also beat Mac-Donnell, who came third but lost to both de Vere and Blackburne.

The win against Neumann is an excellent example of Steinitzian play:

White: Steinitz. Black: Neumann. Vienna Gambit.
1. P-K4,P-K4; 2. Kt-QB3,Kt-QB3; 3. P-B4,PxP;
4. P-Q4,Q-R5 ch; 5. K-K2,P-Q3; 6. Kt-B3,B-Kt5;
7. BxP,BxKt ch; 8. KxB,KKt-K2; 9. B-K2,0-0-0;
10. B-K3,Q-B3 ch; 11. K-Kt3,P-Q4; 12. B-Kt4 ch,K-Kt1;
13. P-K5,Q-Kt3; 14. K-B2,P-KR4; 15. B-R3,P-B3;
16. PxP,QxBP ch; 17. Q-B3,QxQ ch; 18. PxQ,P-KKt3;
19. Kt-K2,Kt-B4; 20. BxKt,PxB; 21. P-B3,B-Q3;
22. B-B4,K-B1; 23. KR-KKt1,K-Q2; 24. R-Kt7 ch,Kt-K2;
25. QR-KKt1,K-K3; 26. BxB,RxB; 27. Kt-B4 ch,K-B3;
28. Kt-Q3,R-Kt3; 29. P-Kt3,R-R3; 30. Kt-K5,R-Kt4;
31. P-QR4,R-R4; 32. P-Kt4,R-R3; 33. Kt-Q7 ch,K-K3;
34. Kt-B5 ch, resigns (Diagram 38).

This game was also an example of the force of Steinitz's more paradoxical play. Notice, however, that although the White King is advanced almost into the thick of the fray, he has taken good care to have more minor pieces developed than Black, so that in this instance there is no real danger for the King.

In the Paris tournament, Steinitz again revealed a certain vulnerability against the better players. It was a curious occasion, with a mixture of very good and very bad players, and with relics of the old system of play in the fact that draws were not counted. The first-prize winner was a Hungarian professional, Ignatz Kolisch, 20 points. He was followed by Simon Winawer, 19, Steinitz, 18, Neumann, 17 and Cecil Valentine de Vere, 14. Then came an assortment of eight enthusiastic amateurs, some gifted, and others, like Morphy's boyhood friend, Eugene Rousseau, who came bottom, not so gifted.

But the top five constituted quite a representative cross-section of the world's leading players. Winawer, whose influence on the progress of opening theory has been somewhat neglected and under-estimated by chess historians, was a strong Polish master

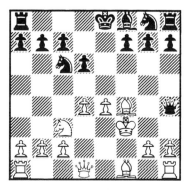

38: Position after .White's 8th move.

who made both his first appearance and his name in international chess at this tournament. It was he who introduced the so-called Winawer variation of the French Defence (1. P-K4,P-K3; 2. P-Q4,P-Q4; 3. Kt-QB3,B-Kt5), a dynamic line based on deep strategical ideas, which was to prove of lasting importance.

This was the greatest success in the chess career of Ignatz Kolisch, a Hungarian professional. It was also his last. The next year, Baron Rothschild of Vienna, who was a generous chess patron, enabled him to take up a new career—as a banker. He prospered exceedingly, eventually himself becoming a baron of the Austro–Hungarian Empire, and a noted patron of chess in his turn.

For a little while Steinitz refrained from competitive play and, during this interval, it was apparent from the results of a number of small international tournaments in Germany that Anderssen's bolt was by no means shot. A new name too was arising, that of Johannes Hermann Zukertort, a player of enormous gifts who was to prove a most dangerous rival to Steinitz.

It was Anderssen, however, who was to win the great tournament at Baden-Baden in 1870, just half a point ahead of Steinitz. This was a double-round event with a time limit of twenty moves an hour controlled by chess clocks known as the *Schwarzwald* (Black Forest) type. Steinitz lost both his games to Anderssen and was also beaten by Blackburne. He, along with Neumann, came half a point below Steinitz and was beginning to achieve the fine tournament results which earned him the name of the 'Black Death' in Europe.

At length, in London in 1872, Steinitz won first prize in an international tournament of some importance. He had 7 points, ahead of Blackburne, 5, and Zukertort, 4. In the same year he beat Zukertort easily in a match by 7 + 1– 4 = . Clearly, Zukertort, who was some six years younger, was not yet remotely his peer.

Another, and still more important success for Steinitz came in Vienna in 1873, when he was first ahead of Blackburne, Anderssen, Samuel Rosenthal, Henry Edward Bird, L. Paulsen and six more masters. The event was run on an unusual and complicated system: in order to obtain the full point, players had to win matches of three games against each other. Naturally, two wins sufficed and this was the case in the majority of matches. But there occurred the strange anomaly by which Blackburne won more games than Steinitz (twenty to his eighteen) and beat him in their individual match by $2\frac{1}{2}$–$\frac{1}{2}$, yet only tied with him for first place. Steinitz beat him in the play-off by 2–0.

Steinitz also defeated his old rival, Anderssen, with two straight wins in the Vienna tournament. One is a game so modern in spirit that it might have been played yesterday:

White: Steinitz. Black: Anderssen. Queen's Gambit Declined.

1. P-Q4,P-Q4; 2. P-QB4,P-K3; 3. Kt-QB3,Kt-KB3;
4. B-Kt5,B-K2; 5. P-K3,0-0; 6. Kt-B3,P-QKt3;
7. B-Q3,B-Kt2; 8. 0-0,QKt-Q2; 9. PxP,PxP; 10. R-B1,P-B4;
11. PxP,PxP; 12. Q-R4,Kt-K5; 13. BxKt,PxB;
14. KR-Q1,BxB; 15. KtxB,QxKt; 16. RxKt,KR-Kt1;
17. Q-Kt3,B-B3; 18. QxP ch,K-R1; 19. P-KR4,Q-Kt5;
20. RxP,RxR; 21. QxR,RxP; 22. QxP,Q-K3;
23. R-Q1,P-R3; 24. R-Q6,Q-B2; 25. Kt-Q1,R-K7;
26. K-B1, resigns (Diagram 39).

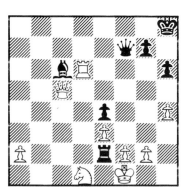

39: Final position.

The quiet piece of humour in the final move, with the King attacking the Rook, would have appealed to the great Aron Nimzowitch, but this game was played thirteen years before he was born.

This was Anderssen's last tournament for some time. He was to have another burst of chess activity shortly before his death, but by now, at the age of fifty-five, he was feeling the strain. Yet he did well in this event and, in the following position against Paulsen, produced a charming combination (Diagram 40).

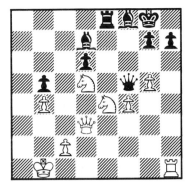

40: Black (L. Paulsen); White (Anderssen) to play.

Now he won by 34. Kt(K4)–B6 ch,PxKt; 35. KtxP ch, K–B2; 36. RxP ch,B–Kt2; 37. RxB ch,KxR; 38. KtxR ch,K–B1; 39. QxQ ch,BxQ; 40. KtxP,B–Q2; 41. Kt–K4,K–Kt2; 42. Kt–Kt3,K–B2; 43. P–B5,K–K2; 44. K–B1,K–Q3; 45. P–Kt6,B–K1; 46. K–Q2,K–Q4; 47. K–Q3,K–K4; 48. K–K3,K–Q4; 49. K–B4,K–B5; 50. Kt–K4,KxP; 51. Kt–Q6,B–B3; 52. P–B6,K–B6; 53. KtxP ch,BxKt; 54. P–B7, resigns.

In 1874 *The Field* decided to institute a chess column and invited Steinitz to be its editor. In accepting the invitation he must have been conscious of the opportunity this gave him to express his ideas in writing as well as over the board. To do this it was necesary for him to devote time to study and to elaborating his new methods; for about ten years, therefore, with the exception of a match against Blackburne, which he won by 7–0 in 1876, he did not take part in competitive chess. By dint of hard work he made *The Field* column a household word among the world's chessplayers. He also made many enemies, as I have said, since his vitriolic pen spared nobody. It was in *The Field* that he first enunciated the principles of modern chess, talked about the power of two Bishops and made the reference to the accumulation of small advantages, which has become famous.

For the first part of this period of Steinitz's absence there were, in fact, few tournaments and those were small. Then in 1877 a jubilee tournament was held in Leipzig to celebrate Anderssen's fiftieth year of playing chess. First prize was won by Louis Paulsen, half a point ahead of Anderssen and of Zukertort, whose career was on the rise. In 1878 in a big tournament in Paris, after coming equal first with Winawer ahead of Blackburne, he won the play-off by 3–1. Anderssen also played in this event, but he did only respectably, coming halfway down the list. He was already unwell, and he died a few months later on 13 March, 1879.

With his death, there passed away a whole era of the game. A magnificent combinationalist, he had that quality which the Germans call '*genial*', for which there is no good translation. It derives from genius but it has a warmth that is sometimes lacking from that cold epithet. No one ever spoke critically of him and he was a noble gentleman in the best sense of those two words.

In the new era, with Steinitz temporarily out of action, the lead passed into the hands of Zukertort and, as far as tournaments were concerned, into those of Blackburne. Both were remarkable and colourful figures.

Joseph Henry Blackburne, who was the slightly older of the two, was born in Manchester on 10 December, 1841. He learned chess in his late teens, his interest having been aroused first by a simultaneous display given by Paul Morphy and then by a blindfold display by Louis Paulsen. He himself was an attacking player who excelled in combination play and in the end-game; when he brought off some fine coup, he used to call it 'a little bit of Morphy'. He also became

Sixteen of the leading players of the world in 1886. Left to right, back row: Mackenzie, Kolisch, Bird, Rosenthal, Norwood-Potter, Shallop, Paulsen; middle row: Winawer, de Rivière, Mason, MacDonnell, Gunsberg; front row: Blackburne, Steinitz, Zuckertort, Englisch.

expert in giving simultaneous displays, sometimes blindfold, sometimes not.

Many are the stories of his wit and prowess at displays. Perhaps the most famous was the occasion when he picked up a glass of whisky which one of his opponents had at the side of his board. He drank the whisky, made his move and walked happily on. His opponent refilled the glass and when Blackburne returned and was about to pick it up again, the man stopped him. Said Blackburne, 'I saw a glass of whisky en prise and took it en passant.' That he was fond of whisky is also indicated by some evidence at my old school, which had a long chess-playing tradition. We possessed minutes of the chess-club going back to the latter half of the nineteenth century, and one page was devoted to a visit and a simultaneous display by Blackburne. At the bottom, the secretary had written, 'Mr. Blackburne's fee was a guinea and a bottle of whisky.' A story of his skill is to be found in Graham's *Mr Blackburne's Games at Chess*. During a game, someone came to him, said that Mr X was anxious to get away to catch a train and asked if he would, therefore, please accept the offer of a draw. 'Ah,' said Blackburne, 'let me see.' Then he announced a mate in six moves, adding, 'And now the gentleman can catch his train.'

Blackburne was a gifted tournament player who scored many successes and has thus far been the only Englishman to win first prize outright in a great tournament. He was less at home in matches and lost many, even to players whom he frequently beat in tournaments. On the whole his strength lay in open play and his weakness in close. He was not quite versatile enough to come into consideration for the highest honours of a world championship, but he could certainly hold his own in tournaments in any company.

Zukertort, on the other hand, rose to the point where it was obvious that he was a challenger for the world title. A figure of mystery as far as his antecedents were concerned, born either in Riga or in Lublin on 7 September, 1842, he settled in England in the 1870s and became naturalized. He claimed to have obtained a doctorate of medicine at Breslau University in 1865, to have been in the Prussian army in the wars against Denmark, Austria and France (it is not clear what he was doing in the Prussian army if he was born in either Lublin or Riga), to have been a first-class shot, an excellent fencer and, on some occasions, a professional journalist. The number of languages he spoke ran to eleven or more. This at least can be substantiated—he was an excellent blindfold chessplayer.

He too was a very fine combinationalist, and he had more experience and command of close positions than, say, Blackburne. His weakness was a variability that was due to a highly-strung nervous system. He was a great player who might well have become a most worthy world champion had his life-span not more or less coincided with that of a still greater figure, Wilhelm Steinitz. Indeed, it is arguable that in skill and ability he was the equal of Steinitz, but that he was handicapped by being physically weaker. It is unfortunate, but nevertheless one of the hard facts of life among chessmasters, that physical matters played an all-important role in something which, ideally speaking, should concern and depend upon the mind only.

During this interesting period in chess history—roughly the 1880s—when international tournaments were being held on a really big scale in Europe, these two players were constantly among those who took the leading places. Blackburne achieved the greatest triumph of his career in the great international tournament in Berlin in 1881, where he was first with fourteen points out of a possible sixteen, no less than three points ahead of the second-prize winner, Zukertort. In this tournament a new name appeared, that of the great Russian master, Mikhail Ivanovitch Tschigorin, who was equal third and fourth with Winawer, with ten-and-a-half points. This exciting player, a romantic if ever there was one, was to exert a profound influence on the course of opening theory—considerably more in the twentieth century than he did in the nineteenth. Russian players look to him, more than to any other Soviet player of our time, almost as their patron saint.

In 1882 Steinitz, the world champion, returned to the arena, and at once the effect of his long pondering over modern strategy became apparent in his play. Thanks to the financial backing of Kolisch, now Baron Kolisch and a rich man, a strong double-round tournament of eighteen players was held in Vienna that year. Steinitz tied with Winawer for first place with twenty-four points, and shared the top two prizes with him after a play-off had ended all square, each player winning a game. James Mason, an American master who lived in London for most of his life, was third with twenty-three points. He was eventually to produce a fine work on chess, 'The Art of Chess' (1895), which, thanks to his easy natural style of writing, became a classic and can still be read with profit and entertainment.

Zukertort was equal fourth with the American master, George Henry Mackenzie, in the Vienna tournament and in the following year came his best tournament result at the great London International Tournament of 1883. This too was a double-round tournament which included most of the leading masters. It was endowed with a prize-fund of £1,100 which, for the time, was unprecedented in its magnitude. Zukertort led from the start and was assured of first prize with two weeks to go when his score of twenty-two points was beyond the reach of any other competitor. But he had been sustaining himself by the use of drugs and practically collapsed towards the end, losing his last three games. Thus, the high point in his tournament career was also to be his last tournament success.

Steinitz, who like Zukertort did not draw a single game, was second with 19 ahead of Blackburne 16½, Tschigorin (also no draws!) 16, Englisch, Mackenzie and Mason, 15½, Rosenthal, 14, Winawer, 13, Bird, 12, Noa, 9½, Sellman, 6½, Mortimer and Skipworth 3. The two bottom-placed players are worthy of note. Mortimer was a very successful writer of farces for the stage and the Reverend A. B. Skipworth was probably the most belligerent of all the nineteenth-century English chess reverends. It was a remarkable tournament, too, for the scarcity of draws. Out of the 182 games played, only seven were drawn!

Much the most striking game was Zukertort's win over Blackburne, an anthology piece with almost as dramatic a turn of events as ever has been witnessed in tournament chess:

White: Zukertort. Black: Blackburne. Queen's Gambit Declined.

1. P-QB4,P-K3; 2. P-K3,Kt-KB3; 3. Kt-KB3,P-QKt3;
4. B-K2,B-Kt2; 5. 0-0,P-Q4; 6. P-Q4,B-Q3; 7. Kt-B3,0-0;
8. P-QKt3,QKt-Q2; 9. B-Kt2,Q-K2; 10. Kt-QKt5,Kt-K5;
11. KtxB,PxKt; 12. Kt-Q2,QKt-B3; 13. P-B3,KtxKt;
14. QxKt,PxP; 15. BxP,P-Q4; 16. B-Q3,KR-B1;
17. QR-K1,R-B2; 18. P-K4,QR-B1; 19. P-K5,Kt-K1;
20. P-B4,P-K3; 21. R-K3,P-B4; 22. PxP e.p.,KtxP;
23. P-B5!,Kt-K5; 24. BxKt,PxB; 25. PxKtP,R-B7;
26. PxP ch,K-R1; 27. P-Q5 dis ch,P-K4;
28. Q-Kt4!,R(B1)-B4; 29. R-B8 ch,KxP; 30. QxP ch,K-Kt2;
31. BxP ch,KxR; 32. B-Kt7 ch, resigns (Diagram 41).

The game in the last ten moves is most richly orchestrated; but note how old-fashioned it appears in contrast to Steinitz's Queen's Gambit against Anderssen at Vienna ten years earlier! Rejecting his doctor's advice to give up serious chess, Zukertort left England for prolonged tours, first of the United States and Canada, and then of Europe. Meanwhile his supporters and admirers were asserting that, after his London performance, he was the true world champion. His advocates included the many enemies Steinitz had made, among them Leopold Hoffer, editor of the *Chess Monthly*. The magazine vigorously espoused Zukertort's cause and pursued Steinitz with obloquy and contempt. These assertions were to be put to the test three years later, and were, alas, to prove the death of poor Zukertort.

Steinitz himself, disgusted with the attacks made on him by his English critics, and under the false impression that it would be easier to earn his living in the United States, left for New York shortly after the London tournament, with a bitter remark to the effect that he would rather die in America than live in England. His arrival in America was, as we shall see, a powerful spur to chess life there.

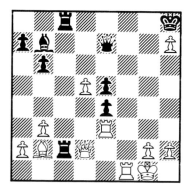

41: Position after Black's 27th move.

Two more important tournaments were held during this period, one in Nuremburg in 1883, and the other in Hamburg in 1885, both under the auspices of the German Chess Federation. In Nuremburg, Winawer was first with fourteen points out of eighteen, half a point ahead of Blackburne. At Hamburg, Isidor Gunsberg was first with twelve points out of seventeen, Blackburne again coming second half a point below him. Gunsberg, who came to England early in life from Budapest, was one of the players who worked the chess automaton, Mephisto. Later in his career he was to get as far as playing matches for the world championship, but it is doubtful if his strength was of this quality. He was active as a journalist for many years and, as a youth, I saw him in this capacity at an international tournament in Canterbury; this was only a year before his death, in 1930.

A most important newcomer in the Hamburg event was Dr Siegbert Tarrasch, who came second, equal with Blackburne and three others. Of him much more anon; but for the moment it is sufficient to say that his writings and his games were to have just as much influence on the course and progress of chess theory as were those of Tschigorin. Later on these two were to take part in matches for the world title.

It was, however, Zukertort who, in 1886, was unwise enough to challenge Steinitz for the world championship. He must have been fully aware of the risk to his health that such a match must entail. In the first place, the contest would inevitably be of long duration, for the victor would be the first person to win ten games, draws not being counted. Secondly, the match was due to be played in three different places, two of which, St Louis and New Orleans, were considered to have climates troublesome to Europeans. Finally there was the fact that his health had already once before broken down under the strain of a long tournament, and the contest with Steinitz was likely to be just as arduous as that one, if not more so.

At first the match went well for the challenger. Indeed, at the end of the series in the first city of play, New York, he was leading by four to one. But the other two venues proved disastrous for him. By the end of the St Louis series his opponent had won as many as he, and in New Orleans (the home of Paul Morphy), Steinitz attained his ten games without Zukertort's having added more than one to his total. Thus the world champion retained his title with a score of 10+ 5− 5=.

There was no arguing against such figures, although Zukertort on his return blamed it all on the climate, an excuse that has often been given in such cases. It seems that he hoped for a return match under more favourable conditions, one, which, in his own words, would be 'not for a trial of constitution, but for a trial of chess skill'. He never got his match; within two years he was dead.

On his return to England, however, he took part in two small tournaments, coming equal seventh with Mackenzie in one in London which was won by Blackburne, and faring rather better in a weaker tournament at Nottingham, where he was equal third with Gunsberg, below Burn and Schallopp. He came equal fourteenth in 1887 in a big tournament of the German Chess Federation at Frankfurt-am-Main, which was won by Mackenzie with 15 points ahead of Blackburne and Weiss, 13½, von Bardeleben 13, Berger and Tarrasch, 12. He was fourth in a smaller tournament in London, also in 1887, which was won jointly by Burn and Gunsberg. He died the next year, on 20 June, of cerebral haemorrhage, following a game of chess at Simpson's Divan.

Once established in the United States, Steinitz set about creating a literary outlet with which he could assail old-established theory and replace it by his own. For this purpose he founded the *International Chess Magazine* and edited it from January 1885 to December 1891. The magazine was almost entirely written by Steinitz, and it says much for his literary ability that it still makes very good reading. Later too he wrote *The Modern Chess Instructor,* which was published in two parts; the first is a large volume, the second is tiny and hard to come by. He also wrote and published in 1889 a tournament book of considerable merit about the Sixth American Congress. This was a strong double-round tournament in which twenty players competed. Steinitz himself did not do so, since he was too busy organizing the event. First prize was shared between Tschigorin and Weiss, ahead of Gunsberg, Blackburne and Burn, in that order.

Earlier in that year had come a really severe test for Steinitz, in the shape of a match for the title of world champion against the Russian giant, Tschigorin. This was not merely a rivalry of personal skills, but also a clash between two schools of thought—between Tschigorin, the romantic, and Steinitz, the classical. This terminology may surprise those who are accustomed to thinking, along with Réti, that the terms should be used chronologically to describe successive schools, and that the romantic succeeds the classical. But Réti was wrong to adopt this rigid if convenient form of classification. In reality, classical and romantic players exist contemporaneously. Not only do they not succeed each other, but one can discern traces of romanticism in the classical and vice versa. One can, for example, think of a number of superb players of our time who are romantic, but who certainly do not pertain to the Anderssen period. Equally, one can enumerate a number of players who believe in classicism in chess, but who would be at an utter loss to find themselves in the classical Tarrasch period of the nineteenth century.

The match with Tschigorin took place early in the year of 1889 in Havana, and Steinitz won it comfortably enough by about the same margin with which he had beaten Zukertort (10+ 6– 1=, i.e. the same number of wins, but one more loss and many fewer draws). The tenth match-game was typical. Tschigorin employed his famous defence to the Queen's Pawn, which has been named after him. But the calm way in which Steinitz rejected it in favour of some line and method which has become everyday practice nowadays, is indeed impressive:

White: Steinitz. Black: Tschigorin. Queen's Gambit Declined. Tschigorin Defence.

1. Kt-KB3,P-Q4; 2. P-Q4,B-Kt5; 3. P-B4,Kt-QB3;
4. P-K3,P-K4; 5. Q-Kt3,BxKt; 6. PxB,KpxP; 7. BPxP,Kt-K4;
8. PxP,Kt-Q2; 9. Kt-B3,Q-K2 ch; 10. B-K3,Q-Kt5;
11. Q-B2,KKt-B3; 12. B-QKt5,R-Q1; 13. o-o-o,P-QR3;
14. B-R4,B-K2; 15. KR-Kt1,P-KKt3; 16. B-R6,P-QKt4;
17. B-Kt3,Kt-Kt3; 18. KR-K1,K-Q2; 19. B-KB4,R-QB1;
20. P-QR3,Q-R4; 21. B-Kt5,Kt-Kt1; 22. BxB,KtxB;
23. Kt-K4,R-QKt1; 24. Kt-B6 ch,K-Q1; 25. RxKt,KxR;
26. QxP ch,Kt-Q2; 27. QxQ, resigns (Diagram 43).

Steinitz was the moving spirit in the New York 1889 tournament,

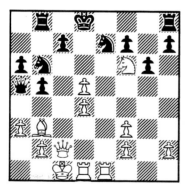

43: Position after Black's 24th move.

Dr Lasker (left) playing against Dr Tarrasch (right).

and of the limited edition of tournament books produced, six were allocated to him; of one of them I am the proud possessor.

In 1889 a strong international tournament was also held by the German Chess Federation at Breslau, and was easily won by Tarrasch. At the same time as Tarrasch was winning the chief tournament, a young man of twenty-one, named Emanuel Lasker, was winning the master title in the Major Tournament of the Congress. The following year this same young man won a celebrated game in the first international tournament ever to be held in the Netherlands (at Amsterdam, and he came second to Burn). His game was against Bauer, with a lovely double Bishop sacrifice:
White: Lasker. Black: Bauer. Bird's Opening.

1. P-KB4,P-Q4; 2. Kt-KB3,P-K3; 3. P-K3,Kt-KB3;
4. P-QKt3,B-K2; 5. B-Kt2,P-QKt3; 6. B-Q3,B-Kt2;
7. Kt-B3,0-0; 8. 0-0,QKt-Q2; 9. Kt-K2,P-B4; 10. Kt-Kt3,Q-B2;
11. Kt-K5,KtxKt; 12. BxKt,Q-B3; 13. Q-K2,P-QR3;
14. Kt-R5,KtxKt; 15. BxP ch,KxB; 16. QxKt ch, K-Kt1;
17. BxP,KxB; 18. Q-Kt4 ch,K-R2; 19. R-B3,P-K4;
20. R-R3 ch,Q-R3; 21. RxQ ch,KxR; 22. Q-Q7,B-KB3;
23. QxB,K-Kt2; 24. R-KB1,QR-Kt1; 25. Q-Q7,KR-Q1;
26. Q-Kt4 ch,K-B1; 27. PxP,B-Kt2; 28. P-K6,R-Kt2;
29. Q-Kt6,P-B3; 30. RxP ch,BxR; 31. QxB ch,K-K1;
32. Q-R8 ch,K-K2; 33. Q-Kt7 ch,KxP; 34. QxR,R-Q3;
35. QxRP,P-Q5; 36. PxP,PxP; 37. P-KR4,P-Q6;
38. QxQP, resigns (Diagram 44).

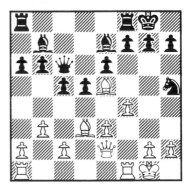

44: Position after Black's 14th move.

The idea of this combination was taken up and repeated by many chessmasters in both the nineteenth and twentieth centuries.

The rise of these new young talents and the challenge they offered to Steinitz to prove that he was world champion in tournament chess as well as in match play, could not have escaped his notice. But for the time being he contented himself with meeting the more or less established figures of the chess-world in single combat. He could not hope to put off competing against the younger stars forever; in fact, he never was to play a match against Tarrasch who, on his tournament results, was the obvious candidate for role of challenger. The real danger, as we shall see, lay in another quarter.

Meanwhile, at the turn of the year 1890–91, he took on Isidor Gunsberg in a match for the world championship, bearing in mind that he owed Tschigorin a return match. Gunsberg, whose match record was much more distinguished than his tournament results (he had beaten both Blackburne and Bird in matches with remarkable ease and even drawn a match with Tschigorin at Havana in 1890 by 9+ 9– 6=), put up a better resistance to Steinitz than Tschigorin had done, but in the end Steinitz won by 6+ 4– 9=.

His next enterprise struck devastatingly at both his pride and his pocket. In his *Modern Chess Instructor,* published in 1890, he had given some analyses (among others) on the Two Knights' Defence (1. P-K4,P-K4; 2. Kt-KB3,Kt-QB3; 3. B-B4,Kt-B3; 4. Kt-Kt5,P-Q4; 5. PxP,Kt-QR4; 6. B-Kt5 ch,P-B3; 7. PxP,PxP; 8. B-K2,P-KR3; 9. Kt-R3,) and on the Evans' Gambit (1. P-K4,P-K4; 2. Kt-KB3,Kt-QB3; 3. B-B4,B-B4; 4. P-QKt4,BxP; 5. P-B3,B-R4; 6. O-O,Q-B3; 7. P-Q4,Kt-R3), maintaining that White stood better in the first case, and that Black was better in the second. Tschigorin maintained the contrary and they played a cable match with these two variations for a stake of 750 dollars. The Russian won both games and the blow to Steinitz's finances was heavy and lasting.

So, when the opportunity of a new match with Tschigorin came along he accepted it readily. The conditions were a little different. The victor was to be the man who won ten games; but if the score stood at 9-all, then only three more deciding games would be played. The match was played from 1 January, 1892 to 28 February in Havana. This time Tschigorin, the challenger, played better and it was touch and go. He took the lead from the start and Steinitz had to work dreadfully hard to restore the balance. At one moment the score stood 5–3 in Tschigorin's favour. Then the tide began to flow in the world champion's direction. After twenty games, the match stood all square with each player having won eight. Then, after a draw, Steinitz won the twenty-second game; now he was ahead by 9–8. For the twenty-third game a record audience of 1,900 assembled and, with Tschigorin playing a King's Gambit for the first time in the match, play went as follows:

White: Tschigorin. Black: Steinitz. King's Gambit Accepted.

1. P-K4,P-K4; 2. P-KB4,PxP; 3. Kt-KB3,Kt-KB3;
4. P-K5,Kt-R4; 5. B-K2,P-KKt3; 6. P-Q4,B-Kt2; 7. O-O,P-Q3;
8. Kt-B3,O-O; 9. Kt-K1,PxP; 10. BxKt,PxB; 11. PxP,QxQ;
12. KtxQ,Kt-B3; 13. BxP,B-B4?; 14. Kt-K3,B-K5;
15. Kt-B3,KR-K1; 16. Kt-Kt5,B-Kt3; 17. Kt-Q5,BxKP;
18. KtxP,BxKt; 19. BxB,QR-B1; 20. B-Kt3,Kt-Q5;
21. P-B3,Kt-K7 ch; 22. K-B2,P-R5; 23. B-Q6,Kt-Q5;
24. PxKt,R-B7 ch; 25. K-Kt1,R(K1)-K7; 26. QR-K1,RxP ch;

*Late eighteenth century
European chessmen; the white
pieces are in bone, the black in
horn.*

A game of chess—Lord Grey playing King William IV during the Reform Bill controversy; from Doyle's Political Sketches, *1832.*

27. K-R1,K-Kt2; 28. R-K8?,P-B4; 29. Kt-K6 ch,K-B3;
30. R-K7,R(Kt7)-K7; 31. P-Q5,R(B7)-Q7; 32. B-Kt4? ,RxP ch;
33. K-Kt1,R(Q7)-Kt7 mate (Diagram 45).

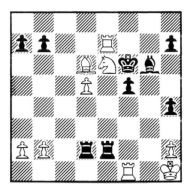

45: *Position after Black's 31st move.*

The game was typical of such world championship contests in that the tension of the moment made both players perform far below their usual standards. So, here, Black should have played 13. .,KtxP with marked advantage; White could have won by 28. B-K5 ch, and, instead of the hideous mistake allowing mate, he could have retained an advantage by 32. RxKtP. Throughout the game, too, Steinitz disdained a draw and played for more (he should have got less).

If America (including Cuba) was the home of matches, Europe was the centre where nearly all the important tournaments were played. In these, Tarrasch scored constant and magnificently impressive successes. At Manchester in 1890 he was first with 15½, Blackburne coming second with 12 points. At Dresden in 1892 he was again first, this time 'only' 1½ points ahead of his nearest rivals. And at Leipzig in 1894 he was first with 13½, ahead of Lipke, 13, Teichmann, 12, Blackburne and Walbrodt, 11½, Janowski and Marco, 10½ etc. There were some important new names on this list. Teichmann was to develop into one of the strongest German masters. Janowski, a brilliant Polish–Jewish player, was to become a candidate for world championship honours and Marco was to be one of the greatest annotators of all time in his writings in the *Wiener Schachzeitung.*

It seemed obvious to everyone that Tarrasch was the natural challenger for the world title and the Havana Chess Club started negotiations to that effect. But there were complications. Tarrasch was a practising doctor of medicine and there were difficulties about the amount of time he could spend away from his work. Then, too, although he was obviously one of the greatest tournament players of all time, he was not so sure of himself in matches. In 1893 he drew a match with Tschigorin at St Petersburg by 9+ 9– 4—. This too must have given him pause. In any case, he hesitated, and in so doing it may well be that he missed a favourable tide. As we shall see, another fine player stepped in and took the potential and actual honours from him.

Whether world champion or no, Tarrasch is still one of the chess immortals and deserves, or rather demands, a special mention in any history of the game. Siegbert Tarrasch was born on 5 March, 1862 in Breslau. He became a doctor, practising first in Nuremburg and then in Munich. We have traced his tournament career so far in all its glory. Had there been two world championship titles, one for matches and the other for tournaments, there is no doubt that by 1894 he would have been termed the world champion for tournament play.

Magnificent though he was at the board, however, it is probable that he will be remembered more for his writings, which deservedly earned him the title of *praeceptor Germaniae* (the teacher of Germany); indeed this might also have been phrased *praeceptor mundi* (the teacher of the world). He wrote with a keen clarity and a fine sense for the feeling and sound of words which has never been excelled by any chess author.

In two great books *Dreihundert Schachpartien* (Leipzig 1895) and *Die Moderne Schachpartie* (Nurnberg 1912), he gave a complete picture of the classical player and demonstrated how methodical

Tarrasch photographed during the 1895 Hastings Tournament, which aroused great local interest.

logic could produce works of art in chess. A later book, *The Game of Chess,* as it was known in the English translation, which appeared in 1935, a year after his death, showed a decline in his powers of judgment; by then, the methodical logic had become dogmatic prejudice. But the bulk of his writings will stand the test of time.

Modern judgements, in reaction against his formulation of basic principles, have tended to underestimate his contributions to the game. He, more than anyone of his era, more even than Steinitz, widened, deepened and popularized the scope of opening theory. For Tarrasch, by means of his logical and methodical approach to the problems of the openings, made their study scientific, and the application of opening knowledge became entirely reasonable and comprehensible (this was most important for the popularization of the game) to the average human intelligence. Here again we see the processes of civilization at work. The professional classes, and Dr Tarrasch was essentially of these, had by this time become the new leaders of society in the best sense. The middle classes had triumphed and the aristocracy was on its way out.

But it should not be thought for one moment that his essentially classical approach deprived him of the warm humanity which is commonly (and in many cases mistakenly) ascribed to the romantic. Consider his following famous passage, of which the last sentence in particular is so true that one never tires of it:

> Chess is a form of intellectual productiveness; therein lies its peculiar charm. Intellectual productiveness is one of the greatest joys—if not the greatest one—of human existence. It is not everyone who can write a play, or build a bridge, or even make a good joke. But in chess, everyone can, everyone must, be intellectually productive and so can share in this select delight. I have always the slight feeling of pity for the man who has remained ignorant of love. Chess, like love, like music, has the power to make men happy.

With all his passion for chess and all his skill, it might be wondered why he never became world champion. There were two reasons. The first was that he was essentially an amateur who put his profession ahead of the game for most of his life. The second was that his period of playing coincided to a large extent with that of another and younger genius named Emanuel Lasker.

Lasker who, like Tarrasch, was a German Jew, was born in Berlinchen on 24 December, 1868. He was six years younger than Tarrasch and thirty-two years younger than the world champion, Steinitz. As a child he already evinced brilliance at both mathematics and chess. Although his parents tried to separate him from the game's temptations, it was chess that truly attracted him, and he became a professional. His first steps to masterhood have already been mentioned and by the time we take up his story again he had left Germany for England. There he was immediately successful, winning matches overwhelmingly against Blackburne and Bird; in 1892 he won a tournament in London ahead of all the best English players, with Blackburne in second place.

Like Steinitz, he left England for America, and there he played in a tournament involving most of the leading masters in the United States (including the young Harry Nelson Pillsbury) and succeeded in winning all thirteen games. Prior to this he had had the impertinence (so it must have seemed to Tarrasch) to challenge the great praeceptor to a match. Tarrasch refused, saying, '*Der junge Mann soll erst durch grossere Siege in internationalen Turnieren den Nachweis erbringen, das er das Recht hat, mit einem Mann wie mir zu spielen.*' (The young man should first furnish the evidence by greater victories in international tournaments that he has the right to play with a man like me.)

Nothing daunted, the 'young man' launched a *défi* to the world champion himself, which was accepted. The match, the winner of which was the first to win ten games, was held in three cities, New York, Philadelphia and Montreal from 15 March to 26 May, 1894. In the earlier part the two were even, but as the match progressed, Steinitz tired; he gave way more and more and in the end Lasker triumphed by 10+ 5– 4=.

Suddenly, and most unexpectedly, the chess-world had a new champion and it was incredulous. Experts felt that in real strategic capacity Steinitz was far superior, and attributed Lasker's victory to his stronger physique, which was due to his being the younger by thirty-two years. Kurt von Bardeleben made this clear in an article in the *Deutsche Schachzeitung* in 1894. He acknowledged Lasker's skill in defending bad positions but implied that a true world champion would not get into such positions in the first place. Still worse, he censured Lasker for his lack of attacking spirit and for his colourless kind of combinations. Then he returned again to the theme that Lasker was far better in defence, adding that he knew that passive defence was no good.

The general reaction to the match seems to have been that Lasker triumphed tactically, and that this was the result of Steinitz's not having been able to give the game the concentration and vigour he had bestowed on it in the past.

That Steinitz was not exactly past it, however, he demonstrated in a tournament in New York that year, in which he was easily first with $8\frac{1}{2}$ points out of 10, losing only to Albin who came second with $6\frac{1}{2}$ points. Pillsbury, who was one of Steinitz's pupils, also played in this event, but came halfway down the table with 5 points.

Lasker, meanwhile, with the chess-world unconvinced that he was its best player, was behoven to take steps to prove his mastery. The obvious way was by means of tournament play, since it was here that Tarrasch, with considerable justice, was regarded as supreme. The opportunity soon presented itself and it came in England, the country which had welcomed both Steinitz and Lasker when they were talented, striving, young and poor.

The town of Hastings, in Sussex on the south-east coast, had a thriving chess club and a number of enthusiasts who were prepared to work hard for the cause of chess. Chief of these was H. E. Dobell, whom I knew when I was a boy; he was a gentle, charming, wise old man with a passion (which I shared) for chess and music. It was thanks to his enthusiasm that Hastings was to become a centre for both these pursuits. He conceived the idea of a great tournament that was to include every single one of the world's best players. The world champion must be there; so must the ex-world champion, Steinitz, and all the candidates for the title, such as Tarrasch, Tschigorin, Janowski, Blackburne and Gunsberg. All the young hopefuls must be there too, in case one of them was a future world

Emanuel Lasker.

champion. So there were Teichmann, Schlechter, Walbrodt, Marco
—and a long shot, Pillsbury.

Who would emerge victor? I suppose that if a general question-
naire had been circulated, the votes would have given an order something like this: Tarrasch, Tschigorin, Steinitz, Lasker. And they
would not have been all that wrong—if they had been voting for the
second, third, fourth and fifth places.

The struggle for the top prize was intense and, although it might
seem that the players I have singled out belonged to a special elite
class, of the twenty-two competitors only the bottom two, Tinsley
and Vergani, failed to score against the top five. In the end it was
Harry Nelson Pillsbury, then twenty-three years old, who won first
prize with a score of 16½ points, just ahead of Tschigorin 16, Lasker
15½, and then—a significant interval—Tarrasch 14 and Steinitz 13.
Pillsbury lost to both Tschigorin and Lasker, but beat Tarrasch and
Steinitz. There is a pathetic story of how Steinitz, after losing to
Pillsbury, lamented with tears to a friend, 'They are all beating me
now, even my pupil.'

Lasker's third place was on the whole reassuring. True, it was not
a first, but he was above both Tarrasch and Steinitz, and he had
beaten the winner, Pillsbury, in their individual game. Curiously
enough, this was the first important tournament in which he had
taken part. More practice was necessary, and after that, it was clear,
he would become a very great tournament player.

Nor should Steinitz have been so disappointed with his performance. He was an old and fairly sick man and it was a tribute to
his essential greatness as a player that he figured as high as he did in
this event which was certainly the strongest of its kind up to the
year when it was played. By a touching stroke of fate, he won the
first brilliancy prize, thus reverting to the days of his youth, when
he was termed so neatly the 'Austrian Morphy'. I give the game,
which is in the fine old romantic style:

White: Steinitz. Black: Kurt von Bardeleben. Giuoco Piano.

 1. P-K4,P-K4; 2. Kt-KB3,Kt-QB3; 3. B-B4,B-B4;
 4. P-B3,Kt-B3; 5. P-Q4,PxP; 6. PxP,B-Kt5 ch; 7. Kt-B3,P-Q4;
 8. PxP,KKtxP; 9. o-o,B-K3; 10. B-KKt5,B-K2;
11. BxKt,QBxB; 12. KtxB,QxKt; 13. BxB,KtxB;
14. R-K1,P-KB3; 15. Q-K2,Q-Q2; 16. QR-B1,P-B3;
17. P-Q5,PxP; 18. Kt-Q4,K-B2; 19. Kt-K6,KR-QB1;
20. Q-Kt4,P-KKt3; 21. Kt-Kt5 ch,K-K1; 22. RxKt ch,K-B1;
23. R-B7 ch,K-Kt1; 24. R-Kt7 ch,K-R1; 25. RxP ch, resigns
(Diagram 46).

At the position given here, von Bardeleben left the board, the room
and the Brassey Institute where the tournament was held. Since he
was not seen again in the playing hall, and since he was well known
for his unsportsmanlike behaviour, it was assumed that this was his
tactful way of resigning. In his absence Steinitz announced a mate
in ten moves as follows:

25. .,K-Kt1; 26. R-Kt7 ch,K-R1; 27. Q-R4 ch,KxR;
28. Q-R7 ch,K-B1; 29. Q-R8 ch,K-K2; 30. Q-Kt7 ch,K-K1;
31. Q-Kt8 ch,K-K2; 32. Q-B7 ch,K-Q1; 33. Q-B8 ch,Q-K1;
34. Kt-B7 ch,K-Q2; 35. Q-Q6 mate.

The tournament aroused great interest in Hastings and drew
packed audiences at the Institute, which is about a quarter of a mile
away from the White Rock Pavilion where the present Hastings

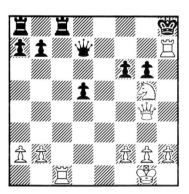

46: Final position.

tournaments are held. (The Pavilion was not then in existence.) Sir George Thomas once told me that he had acted as a demonstration boy at this event. For the information of the uninitiated, it is the practice at big international events to show the progress of the games on wall-boards manned by volunteers.

Despite the excitement it aroused, however, the Hastings tournament had not really answered the questions about the world championship in a satisfactory way. So the St Petersburg Chess Club invited the top five players of the Hastings event to play a match-tournament in their club. The idea was to choose a worthy challenger for the world title, and no doubt the organizers hoped that this would be Tschigorin. Tarrasch refused the invitation, which improved the chances of Tschigorin's qualifying for a title match. But he was out of form and the contest resolved itself into a fight between Lasker and Pillsbury.

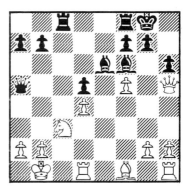

47: *Position after White's 17th move.*

The Hastings victor led for the first part of the tournament, but the turning point came at the beginning of the second half, when Lasker won a magnificent game against the American. He never looked back from that moment and won the first prize with a couple of points to spare over the former world champion, Steinitz. The final scores were Lasker 11½, Steinitz 9½, Pillsbury 8 and Tschigorin 7. Players met each other six times; Lasker beat Steinitz by 4–2, lost to Pillsbury by 2½–3½ and beat Tschigorin by 5–1.

The historic game that was the turning point contained a combination starting on the seventeenth move which dispelled once and for all the myth of the new world champion's deficiency in that sphere of chess.
White: Pillsbury. Black: Lasker. Queen's Gambit Declined. Semi-Tarrasch Defence.

  1. P-Q4,P-Q4; 2. P-QB4,P-K3; 3. Kt-QB3,Kt-KB3;
  4. Kt-B3,P-B4; 5. B-Kt5,PxQP; 6. QxP,Kt-B3; 7. Q-R4,B-K2;
  8. 0-0-0,Q-R4; 9. P-K3,B-Q2; 10. K-Kt1,P-KR3;
11. PxP,PxP; 12. Kt-Q4,0-0; 13. BxKt,BxB; 14. Q-R5,KtxKt;
15. PxKt,B-K3; 16. P-B4,QR-B1; 17. P-B5,RxKt!;
18. PxB,R-QR6; 19. PxP ch,RxP; 20. PxR,Q-Kt3 ch;
21. B-Kt5,QxB ch; 22. K-R1,R-B2; 23. R-Q2,R-B5;
24. KR-Q1,R-B6; 25. Q-B5,Q-B5; 26. K-Kt2,RxP;
27. Q-K6 ch,K-R2; 28. KxR,Q-B6 ch; 29. K-R4,P-Kt4 ch;
30. KxP,Q-B5 ch; 31. K-R5,B-Q1 ch; 32. Q-Kt6,BxQ mate
(Diagram 47).

This remarkable game had a remarkable sequel in the United States of America in the Cambridge Springs Tournament of 1904, which was the last Pillsbury played in. He died prematurely at the age of thirty-four in 1906.

If there were those who still argued that St Petersburg 1896 was not sufficient proof of Lasker's tournament prowess, since this was a match-tournament rather than a tournament pure and simple, then these doubts were soon dispelled. After some six months he took part in an immensely strong tournament at Nuremburg (from 20 July to 10 August, 1896) and won first prize in no uncertain fashion with 13½ points. He was followed by Maroczy 12½, Pillsbury and Tarrasch 12, Janowski 11½, Steinitz 11, Schlechter and Walbrodt 10½, Schiffers and Tschigorin 9½, Blackburne 9, Charousek 8½, Marco 8, Albin 7, Winawer 6½, Porges and Showalter 5½, Schallopp 4½ and Teichmann 4.

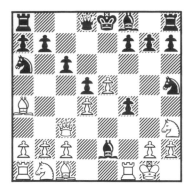

48: Position after Black's 11th move.

Of the big five, Pillsbury and Tarrasch had still kept well up in the table. Steinitz had sunk a little and Tschigorin even more. Two Hungarian newcomers caught the eye. One was Geza Maroczy, who had gained the master title by winning the minor tournament at Hastings in 1895 and who was to form part of what one might term the iron age, which reinforced the theories of Tarrasch with still greater bulwarks and demarcation lines. The other was Rudolf Charousek, then twenty-three, possibly the most gifted of all Hungarian players. In his tragically short life (he died of tuberculosis in 1900) he shone with a brilliance that has never been excelled. His keenness to improve was illustrated by the story that, as a poverty-stricken boy, he borrowed the vast tome of Bilguer's *Handbuch* and copied it all out by hand.

How rapidly he was improving was shown later in the same year when, playing radiant chess, he tied for first place with Tschigorin in a very strong, if smaller, international tournament at Budapest, with 8½ points out of 12. Pillsbury came next with 7½, followed Janowski and Schlechter 7, Walbrodt and Winawer 6½, Tarrasch 6 and five others. Tschigorin won the play-off for first prize by 3–1. Charousek was a great exponent of the King's Gambit which he played with a rare understanding. Here is his win with the opening against Tschigorin in the tournament:

White: Charousek. Black: Tschigorin. King's Bishop's Gambit.
1. P-K4,P-K4; 2. P-KB4,PxP; 3. B-B4,Kt-QB3; 4. P-Q4,Kt-B3; 5. P-K5,P-Q4; 6. B-Kt3,B-Kt5; 7. Q-Q3,Kt-KR4; 8. Kt-KR3,Kt-Kt5; 9. Q-QB3,Kt-R3; 10. 0-0,B-K7; 11. B-R4 ch,P-B3; 12. BxP ch,PxB; 13. QxP ch,K-K2; 14. KtxP,KtxKt; 15. BxKt,P-KR3; 16. Kt-QB3,B-B5; 17. P-K6,R-B1; 18. B-B7!,PxP; 19. BxQ ch,RxB; 20. Q-Kt7 ch,R-Qt2; 21. R-B7 ch,KxR; 22. QxR ch,B-K2; 23. R-K1,R-K1; 24. P-QKt3,K-B1; 25. PxB, resigns (Diagram 48).

This game is well worth studying as an illustration of the extension and deepening of Morphy's ideas, in particular White's fourteenth and seventeenth moves; the eighteenth was pure Charousek. In fact, since Tschigorin, who could also be an obstinate reactionary where some open games were concerned, played here in a rather old-fashioned style, the contest could well have been an addendum to the Morphy–Anderssen match.

At the end of 1896 Steinitz got his chance to regain his title in a match which again was to go to the first to win ten games, and which was held in Moscow from 7 November, 1896 to 14 January 1897. From the first it was an unmitigated disaster for the ex-world champion. The score by which Lasker won the match, 10+ 2– 5=, was so shattering that Steinitz had a nervous breakdown and had to go to a Moscow sanatorium to recover. This really was the end. He made some sort of a come-back in 1898 with a good fourth place at Vienna and a fifth at Cologne, but London 1899 was a tragedy: he came eleventh, below all the recognized masters. He returned to New York, his mind gave way and he died on 12 August, 1900.

It was perhaps fitting that he died when the century, which he had so dominated as a chess-thinker, was at an end. Steinitz, more than anybody else in the history of the game, more even than Philidor, was a conscious innovator in both theory and practice on the broadest scale. After him, the way in which chessmasters looked at the game, its aims and its demands, was different. It was as though he brought distant objects in, to nearer and more precise vision by means of a mind of telescopic power. That he died a disappointed and even disorientated man was inevitable. All world champions, when they lose the title, suffer this sea-change. His memorial exists in the theories, especially on the openings and early middle-game, which are now accepted as part and parcel of the game.

I must return to the year 1897, for that was when an international women's tournament was held for the first time. London was the venue and, appropriately enough, first prize went to an English lady, Miss Mary Rudge. There were twenty competitors, and Lady Thomas, Sir George Thomas's mother, must have been a reasonably good player since she finished equal sixth.

In the same year Charousek scored another success with a first place in the important Berlin tournament. A very strong double-round tournament, the Kaiser-Jubilee, at Vienna in 1898, ended in a tie between Tarrasch and Pillsbury with 27½, two points ahead of the next player, Janowski. That year at Cologne, Amos Burn, an English grandmaster who anticipated modern opening methods by playing the King's Indian Defence, was first with 11½ points, ahead of Charousek, W. Cohn and Tschigorin 10½, Steinitz 9½, Schlechter and Showalter (an excellent American master) 9, Berger (the great end-game theorist) 8, etc.

The great American master, Frank Marshall, made his initial appearance on the international scene when he came first in London in 1899. This was, however, a minor tournament; in the main event, a double-round affair of great strength, Lasker scored a triumph in coming first with 23½ points, far ahead of Janowski, Maroczy and Pillsbury 19, etc. In addition he was awarded the brilliancy prize for his win over his old rival, Steinitz:

White: Steinitz. Black: Lasker. Vienna Game.

1. P-K4,P-K4; 2. Kt-QB3,Kt-KB3; 3. P-B4,P-Q4;
4. P-Q3,Kt-B3; 5. BPxP,QKtxP; 6. P-Q4,Kt-Kt3;
7. PxP,KtxP; 8. KtxKt,QxKt; 9. Kt-B3,B-Kt5; 10. B-K2,0-0-0;
11. P-B3,B-Q3; 12. 0-0,KR-K1; 13. P-KR3,B-Q2;
14. Kt-Kt5,Kt-R5; 15. Kt-B3,KtxP!; 16. KxKt,BxP ch;
17. K-B2,P-KB3; 18. R-KKt1,P-KKt4; 19. BxP,PxB;
20. RxP,Q-K3; 21. Q-Q3,B-B5; 22. R-R1,BxR;
23. KtxB,Q-B3 ch; 24. B-B3,B-B4; 25. KtxP,Q-Kt3;
26. Q-Kt5,P-B3; 27. Q-R5,R-K2; 28. R-R5,B-Kt5;
29. R-KKt5,Q-B7 ch; 30. K-Kt3,BxB; White resigns
(Diagram 49).

Lasker had another remarkable victory in the tournament held in Paris in 1900, in conjunction with the World Exhibition. It was a major event which was made even more arduous by the fact that, in order to avoid the so-called 'remis-tod' (death draw), the first draw did not count and a second game had to be played. The world champion came first with 14½ points, ahead of Pillsbury 12½, Maroczy and Marshall 12. In another strong tournament that year in Munich, there was a triple tie for first place among Pillsbury, Maroczy and Schlechter with 12 points each.

Now Lasker retired from the fray to devote himself again to mathematical studies, and in 1902 he obtained a brilliant doctorate at the University of Erlangen. As a mathematician he was eventually to earn the respect of Einstein and he was probably the best mathe-

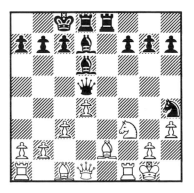

49: Position after White's 15th move.

matician among all the grandmasters in the history of the game. In consequence, his appearances in the chess world became rarer. But, or perhaps therefore, he was still to have many successes.

In 1901 a series of noteworthy tournaments commenced at Monte Carlo. In the first of these a complicated system of scoring was used, by which with the first draw players each received $\frac{1}{4}$ point; they played again and the winner received half a point, or, if the game was again drawn, then each player earned another $\frac{1}{4}$ point. This tournament was won by Janowski ahead of Schlechter. The 1902 tournament, with the same rules, was won by Maroczy with $14\frac{3}{4}$ points, ahead of Pillsbury $14\frac{1}{2}$ and Janowski 14. In 1903 there was a return to the normal scoring and a strong double-round tournament was won by Tarrasch with 20 points followed by Maroczy 19, Pillsbury $18\frac{1}{2}$, and Schlechter 17. A much smaller double-round tournament in 1904 was won by Maroczy $7\frac{1}{2}$, ahead of Schlechter 7 and Marshall $6\frac{1}{2}$.

The early 1900s was a rich period in tournaments. At Hanover in 1902, Janowski was first with $13\frac{1}{2}$, ahead of Pillsbury 12; the Yorkshire schoolmaster, H. E. Atkins (potentially perhaps the most talented of British masters), making one of his rare international appearances, came third with $11\frac{1}{2}$. It was at this event that Pillsbury, one of the finest blindfold players of all time, gave a simultaneous blindfold display against the players in the *Hauptturnier* with a score of $3+$ $7-$ $11=$. The magnitude of this performance will be realized when one knows that the winner of a *Hauptturnier* was recognized as a master, and that these events usually contained a strong sprinkling of future grandmasters.

Tschigorin won a Russian tournament at Kiev in 1903 with 15 points in an event which contained a number of future famous chessplayers: Bernstein 14, Jurevitch $13\frac{1}{2}$, Salwe 13, Rubinstein $11\frac{1}{2}$ and many more who were to become the basis of the eventual expansion of Russian chess. In the same year a Gambit tournament was held at Vienna in which the opening moves 1. P-K4,P-K4; 2. P-KB4,PxP; were prescribed. It was won by Tschigorin, with Marshall in second place.

In 1904 a strongly-contested international tournament saw the return of Lasker. But it was Marshall who was the hero of this event, which was held at Cambridge Springs in the United States. The Americans made great efforts to procure the best players from Europe, not only to give the occasion special éclat, but, since they had invited the world champion, also in the hopes of finding a challenger-designate for the title. Lasker came; so did Tschigorin, Schlechter and Janowski; but neither Tarrasch nor Maroczy was available. Still, the tournament was a strong one and Frank Marshall, then twenty-seven, who won it with the remarkable score of thirteen points out of fifteen, achieved the best performance of his career. He went through the tournament without a defeat, whereas Lasker lost both to Schlechter and Pillsbury. Only by a typical fighting effort in the last round, when he beat Janowski, did the world champion manage to attain a comparatively respectable position by tying with Janowski for second place with eleven points.

An ivory Portuguese chess set;
Macao, c. 1840.

Overleaf: Chinese ivory chess
pieces, c. 1850

Overleaf: Cantonese ivory pieces,
c. 1860.

A European barleycorn chess-set,
1870–80.

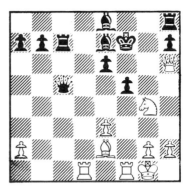

50: *Position after Black's 24th move.*

Pillsbury, already a sick man, came low—equal eighth with Mieses, with seven points. This was the last tournament in which he was to play. His health deteriorated and he died on 17 June, 1906, at the age of thirty-four. It was sad that so fine a talent should have been cut short in its prime. But, despite the brevity of his life-span as a player, he had contributed something important and lasting to the development of chess. Like Morphy before him and Fischer after him, he endowed the game with a fresh dynamism. In this connection, it is significant that chess has constantly received such impetus from the New World.

It will perhaps be remembered that, in describing Pillsbury's loss to Lasker at St Petersburg, 1895–6, I earlier referred to a sequel at Cambridge Springs. Pillsbury realized that his seventh move in that game (Q-KR4) had been a mistake, and had worked out a different and winning line which he held in reserve for Lasker. Now, nine years later, he used it with effect:

White: Pillsbury. Black: Lasker. Queen's Gambit Declined, Semi-Tarrasch Defence.

1. P-Q4,P-Q4; 2. P-QB4,P-K3; 3. Kt-QB3,Kt-KB3;
4. Kt-B3,P-B4; 5. B-Kt5,PxQP; 6. QxP,Kt-B3; 7. BxKt,PxB;
8. Q-R4,PxP; 9. R-Q1,B-Q2; 10. P-K3,Kt-K4;
11. KtxKt,PxKt; 12. QxBP,Q-Kt3; 13. B-K2,QxP;
14. 0-0,R-B1; 15. Q-Q3,R-B2; 16. Kt-K4,B-K2;
17. Kt-Q6 ch,K-B1; 18. Kt-B4,Q-Kt4; 19. P-B4,PxP;
20. Q-Q4,P-B3; 21. QxBP,Q-QB4; 22. Kt-K5,B-K1;
23. Kt-Kt4,P-B4; 24. Q-R6 ch,K-B2; 25. B-B4!,R-B3;
26. RxP ch,QxR; 27. R-B1,QxR ch; 28. KxQ,B-Q2;
29. Q-R5 ch,K-Kt1; 30. Kt-K5, resigns (Diagram 50).

A beautiful swan song!

The tournament has been commemorated in opening theory, since the Cambridge Springs variation of the Queen's Gambit derives its name from having been employed here.

(1. P-Q4,P-Q4; 2. P-QB4,P-K3; 3. Kt-QB3,Kt-KB3;
4. B-Kt5,QKt-Q2; 5. P-K3,P-B3).

Marshall's outstanding victory in this event put him in the running (along, of course, with Tarrasch) for a match for the world championship. But his ensuing results were somewhat disappointing. In the important double-round international tournament at Ostend in 1905 he came low—equal seventh to ninth with Burn and Leonhardt, with 12½ points. The tournament was won by Maroczy with 19½, and Janowski and Tarrasch tied for second place with 18.

Marshall did better at another big tournament, at Barmen, in Germany, in the same year, which was won by Janowski and Maroczy, who were equal first with 10½ points each. He came next with 10 points, above Bernstein and Schlechter. But at the end of 1905 he was annihilated in a match by Tarrasch, who scored 8+ 1– 8=. A good first place at Scheveningen was followed by another failure at Ostend, in 1906, where he came seventh with 16½ points, first prize in the event going to Schlechter with 21 points. Then he scored another fine success, at Nuremburg in 1906, where he won first prize without losing a game, with 12½ points, ahead of Duras 11, Forgacs and Schlechter 10½. This time Tarrasch was only equal ninth to eleventh with 7½.

So at last on 26 January, 1907, the match between Lasker and Marshall for the world title commenced in New York. Conditions for the contest were the same as those for the Tarrasch-Marshall match. Marshall's American supporters, who imagined that he might well win, were soon disappointed. This time he received even more summary treatment than in the match with Tarrasch. He did not win a single game and Lasker won the match by 8+ 0– 7=. Splendid player though Marshall undoubtedly was, when it came to match-play he was not in the same class as Lasker.

This left Tarrasch as the obvious candidate for a title-match. But, suddenly, there emerged a fresh and most powerful force from Poland, Akiba Rubinstein, who was twenty-five years old. The international tournament at Karlsbad in 1907 was an interesting mixture of old and new masters. To our modern eyes it comprised practically all the grandmasters of the early twentieth century; but at the time some of the names of the competitors must have seemed experimental. The first prize went to one of the newest of these, the Polish-Jewish player, Rubinstein. Maroczy was second with $14\frac{1}{2}$, followed by Leonhardt $13\frac{1}{2}$, and Nimzowitsch and Schlechter $12\frac{1}{2}$. Marshall came equal eleventh and twelfth with Dus-Chotimirsky with 10 points, Janowski was even lower with $8\frac{1}{2}$, and only three places from the bottom was Tschigorin with $7\frac{1}{2}$.

The newcomer had enormous gifts. He played the openings like an angel and the endings like a god. This was the result of intense and arduous study which began considerably later in life than with the usual grandmaster; he did not learn the game until he was sixteen. He was born at Stawiski in Poland on 12 December, 1882, and was destined to become a rabbi—but chess got in the way. The story goes that at the age of seventeen, he presented himself in the café where the Polish champion, Salwe, reigned supreme, played some games against him and lost every one. He then disappeared and was not seen for a year. On his re-emergence, he beat Salwe repeatedly. He is reputed to have won a match against Salwe in 1903, and at Lodz in 1906 he came first in a treble-round tournament with $6\frac{1}{2}$ points, ahead of Tschigorin $5\frac{1}{2}$, Flamberg $3\frac{1}{2}$ and Salwe $2\frac{1}{2}$. In an all-Russian tournament the same year, he was equal second with Blumenfeld below Salwe.

As wonderful a player as he clearly was, it was equally clear that he had no chance of a match for the world title, since he was terribly poor and had no means of raising the vast stake which Lasker required. He was playing again, however, at Ostend in 1907, but in the masters not the grandmasters tournament. Tarrasch won the grandmasters, and Rubinstein tied with Bernstein for top place in the masters.

The great Russian player, Mikhail Tschigorin, who came bottom in that grandmasters tournament, died on 25 January, 1908. He, if anyone, could have been called a romantic player but, it is intriguing to note that he did almost as much to found modern opening theory as did the archpriest, Steinitz, himself.

With Tarrasch's fresh tournament triumph at Ostend in 1907, it was manifest that he should be allowed a chance to play for the world title. Lasker, mindful of the financial difficulties that had beset and practically reduced to insanity his predecessor as world champion, was determined to make as much as he could out of the title. The financial conditions he demanded were, for the time colossal. Nevertheless, the German Chess Federation managed to raise the necessary 17,500 Reichsmark and a match between the mighty

A Marshall–Janowski match seen here with M. Nardus, the rich patron who financed a number of matches in which Janowski played.

opposites was arranged. The one, the world champion, was pragmatic, more concerned with tactical considerations of right or wrong than with the eternal verities; the other, the challenger, was so passionately devoted to the basic principles that it amounted to dogmatism. The contest began on 17 August, 1908 in Düsseldorf and was continued in Munich on 1 September.

As in the previous matches, the first to win eight games would be the victor. It was highly instructive to see how Lasker adapted his style to deal with Tarrasch. With Marshall he had not, on the whole, taken risks but had sought to lead the game along quieter paths. With Tarrasch, on the other hand, he deliberately went in for unfathomable complications. This was not merely on the grounds that his opponent was over-addicted to the enunciation—almost to the worship—of principles, but also from a feeling that with Tarrasch some six years older (the doctor was born in 1862, Lasker in 1868) he would tire the more rapidly under the stress and strain of complications, particularly if they were hazardous.

One should not under-estimate the great powers of so remarkable a personality as Dr Tarrasch. Had the match been played ten years earlier, when Tarrasch was in his prime and when perhaps Lasker had not quite reached his peak, the story and the result might have been different. As it was, the world champion won by the convincing score of 8+ 3– 5= and Tarrasch's real hopes of becoming world champion were forever dashed.

A fascinating example of the contrast between the two which I have mentioned is furnished by the fourth game of the match: White: Tarrasch. Black: Lasker. Ruy Lopez, Steinitz Defence by transposition.

1. P-K4,P-K4; 2. Kt-KB3,Kt-QB3; 3. B-Kt5,Kt-B3; 4. o-o,P-Q3;
5. P-Q4,B-Q2; 6. Kt-B3,B-K2; 7. R-K1,PxP; 8. KtxP,KtxKt;
9. QxKt,BxB; 10. KtxB,o-o; 11. B-Kt5,P-KR3; 12. B-R4,R-K1;
13. QR-Q1,Kt-Q2; 14. BxB,RxB; 15. Q-B3,R-K4!;
16. Kt-Q4,R-QB4; 17. Q-QKt3,Kt-Kt3; 18. P-KB4,Q-B3;
19. Q-KB3,R-K1; 20. P-B3,P-QR4; 21. P-QKt3,P-R5;
22. P-QKt4,R-B5; 23. P-Kt3,R-Q1; 24. R-K3,P-B4;

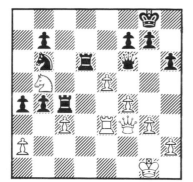

51: Position after White's 27th move.

25. Kt-Kt5,PxP; 26. RxP,RxR; 27. P-K5,RxKBP!;
28. KtPxR,Q-Kt3 ch; 29. K-R1,Q-QKt8 ch; 30. K-Kt2,R-Q7 ch;
31. R-K2,QxP; 32. RxR,QxR ch; 33. K-Kt3,P-R6;
34. P-K6,Q-K8 ch; 35. K-Kt4,QxP ch; 36. P-B5,Q-B5 ch;
37. Kt-Q4,P-R7; 38. Q-Q1,Kt-Q4; 39. Q-R4,KtxP;
40. Q-K8 ch,K-R2; 41. K-R5,P-R8=Q; White resigns
(Diagram 51).

The game is worthy of close study since it contains much of the Laskerian way of chess life and thought. The opening is treated in an essentially practical manner without any preconceived ideas. To that extent, Lasker was averse to strict basic principles. And yet he does, by an almost intuitive mastery of the subject, contrive to give himself possibilities of ingenious counter-attack. From the tactical point of view note, in particular, the wholly Laskerian use of the Rook in the middle-game (his fifteenth and sixteenth moves culminating in his twenty-seventh move) in which practical ingenuity is raised to a peak of brilliance. Many years later, in the 1960s, I was partnering the former world champion, Mikhail Tal, in a consultation game and he astonished me by a manoeuvre in the middle-game of the Rook to KKt4 and then over to the centre. It is more than probable that he got his idea from studying Lasker's play.

The path of a world champion is not exactly strewn with rose petals. As soon as Tarrasch was disposed of, other rivals immediately appeared on the scene. One in particular, modest and retiring in personality though he was, made his presence felt in tournament play. This was the Viennese, Karl Schlechter, about whose style of play Richard Réti, in his *Modern Ideas in Chess*, wrote with 'poetic fervour' (as I said in my foreword to the second edition, published in 1943). He called Schlechter's development in the game 'one harmonious evolution' and concluded as follows:

> By the time we shall have grown weary of the blatant combinations of the old masters and the over-subtle positional plans of the new ones, we shall still delight in immersing ourselves in Schlechter's games, in which, side by side with the greatness and simplicity of nature, the grace and airiness of Viennese music are often reflected.

Schlechter emerged at the top in two great international tournaments in 1908: in Vienna, where he came equal first with Duras and Maroczy with 14 points, a point ahead of Rubinstein; and in Prague, where he was again equal first with Duras, this time with $13\frac{1}{2}$ points, half a point ahead of Vidmar, and again a point ahead of Rubinstein. Vienna saw the first appearance of Richard Réti in the international field. A student of twenty who was referred to at the time as a promising amateur, he was very much out of his depth, and came bottom with $1\frac{1}{2}$ points.

Lasker participated again in 1909, when a historic tournament in memory of Tschigorin was held in St Petersburg. Although he had a long series of wins, he had a loss to Rubinstein which meant that he tied with him for first place, with $14\frac{1}{2}$ points out of 18. Schlechter had a semi-failure in this tournament, but won first prize in a strong and interesting one in Hamburg the following year. It was the first international tournament in which the Russian, Alexander Alekhine, took part and since he was then only eighteen, he did well to come

Carl Schlechter, photographed here during the 1895 Hastings Tournament.

eighth in such company, three points below the first-prize winner. He finished half a point ahead of Tarrasch who had the mortification of being the only player to lose to the English master, F. D. Yates, against whom he had lodged an official objection on the grounds that Yates was not strong enough to play in such a tournament.

Meanwhile pourparlers had been going on regarding a match for the world championship between Lasker and Schlechter. A good deal of mystery and confusion attends these initial arrangements and I doubt whether we shall ever get positive assurance as to what these were. One account states that the match was going to be a bigger one than usual and that the agreement was that Schlechter, in order to win the title, would have to win by a margin of two games, the idea being that when and if each had won nine games, the match should be declared drawn without putting the matter to the test of a further single game.

But when sufficient money was not forthcoming to finance a long match, it was decided to hold a shortened match of ten games only. Now comes the difficult part of the problem. Was this rule of the challenger having to win the match by a two-game margin abandoned in view of the adoption of a fixed number of games, and that a small number? It would seem logical for this to have happened and contemporary accounts of the match all assume that it was a straightforward affair of one man's winning by the odd point if necessary. Neither player ever denied this version, and although Schlechter died in 1918, only eight years after the match, Lasker lived on into the period of World War II, and had ample time and opportunity to deny this account had he pleased.

If the match did indeed depend on the odd game, Lasker had the narrowest of escapes. At the end of the ninth game, eight had been drawn and Schlechter had won one. All he needed to do to win the match was to draw the tenth game, and he had obtained the favourable position shown below after thirty-five moves. He had Black and now, instead of maintaining a distinct advantage by either 35. .,R–Q1 or 35. .,Kt–Q3, he thought he saw a quick win by 35. .,RxP (Diagram 52). Play continued. 36. BxR,RxB; 37. R–B8 ch,B–B1; 38. K–B2,Qp–R7 ch; 39. K–K1,Q–R8 ch. This is the mistake; instead he should have played 39. .,Q–R5 ch, when White would have had to submit to a draw by perpetual check. In that case, Schlechter would have won the match and become world champion (providing the above version of the conditions of the match is correct) and the history of world chess would have been changed. Had he become world champion, there is a strong likelihood that he would not have died in 1918 after the privations of the enemy blockade. Who knows then to what extent his own chess art would have been enhanced?

After the text-move White eventually escaped with his King into safety and won on the seventy-first move. Lasker had emerged with his title, but with his reputation seriously sapped and undermined. It is as well that he did not know that a player was coming from the New World who was to do much more to his control of the world championship than undermine it. He was to shatter it forever, but that story I must leave to the next chapter.

Before dealing with other aspects of Lasker's many-sided activities. I should mention that, at about this time, he had some marked match successes against Janowski, the Polish–Jewish grandmaster. The Pole

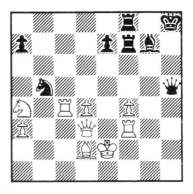

52: Black (Schlechter) to play; White (Lasker).

had considerable financial backing from a patron named Nardus, in Paris, and it was here that the matches took place. In 1909, Lasker won by 7+ 1– 2= and in 1910 his win was even greater, 8+ 0– 3=.

But, sadly, no patron could be found for Akiba Rubinstein and so the world missed the wonderful chance of seeing these two magnificent brains pitted against each other.

There is one aspect of Lasker's creative powers which deserves extensive treatment—his writings. He wrote some works on philosophy which, except in so far as they affect chess, are no concern of this book. Roughly speaking, his was a philosophy of struggle and where he uses it to base some theme of chess on it, alas, it vitiates his chess work. Thus, his *Manual of Chess,* published in London in 1932, is spoiled by the use of a philosophy which strikes one as merely a feeble imitation of an already weak original.

His book on the St Petersburg tournament in 1909, *Der Internationale Schachkongress zu St Petersburg 1909,* Berlin 1909, was very highly praised by Alekhine. I have to say, however, that on examining it, I got the impression that he and I must have been studying different books. It suffers from many vital defects. Crucial variations are, as like as not, regularly left out. The writing is undistinguished, by no means exhaustive and, I regret to say, unrewarding.

But there is one work of his which will be remembered as long as chess is played and that, curiously enough, is his earliest, *Common Sense in Chess,* which was published in London in 1896. Like Réti's *Modern Ideas in Chess,* it was not written originally in book form. It was the product of a lecture tour he made in England in 1895, and it reads like a series of easy talks on the game. It was a little book, only 141 small pages, and had few pretensions. But (or perhaps, therefore,) it was an instantaneous success and was published and read all over the world.

Starting with the concept that chess is the fight between two brains or intellects, he tries to strip the game of anything too pompous in the way of its aim or activity. It is essentially, he says, a fight, but a fight in which the scientific, the artistic, the purely intellectual element, holds undivided sway. This is his chief principle and I doubt whether any chess enthusiast would quarrel with it nowadays. Once he has laid this down, he deals with what one might call the tools of the trade in typically practical fashion. There are chapters on development, on specific openings, on attack and defence and (the last three chapters) on the endings.

It is difficult to say which, if any, of these sections is the best. Perhaps, since work on the openings is always bound to be, to a great extent, a matter of fashion and therefore evanescent, the earlier part of the work is not so vitally important as the later. Probably, in view of Lasker's great accomplishment as an end-game player, one ought to plump for the last part. One remark alone, on Pawns, contains so much wisdom in so little space that it must be regarded as possibly the wisest remark ever made about what is after all the life-blood of the game: 'A pawn move without a clearly defined purpose is to be blamed.'

I shall be dealing with Lasker's later career in the next chapter. Nevertheless, it is appropriate here to sum up what he was and what he gave to the world. It may seem paradoxical, but, even though he was so many-sided as to be termed the 'Michelangelo of chess', he was essentially *a player*, and, as such, he was essentially practical. Again, this may seem odd in view of his penchant for philosophizing. But he never let his philosophic theories influence or bedevil his play. Hence his enormous successes in both tournament and match play.

He was a wonderful tactician, perhaps the best the world has ever seen. This of course goes very much with his practicality. That he took enormous risks is true; but I imagine he trod the tightrope because he could keep his head better than anyone else. He founded no school, did not noticeably follow any and delighted in challenging and disproving the pedagogic principles of others. And yet— again a paradox—his influence on subsequent great players has been enormous. Quite a number of present-day grandmasters have confessed to me that if anyone influenced them it was Lasker.

chapter 13

Capablanca
and the hypermoderns
from war to war

In 1911, Lasker was world champion. His chief rivals were Rubinstein and Schlechter, who had emerged in the twentieth century, and still from the nineteenth, there was Tarrasch. These, along with Marshall, Duras and Maroczy, constituted a formidable band of players who usually appeared among the leaders in tournament play. Not far behind were Bernstein, Vidmar and Teichmann, as well as a most interesting new wave of players headed by Alekhine, Nimzovitch, Spielmann and Tartakower.

Lasker confined himself to playing at long intervals in carefully selected great tournaments. A good cross-section of the outstanding players of the day was provided by the magnificent second international tournament at Carlsbad in 1911. Twenty-six masters took part, and the German player, Richard Teichmann, at that time leading the not particularly prosperous life of a chess professional in London, had his greatest tournament success. He had inherited a small legacy just before and this relief from care enabled him continuously to play the fine chess of which he was known to be capable. He was first with 18 points, ahead of Rubinstein and Schlechter 17, Rotlevi 16, Marshall and Nimzovitsch $15\frac{1}{2}$, Vidmar 15, Alekhine, Duras, Leonhardt and Tartakower $13\frac{1}{2}$, Spielmann 13, etc. Among the players from a past era were Burn and Salwe who scored 11 points each.

A smaller, but most select, tournament was also held in 1911. This was at the Spanish seaside resort of San Sebastian, and only players who had won first prizes in international tournaments were invited. One exception was made, that of a Cuban named José Raoul Capablanca, who was twenty-two years old, and who was admitted because he had won a match against Marshall in New York in 1909 by the crushing score of 8+ 1– 14=. Some of the players, notably Bernstein, voiced their discontent at the admission of so untried a master. As might have been expected, Capablanca won a brilliancy prize against Bernstein. But what was not anticipated was that he was to win first prize ahead of everyone who mattered in world chess, with the exception of Lasker. Capablanca lost to Rubinstein, but nevertheless came ahead of him with $9\frac{1}{2}$ points. Rubinstein who did not lose a game but drew too many, came equal second with Vidmar, with 9 points, ahead of Marshall $8\frac{1}{2}$, Nimzovitsch, Schlechter

From the binding of the Tournament book of London, 1883 (players do not necessarily belong to the country in the parallel column).

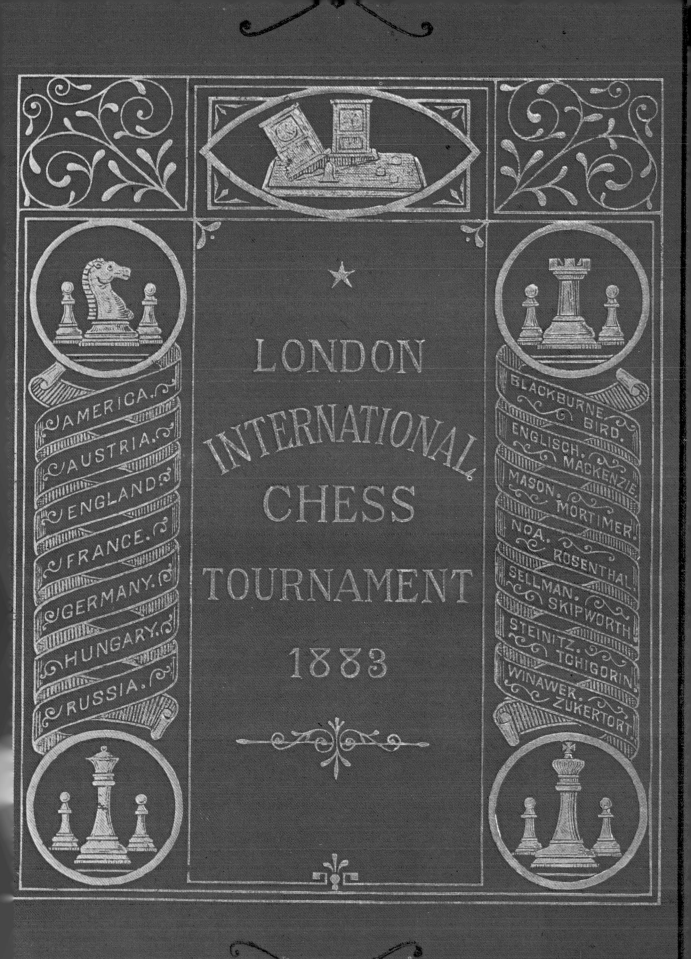

LONDON
INTERNATIONAL
CHESS
TOURNAMENT
1883

AMERICA.
AUSTRIA.
ENGLAND.
FRANCE.
GERMANY.
HUNGARY.
RUSSIA.

BLACKBURNE.
BIRD.
ENGLISCH.
MACKENZIE.
MASON.
MORTIMER.
NOA.
ROSENTHAL.
SELLMAN.
SKIPWORTH
STEINITZ.
TCHIGORIN.
WINAWER.
ZUKERTORT.

A hand-painted 'Napoleonic' set of the twentieth century.

and Tarrasch $7\frac{1}{2}$, Bernstein and Spielmann 7, Teichmann $6\frac{1}{2}$, Janowski and Maroczy 6, Burn and Duras 5, and Leonhardt 4.

This was the game for which Capablanca was awarded the brilliancy prize. It is played with the noiseless efficiency of a Rolls Royce engine:

White: Capablanca. Black: Bernstein. Ruy Lopez.

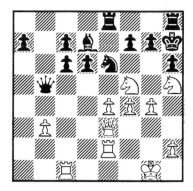

53: Position after Black's 27th move.

 1. P-K4,P-K4; 2. Kt-KB3,Kt-QB3; 3. B-Kt5,Kt-B3;
 4. 0-0,B-K2; 5. Kt-B3,P-Q3; 6. BxKt ch,PxB; 7. P-Q4,PxP;
 8. KtxP,B-Q2; 9. B-Kt5,0-0; 10. R-K1,P-KR3;
11. B-R4,Kt-R2; 12. BxB,QxB; 13. Q-Q3,QR-Kt1;
14. P-QKt3,Kt-Kt4; 15. QR-Q1,Q-K4; 16. Q-K3,Kt-K3;
17. Kt(B3)-K2,Q-QR4; 18. Kt-B5,Kt-B4; 19. Kt(K2)-Q4,K-R2;
20. P-KKt4,QR-K1; 21. P-B3,Kt-K3; 22. Kt-K2,QxP;
23. Kt(K2)-Kt3,QxBP; 24. R-QB1,Q-Kt7; 25. Kt-R5,R-KR1;
26. R-K2,Q-K4; 27. P-B4,Q-Kt4; 28. Kt(B5)xKtP,Kt-B4;
29. KtxR,BxKt; 30. Q-QB3,P-B3; 31. KtxP ch,K-Kt3;
32. Kt-R5,R-Kt1; 33. P-B5 ch,K-Kt4; 34. Q-K3 ch,K-R5;
35. Q-Kt3 ch, resigns (Diagram 53).

The effect of this performance was striking. Almost overnight Capablanca became a candidate for world championship honours and there was talk of Paul Morphy redivivus.

Young José Raoul Capablanca, who thus startled Europe, was born in Havana on 19 November, 1888, and everything about him is legendary except that he really existed. He is reported, at the age of four, to have laughed when his father made an illegal move with his knight. Since he had never been given any chess lessons and had merely acquired his knowledge through watching his father play with a friend, his father asked him what he knew about the game. 'Enough', said the precocious infant, 'to beat you', and he promptly did. At the age of twelve, he beat Cuba's strongest player, J. Corzo, in a match by 4+ 3– 6= and in 1909 he defeated Marshall ignominiously, as I have said. At a tournament in New York in 1910, he came second with $9\frac{1}{2}$ points—half a point behind the victor, Marshall. Now he had won a great international tournament, and later that year he challenged Lasker to a match.

He had reached this height without, according to his own account in *My Chess Career* (1920), having studied any books on opening theory. He did say, however, that a friend of the family had given him books on the endings, and that he liked and read them, but nothing else. If this is true, and I see no reason to doubt it, then certainly Capablanca was quite the greatest natural chess genius in the history of the game. As a player his great virtue was a power to blend tactics and strategy, with a complete mastery of both fields which gave his games a most deceptive air of simplicity. Capablanca had that art which hides art to an overwhelming degree.

Whether Lasker realized how formidable an opponent he was likely to be, or whether he thought that the young man had not yet done enough to earn the right to play him for the world championship (it might have been both), the fact remains that, with a great war aiding him to find excuses, he eluded playing the match for some ten years.

The period just before the outbreak of World War I saw intense international chess activity with a number of really noteworthy tournaments. The year 1912, in particular, was marvellous. There was a tournament at Abbazia (now Opatija) in which the

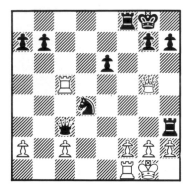

54: Position after White's 23rd move.

King's Gambit had to be played, and this was easily won by that archpriest of the King's Gambit, Rudolf Spielmann. At Budapest Vidmar was first; at Temesvar, in Rumania, it was the pioneer of the hypermoderns, Gyula Breyer (he is reputed by Réti, in *Modern Ideas in Chess,* to have said that after 1. P-K4, White's game is in the last throes). At Stockholm, a future world champion, Alexander Alekhine, came first. In a principally Slavonic tournament held at Wilno, Rubinstein was first. He came first too at a double-round tournament at San Sebastian. Remarkably, for his fourth win in 1912, he came first at Pistyan. A tournament in Breslau saw him come equal first with Duras. It was there that Marshall won his most famous game against Mikhail Lewitzky:

White: Lewitzky. Black: Marshall. French Defence.

1. P-Q4,P-K3; 2. P-K4,P-Q4; 3. Kt-QB3,P-QB4;
4. Kt-B3,Kt-QB3; 5. PxQP,KPxP; 6. B-K2,Kt-B3;
7. o-o,B-K2; 8. B-Kt5,o-o; 9. PxP,B-K3; 10. Kt-Q4,BxP;
11. KtxB,PxKt; 12. B-Kt4,Q-Q3; 13. B-R3,QR-K1;
14. Q-Q2,B-Kt5; 15. BxKt,RxB; 16. QR-Q1,Q-B4;
17. Q-K2,BxKt; 18. PxB,QxP; 19. RxP,Kt-Q5;
20. Q-R5,R(K1)-KB1; 21. R-K5,R-R3; 22. Q-Kt5,RxB;
23. R-Q5,Q-KKt6; White resigns (Diagram 54).

It is said that after the final Queen move the spectators showered the board with gold pieces. The story seems to be apocryphal, but nevertheless *ben trovato.*

Capablanca played in two international tournaments in the Americas in 1913. In the first, in New York, he won first prize with 11 points out of 13, half a point ahead of Marshall; and in the second, in Havana, roles were reversed with Marshall coming first with 10½, half a point ahead of Capablanca.

Then, in September, he was given the post of commercial attaché by the Cuban foreign office and was sent, ostensibly on official duty, to the Cuban Embassy in St Petersburg. In reality, he was a sort of roving ambassador for Cuban chess and his triumphal tour of Europe in this capacity, and in particular of Russia, as memorable in chess history as was the triumphant progress of Alexander the Great in general history. Among those he beat during this tour was the young Alekhine (four years his junior), with a score of 2–0. Nevertheless, it was becoming apparent that Alekhine was the most promising of the younger European players. He won first prize in a tournament at Scheveningen that year, and the following year he was to demonstrate that he was the leading player of another formidable group of young masters in Russia.

By this time Vienna had become the centre of chess in Europe. As the capital of the loose-knit empire of Austro-Hungary it was the natural meeting-place for central European masters. Two tournaments in the Viennese Chess Club in 1913 demonstrated this. In the first, a double-round jubilee event, Spielmann was first with 11 points and the other three prizes were won by Tartakower 10½, Réti 9½ and Schlechter 8. Oddly enough, in the Trebitsch tournament held later in the year, the same four players were in the top four places, but in a different order: Schlechter 14, Spielmann 13½, Tartakower 13 and Réti 12. Among those who occupied an honourable place in this event was Adolf Albin who obtained 9½ points and came sixth. It was after him that the dangerous Albin Counter-Gambit was named (1. P-Q4,P-Q4; 2. P-QB4,P-K4). I have singled

this out since it was characteristic of the exciting and counter-attacking (also, of course, attacking) spirit of central European chess at this stage in the game's development. For example, consider the triumphs of that great master of the attack, Rudolf Spielmann, then, and for some years to come. He was first in an international tournament in Budapest, half a point ahead of Tartakower. Another sign of the times was the frequency of gambit tournaments in which genuine and specified gambits had to be played. It was Spielmann again who won such a tournament in Baden in 1914, and the variations played at that event have formed the basis for much of the theoretical study of the King's Gambit in succeeding years.

Chess had now become popular in Russia and flourished under the patronage of the Tsar, who is reputed to have invented the term 'grandmaster'. In 1914, a great international tournament was planned to take place in St Petersburg. As a preliminary, a tournament was held among the leading Russian players to decide which two would have the right to play in the great event; after a close struggle with the talented Alexander Flamberg, Alekhine and Nimzovitsch emerged as the qualifiers. Another player to make his mark in this event, and who was to become very outstanding indeed, was E. D. Bogoljuboff, who came eighth out of the eighteen who competed.

The great international tournament of St Petersburg duly commenced there on 21 April, 1914. It was run on a novel principle—all-play-all in a preliminary tournament with the first five in that competition playing in a final double-round tournament. The idea

Alekhine, sitting with his back to his opponents, giving a blindfold simultaneous display against twenty-eight leading French players in Paris in 1925. He won 22, drew 3 and lost 3 games.

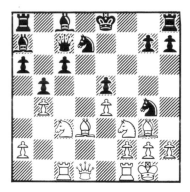

55: Position after Black's 16th move.

was to be revived and employed as late as 1975 in Milan. On both occasions it turned out to have certain distinct drawbacks. The dangers inherent in this method of qualification lie essentially in the temporal nature of the test. If a player is not quite in form in the earlier part of the event, he has no means of recovering by showing his true form at a later stage. Thus, at St Petersburg, to the surprise and disappointment of most experts, Rubinstein failed to get through to the final; another waste was Nimzovitsch's failure to qualify. One more possible disadvantage showed itself clearly in St Petersburg: when a player is outstandingly successful in the preliminary tournament and then does not win the final, there is always a feeling at the back of one's mind that the best player has not won first prize. This still applies even when, as was done at St Petersburg, the results in the preliminaries carry on to and are added to those attained in the finals.

The world champion made an indifferent start in the preliminary tournament and, when he lost to Bernstein in the eighth round, he appeared actually to be in danger of not qualifying for the final. Then, however, he showed what a magnificent fighter he was and managed to qualify fairly comfortably. Capablanca, on the other hand, played like a true world champion and won first place with a margin of one and a half points over the field. The results were as follows: Capablanca 8, Lasker and Tarrasch 6½, Alekhine and Marshall 6, Bernstein and Rubinstein 5, Nimzovitsch 4, Blackburne and Janowski 3½ and Gunsberg 1.

Not only did Capablanca win the tournament but he played chess of wonderful quality and won the first brilliancy prize for the following game:

White: Capablanca. Black: O. Bernstein. Queen's Gambit Declined, Orthodox Defence.

 1. P-Q4,P-Q4; 2. Kt-KB3,Kt-KB3; 3. P-B4,P-K3;
 4. Kt-B3,QKt-Q2; 5. B-Kt5,B-K2; 6. P-K3,P-B3;
 7. B-Q3,PxP; 8. BxBP,P-QKt4; 9. B-Q3,P-QR3;
 10. P-K4,P-K4; 11. PxP,Kt-Kt5; 12. B-B4,B-B4; 13. 0-0,Q-B2;
 14. R-B1,P-B3; 15. B-Kt3,PxP; 16. P-Kt4,B-R2;
 17. BxKtP,RPxB; 18. KtxKtP,Q-Q1; 19. Kt-Q6 ch,K-B1;
 20. RxP,Kt-Kt3; 21. B-R4,Q-Q2; 22. KtxB,QxR;
 23. Q-Q8ch,Q-K1; 24. B-K7 ch,K-B2; 25. Kt-Q6 ch,K-Kt3;
 26. Kt-R4 ch,K-R4; 27. KtxQ,RxQ; 28. KtxP ch,K-R3;
 29. Kt(Kt7)-B5 ch,K-R4; 30. P-KR3,Kt-B1; 31. PxKt ch,KxP;
 32. BxR,RxB; 33. P-Kt3,R-Q7; 34. K-Kt2,R-K7;
 35. P-R4, resigns (Diagram 55).

That Capablanca entered the final stages of the competition one and a half points ahead of the world champion seemed a crippling burden. But (and this is a tribute to Lasker's remarkable and enduring personality), playing wonderful chess, he achieved a plus score against both Capablanca and Alekhine, defeating each by 1½–½. He also won all his games against Tarrasch and Marshall. This brought him ahead of Capablanca by just half a point, and the final scores (including the totals from the preliminary tournament) were Lasker 13½, Capablanca 13, Alekhine 10, Tarrasch 8½, Marshall 8.

For the moment the world champion had fended off the attack on his title, but it was obvious that, sooner rather than later, he would have to defend it in a match against the young Cuban genius. In the finals Capablanca had won one and drawn one game against

Alekhine, and he had won both his games against Marshall. Besides his loss to Lasker, his only other was to the master of classical strategy, Tarrasch, and he at least revenged this by beating him in another game.

It is interesting to see the world champion at work, dealing in his practical way with the problems provided by the Tarrasch Defence, as used by its originator. This was one of the games played in the final:

White: Lasker. Black: Tarrasch. Queen's Gambit Declined. Tarrasch Defence.

1. P-Q4,P-Q4; 2. Kt-KB3,P-QB4; 3. P-B4,P-K3;
4. BPxP,KPxP; 5. P-KKt3,Kt-QB3; 6. B-Kt2,Kt-B3;
7. 0-0,B-K2; 8. PxP,BxP; 9. QKt-Q2,P-Q5; 10. Kt-Kt3,B-Kt3;
11. Q-Q3,B-K3; 12. R-Q1,BxKt; 13. QxKt,Q-K2;
14. B-Q2,0-0; 15. P-QR4,Kt-K5; 16. B-K1,QR-Q1;
17. P-R5,B-B4; 18. P-R6,PxP; 19. QR-B1,R-B1;
20. Kt-R4,B-Kt3; 21. Kt-B5,Q-K4; 22. BxKt,QxB;
23. Kt-Q6,QxP; 24. KtxR,RxKt; 25. Q-Q5,Q-K3;
26. Q-B3,P-R3; 27. B-Q2,Kt-K4; 28. RxR ch,QxR;
29. Q-K4,Kt-Q2; 30. R-QB1,Q-B1; 31. BxP,Kt-B4;
32. Q-Kt4,P-B4; 33. Q-Kt6,Q-B2; 34. QxQ ch,KxQ;
35. B-Kt5,Kt-Q6; 36. R-Kt1,K-K3; 37. P-Kt3,K-Q4;
38. P-B3,P-R4; 39. P-R4,Kt-B4; 40. P-R5,P-Q6;
41. K-B1,P-R5; 42. PxP,KtxP; 43. B-B6,Kt-B4;
44. R-Q1, resigns (Diagram 56).

In the light of this game and its result, and also of the old rivalry between Lasker and Tarrasch, one must marvel at the generosity of Tarrasch's comment, '*Lasker hat für seine Mitwirkung am Turnier vom Komitee eine Riesensumme erhalten: über 4000 Rubel. Ich finde das nicht zu hoch, wenn man solche Partien spielt!*' (For his participation in the tournament Lasker received a most substantial sum: over 4,000 roubles. But, when people play games like that I don't think it too high!)

Mannheim, in Germany, was the scene of another interesting tournament, in which three of the best Russian players took part alongside many interesting central European players and one American, Frank Marshall. It was, alas, never finished. On 1 August. 1914, it was interrupted by the Great War. Eleven rounds had been played out of the seventeen scheduled, and Alekhine was leading with the fine total of nine and a half. The Russian players were interned and played some tournaments among themselves at Triberg throughout the war. But otherwise the number of international tournaments was considerably reduced. Capablanca played in some in New York and won first prize in them all. There was also an interesting double-round contest *à quatre* in Berlin in 1918, which was won by Lasker, ahead of Rubinstein, Schlechter and Tarrasch. Réti won a tournament at Kaschau (Kassa) in east Slovakia in 1918, while Lasker won a match versus Tarrasch in 1916. But in general, it was a lean period in the history of international chess.

And yet it must be observed that great wars actually have an acceleratory effect on the progress of the game. Wherever you get large masses of people together for any length of time (armies or prisoners of war), the number who learn to play and do play increases *à vue d'oeil*. You may say, rightly, that this is all very well in terms of quantity, but what about quality? The answer to that is

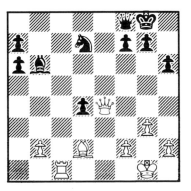

56: Position after Black's 30th move.

that ground which has lain fallow for a long time is more than ready to receive new ideas. So, after the end of every great war there is an immediate upsurge in the interest taken in the game by the ordinary person. In the case of World War I it was the hypermoderns, and in the case of World War II, it was a new dynamic school for which no name has as yet been invented.

We have already mentioned the hypermoderns (Breyer, Nimzovitsch, Réti, Tartakower etc), but before we consider them, there is some unfinished business regarding the world championship. Capablanca won the first international tournament after the war, the so-called Victory tournament, at Hastings in 1919; later he won a match by a very large margin against Kostich, who had come second at Hastings. But what he really wanted was to prove his absolute supremacy, and he again applied to Lasker for a match. The world champion offered to concede the title to him without playing, and there was an immediate outcry throughout the chess-world. Nor was Capablanca himself content to win the title in this limp and bloodless way. A prize fund of $20,000 was collected, of which $11,000 was assured to Lasker win or lose. This he could not resist, and the match duly commenced in Havana in March, 1921.

Its issue was never in doubt and, after fourteen games had been played and the match stood in favour of Capablanca by 4+ 0– 10=, Lasker gave up. Thus ended his long reign of some twenty-seven years as world champion. It was by no means the end of his chess career, however. From time to time he returned to the fray and, despite his increasing years, astonished the chess-world by his magnificent play. But it was the new champion to whom other masters looked as their chief and upon whom they relied to act as their representative and ambassador.

Side by side with match chess, and more important on the whole in demonstrating the progress of the game, was tournament chess. The tournaments of the early 1920s have an especial importance, since they indicated the coming of a new wave, both in theory and praxis. Göteborg 1920 and Berlin 1920 were significant in this respect, the one having been won by Richard Réti and the other by Gyula Breyer. Then, in 1921, Alekhine was first in no less than three tournaments—Budapest, the Hague and Triberg. In Budapest a new and most important name for opening theory made its appearance— that of Grünfeld who came second. It was he who introduced that essentially hypermodern opening, the Grünfeld Defence (1. P-Q4, Kt-KB3; 2. P-QB4,P-KKt3; 3. Kt-QB3,P-Q4).

Alas, in November 1921, a player who had provided a vital spark for this new movement, the Hungarian Gyula Breyer, died at only twenty-seven. A strong memorial tournament to him at Pistyan in 1922 was won by Bogoljuboff with fifteen points, half a point ahead of both Alekhine and Spielmann. Alekhine won the first brilliancy prize in this tournament for the following game:

White: Alekhine. Black: H. Wolf. Queen's Gambit.

1. P-Q4,P-Q4; 2. Kt-KB3,P-QB4; 3. P-B4,BPxP; 4. PxP,Kt-KB3;
5. KtxP,P-QR3; 6. P-K4,KtxKP; 7. Q-R4 ch,B-Q2;
8. Q-Kt3,Kt-B4; 9. Q-K3,P-KKt3; 10. Kt-KB3,Q-B2;
11. Q-B3,R-Kt1; 12. B-K3,P-Kt3; 13. QKt-Q2,B-Kt2;
14. B-Q4,BxB; 15. QxB,B-Kt4; 16. BxB ch,PxB;
17. 0-0,R-R5; 18. P-QKt4,Q-Q1; 19. P-QR3,QKt-Q2;
20. KR-K1,K-B1; 21. P-Q6,Kt-K3; 22. RxKt,PxR;

The British Prime Minister, Bonar Law, with the Mayor of Westminster, watching Capablanca and Euwe in the London Chess Tournament of July 1922.

23. Kt-Kt5,Q-Kt1; 24. KtxKP ch,K-B2; 25. Kt-Kt5 ch,K-B1; 26. Q-Q5,R-Kt2; 27. Kt-K6 ch,K-Kt1; 28. KtxR dis ch,KxKt; 29. PxP,Kt-B3; 30. QxP,R-R2; 31. R-K1,Q-Q3; 32. P-K8-Kt ch,KtxKt; 33. QxKt,QxKt; 34. Q-K5 ch,K-B2; 35. P-KR4,RxRP; 36. Q-K8 ch,K-Kt2; 37. R-K7 ch,K-R3; 38. Q-B8 ch,K-R4; 39. R-K5 ch,K-Kt5; 40. R-Kt5 ch, resigns (Diagram 57).

Well might Tartakower say in his classic work on the hypermoderns, *Die Hypermoderne Schachpartie*, 'Alekhine spielt Sonnenschach.' (Alekhine plays sun-chess).

Wonderful player though Alekhine already was, he had as yet no answer to the majestic powers of Capablanca, as was shown by the Cuban's first appearance as world champion, in a tournament in London in 1922. Capablanca came first with 13 points out of a possible 15, ahead of Alekhine 11½, Vidmar 11, Rubinstein 10½, Bogoljuboff 9, Réti and Tartakower 8½ etc. Nevertheless, the fact that Alekhine came second pointed the way things were going as far as who would be the next challenger for the world championship. Alekhine underlined this by winning a small but strong double-round tournament at Hastings later in the year, just ahead of Rubinstein but a long way above Bogoljuboff, Sir George Thomas, Tarrasch and Yates. These two English masters, F. D. Yates and Sir George Thomas, were to be the chief English representatives in international chess for the next dozen years.

The hypermoderns were much in evidence in a strong tournament at Teplitz-Schönau (northern Bohemia), that year, in which Réti tied with Spielmann for first place with 9 points out of 13, ahead of Grünfeld and Tartakower 8½, Rubinstein 8 etc. Rubinstein more than got his revenge in an even stronger tournament in Vienna, where he came first with 11½ out of 14, followed, at a respectful distance, by Tartakower 10, Wolf 9½, Alekhine, Maroczy and Tarrasch 9, Grünfeld 8, Réti 7½, Bogoljuboff 6½, Spielmann 6, etc.

One other tournament deserves a mention in this year. It was a small affair in New York, in which Edward Lasker came first with 4

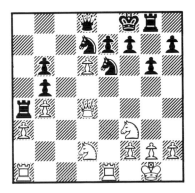

57: Position after Black's 21st move.

points, followed by Jaffe 3, Reshevsky 2½, S. Bernstein and Janowski 2 and Bigelow 1½. The Reshevsky who came third here was the ten-year-old Sammy Reshevsky who, at the age of eight, had already caused a sensation by his ability to play against master players with credit and even success.

I have gone into the tournament play of 1922 in some detail, since it shows to a great extent the activities of the hypermoderns and the measure to which they were successful. But 1922 was also very important from the point of view of hypermodern theory. In that year there appeared in Vienna a small book of 121 pages entitled *Die Neuen Ideen im Schachspiel,* which was published in English under the title, *Modern Ideas in Chess,* the following year. The earlier edition was based on an attack on the ideas and misconceptions of one Franz Gutmayer, but Réti eliminated this from the version that was translated into English, adding much valuable material—on the hypermoderns in particular.

I have already referred to the poetic quality of Réti's work and also observed that I disagree with some of his theories. But whatever I have said in my impudence, I must make it clear that in many ways I regard this work as the best ever written on the game. It did more than any other book to make players realize what vast changes the game had undergone during the centuries when it had already become modern chess. Based as it was on occasional writings, it did not represent Réti's fully considered opinions on the subject. Then, too, that he himself was part and parcel of the movement he described was not necessarily an advantage in terms of objectivity. It is amazing and a tribute to his deep insight that he got as far as he did.

In 1925, some three years after Réti's book, a book by Tartakower, *Hypomoderne Schachpartie,* appeared in Vienna. But for all the wit, charm and erudition which make it such an entrancing pleasure to read, it had nowhere near the influence and effect that Reti's had—on his time and subsequent generations.

Reti was working on a larger, more comprehensive book on the subject, *Masters of the Chess-board,* but unfortunately he died on 6 June 1929 without completing it. He himself counted among the leaders of the hypermodern chess movement, whose adherents included Breyer, Tartakower, Nimzovitsch, Bogoljuboff, Grünfeld, Euwe, Sämisch and even Alekhine, although this brilliant young Russian indignantly denied that he was one of the band, let alone its leader, as some seemed to imply.

All these players had one thing in common. They were looking at chess and its theories with new eyes. There was much talk of their ideas having been derived from Steinitz; but in reality only Nimzovitch could be said to have followed Steinitz's lead. Tschigorin was probably a likelier begetter of their ideas, or rather of the indications that guided them to these ideas. Certainly Euwe and possibly Alekhine owed a great deal to Tarrasch. The rest, Nimzovitch in particular, reacted against Tarrasch, and time has shown they were only partially right in their reactions.

As though to confirm this last observation, Maroczy, whose peak period had been that during which Tarrasch was regarded as the leading theorist, shared first place with Alekhine and Bogoljuboff in the great tournament at Carlsbad in 1923, ahead of such hypermoderns as Grünfeld, Réti, Nimzovitsch, Tartakower and Sämisch.

In 1923, too, there was a welcome return to the arena of the ex-world champion, Emanuel Lasker. He came a good first in an international tournament at Mährisch-Ostrau (Czechoslovakia), a point ahead of Réti, whom he beat in their individual game. He was always a dreaded adversary for the leader of the hypermoderns—possibly because in his pragmatic way he believed in no school and in no movement. There was the chess-board and there were the men. You had to use them to the best of your ability so as to defeat your opponent. Some years after this defeat, when Réti for the first time saw a subway by which to cross the road and avoid the traffic, he was heard to remark that he wished someone would invent a similar subway to avoid Lasker.

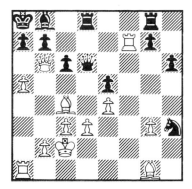

58: Position after White's 25th move.

Rubinstein, who had performed indifferently at Carlsbad, also did badly in this tournament, coming tenth. But he won a most beautiful game which was rightly awarded first brilliancy prize:
White: Rubinstein. Black: Hromadka. King's Gambit Declined.

1. P-K4,P-K4; 2. P-KB4,B-B4; 3. Kt-KB3,P-Q3;
4. Kt-B3,Kt-KB3; 5. B-B4,Kt-B3; 6. P-Q3,B-KKt5;
7. P-KR3,BxKt; 8. QxB,Kt-Q5; 9. Q-Kt3,Q-K2; 10. PxP,PxP;
11. K-Q1,P-B3; 12. P-QR4,R-KKt1; 13. R-KB1,P-KR3;
14. Kt-K2,0-0-0; 15. KtxKt,BxKt; 16. P-B3,B-Kt3;
17. P-R5,B-B2; 18. B-K3,K-Kt1; 19. K-B2,K-R1;
20. R-B3,Kt-Q4; 21. B-Kt1,Kt-B5; 22. Q-B2,B-Kt1;
23. P-KKt3,KtxRP; 24. RxP,Q-Q3; 25. Q-Kt6,R-Q2;
26. B-B5,RxR; 27. BxQ,R-B7 ch; 28. QxR,KtxQ;
29. B-B5, resigns (Diagram 58).

Another landmark in the history of chess came the following year, when there was held the great New York tournament of 1924. Once again Lasker was lured into activity and, with the world champion and every likely candidate for world championship honours also taking part, this double-round event was almost like a trial of strength to determine the leading candidate for a world title match. Capablanca made a poor start and at the end of the first half of the tournament he was equal third with Réti, to whom he had lost, and behind Lasker, who was in stupendous form, and Alekhine. In the second half he did beat Lasker, but he still drew too many. Thus, in the end, Lasker was first with 16 points, above Capablanca 14½, Alekhine 12, Marshall 11, Réti 10½, Maroczy 10, Bogoljuboff 9½, Tartakower 8, Yates 7, Ed. Lasker 6½ and Janowski 5.

Réti won the first brilliancy prize for his game against Bogoljuboff:
White: Réti. Black: Bogoljuboff. Réti Opening.

1. Kt-KB3,P-Q4; 2. P-B4,P-K3; 3. P-KKt3,Kt-KB3;
4. B-Kt2,B-Q3; 5. 0-0,0-0; 6. P-Kt3,R-K1; 7. B-Kt2,QKt-Q2;
8. P-Q4,P-B3; 9. QKt-Q2,Kt-K5; 10. KtxKt,PxKt;
11. Kt-K5,P-KB4; 12. P-B3,PxP; 13. BxP,Q-B2;
14. KtxKt,BxKt; 15. P-K4,P-K4; 16. P-B5,B-KB1;
17. Q-B2,PxQP; 18. PxBP,QR-Q1; 19. B-R5,R-K4;
20. BxP,RxP; 21. RxR,BxR; 22. QxB,RxB;
23. R-KB1,R-Q1; 24. B-B7 ch,K-R1; 25. B-K8, resigns (Diagram 59).

It began to look as though the world champion's natural opponent was the ex-world champion; but for the moment Lasker bided his time.

In 1924, advantage was taken of the fact that an Olympiad was held at Paris to organize a chess Olympiad there, as well. Only amateurs could take part and the winner was the Latvian master,

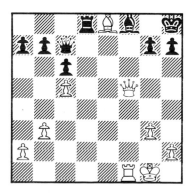

59: Final position.

Mattison. An attempt was also made to hold an international team tournament at the same time, but as the teams varied in number from four to one, it could not be counted as the first genuine international team tournament. That was to come three years later.

The most important achievement of the Paris meeting was the founding, on 20 July, 1924, of the World Chess Federation, known usually as FIDE from the initials of its French name, *Fédération Internationale des Echecs*. The first president of FIDE was Dr Rueb of the Netherlands. Although it was not immediately apparent, this organization was to prove beneficial to the development of world championships, particularly team championships, in the years before the World War II, and also for individual championships somewhat later.

In 1924, a last remaining link with Morphy was cut when the veteran grandmaster, J. H. Blackburne, died on 1 September at the age of eighty-three.

A series of noteworthy tournaments in 1925 witnessed the participation of all the world's leading players. Alekhine had a magnificent success at Baden–Baden, where he came first, unbeaten with 16 points out of a possible 20, $1\frac{1}{2}$ points ahead of Rubinstein. Bogoljuboff was the overwhelming winner at Breslau, with $9\frac{1}{2}$ out of 11, 2 points ahead of Nimzovitsch; and Rubinstein and Nimzovitsch shared first place in the Marienbad tournament. But much the most important tournament that year was that in Moscow, in which the world champion, Capablanca, and the former world champion, Lasker, took part. First, however, went to neither of these. Instead the place was won by the Soviet player, Bogoljuboff, with $15\frac{1}{2}$ points, ahead of Lasker 14 and Capablanca $13\frac{1}{2}$. Capablanca did very well in the group of the top five, where he scored $3\frac{1}{2}$ out of 4 but he lost to two Russians, Iljin-Genevsky and Werlinski. Bogoljuboff, on the other hand, was outstandingly successful against his compatriots, but he stumbled badly against those in the higher echelons of play. There were even rumours of a compact between Bogoljuboff and his compatriots, for they seemed to play with neither heart nor success against him. But that was true, too, of a number of other players, and it would be more charitable and perhaps more fair to assume that he had struck a high peak of form in Moscow. Additional and supporting proof that this was so is shown in the fact that he repeated some of his triumphs in other tournaments away from the Soviet Union, which he was shortly to leave, to take up residence in Germany, where he lived until his death in 1952.

There remained the question of who was going to challenge Capablanca for the world title. Although Lasker did so well whenever he chose to return to battle (remarkably, he chose to return only in very strong events), there seemed less and less chance of his entering the lists for the championship. Three much younger players, Alekhine, Bogoljuboff and Nimzovitsch, were singling themselves out for this. Of the three, Alekhine was the most serious and determined. Bogoljuboff, the eternal optimist, did not really seem to worry overmuch. As for Nimzovitsch, when the issue was eventually decided in a fashion that omitted him altogether, he treated it as a joke and had visiting cards printed on which appeared the words, 'Nimzovitsch, International Master and Crown Prince of the Chess World'.

It was he who scored the first success in 1926, at Dresden. He had a wonderful result with 8½ points out of 9, coming 1½ points ahead of Alekhine. In this tournament he played the best blockade game of all time:

White: P. Johner. Black: Nimzovitsch. Q.P. Nimzovitsch Defence.
1. P-Q4,Kt-KB3; 2. P-QB4,P-K3; 3. Kt-QB3,B-Kt5;
4. P-K3,0-0; 5. B-Q3,P-B4; 6. Kt-B3,Kt-B3; 7. 0-0,BxKt;
8. PxB,P-Q3; 9. Kt-Q2,P-QKt3; 10. Kt-Kt3,P-K4;
11. P-KB4,P-K5; 12. B-K2,Q-Q2; 13. P-KR3,Kt-K2;
14. Q-K1,P-KR4; 15. B-Q2,Q-B4; 16. K-R2,Q-R2;
17. P-QR4,Kt-B4; 18. P-Kt3,P-QR4; 19. R-KKt1,Kt-R3;
20. B-KB1,B-Q2; 21. B-B1,QR-B1; 22. P-Q5,K-R1;
23. Kt-Q2,R-KKt1; 24. B-KKt2,P-KKt4; 25. Kt-B1,R-Kt2;
26. R-R2,Kt-B4; 27. B-R1,QR-KKt1; 28. Q-Q1,PxP;
29. KPxP,B-B1; 30. Q-Kt3,B-R3; 31. R-K2,Kt-R5;
32. R-K3,B-B1; 33. Q-B2,BxP; 34. BxP,B-B4;
35. BxB,KtxB; 36. R-K2,P-R5; 37. R(Kt1)-Kt2,PxP db. ch;
38. K-Kt1,Q-R6; 39. Kt-K3,Kt-R5; 40. K-B1,R-K1;
White resigns (Diagram 60).

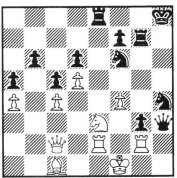

60: Final position.

At the Semmering Panhans tournament in the eastern Alps, Spielmann was first with 13 points, followed by Alekhine 12½, Vidmar 12, Nimzovitsch and Tartakower 11½. But it was Alekhine who more and more was emerging as the natural challenger for the world title. At Kecskemet, Hungary, in 1927 he came first, half a point ahead of Nimzovitsch and L. Steiner, and he won a short but very toughly contested match with the Dutch master, Max Euwe, by 3 + 2 5=.

Then came the final test in New York, when Capablanca played against a selected number of likely candidates. The arrangement was in the form of a match-tournament, in which each player played against the other four times. Alekhine, Nimzovitsch, Spielmann, Vidmar and Marshall accepted invitations. Bogoljuboff, however, sent a telegram saying that, instead of a mediocre tournament, he suggested a match between himself and Capablanca.

The event was an overwhelming triumph for Capablanca, who came first with 14 points, followed by Alekhine 11½, Nimzovitsch 10½, Vidmar 10, Spielmann 8 and Marshall 6. Capablanca did not lose a game and won every match. There were four best-game prizes and the first went to Capablanca for the following beautiful game:
White: Capablanca. Black: Spielmann. Queen's Gambit Declined.
1. P-Q4,P-Q4; 2. Kt-KB3,P-K3; 3. P-B4,Kt-Q2;
4. Kt-B3,KKt-B3; 5. B-Kt5,B-Kt5; 6. PxP,PxP;
7. Q-R4,BxKt ch; 8. PxB,0-0; 9. P-K3,P-B4; 10. B-Q3,P-B5;
11. B-B2,Q-K2; 12. 0-0,P-QR3; 13. KR-K1,Q-K3;
14. Kt-Q2,P-QKt4; 15. Q-R5,Kt-K5; 16. KtxKt,PxKt;
17. P-QR4,Q-Q4; 18. PxP,QxB; 19. BxP,R-QKt1;
20. PxP,R-Kt4; 21. Q-B7,Kt-Kt3; 22. P-R7,B-R6;
23. Kt-Kt1,RxR; 24. RxR,P-B4; 25. B-B3,P-B5; 26. PxP,
resigns (Diagram 61).

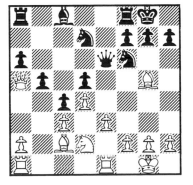

61: Position after White's 15th move.

Alekhine, having come second in New York, had earned the right to play Capablanca for the title. The match for the world championship duly commenced on 16 September, 1927 at Buenos Aires. The winner would be whoever won six games, draws not counting. Practically every expert, with the solitary exception of Reti, expected a Capablanca victory, so they got a rude shock when Alekhine won the first game with a French Defence. But Capablanca soon struck back, and at one moment was leading by 2–1. Then, Alekhine, playing in a style reminiscent of Capablanca himself gradually wore down the opposition. He finished victor with the 34th game by 6+ 3– 25=. It was a firm and convincing result. Against such a score there could be no cavil or suggestion of luck. It is undoubtedly true that Capablanca had not prepared for the match to anything like the extent Alekhine had. It was not in his nature so to do. He at once however began to prepare for a return match, but he was to find it was not so easy to bring Alekhine to the sticking point.

Meanwhile, in London, there had taken place the first genuine international team tournament. Sixteen countries participated, and the champions were Hungary, with a team consisting of Maroczy, Nagy, Vajda, A. Steiner and Havasi. Denmark were second and England third. The following year at the Hague a return was made to the formula of the amateur world championship and this was won by Euwe. There was also a team tournament in which Hungary again came first with the same team as before, with the exception of Maroczy. The United States were second and Poland third.

After he had lost the world title, Capablanca, in an effort to force Alekhine to allow him a match, played in many more tournaments; on the other hand, there was a distinct pause in Alekhine's tournament activities. The ex-world champion took part in no less than three international tournaments in 1928 alone. In the one which was to have the most bearing on the question of a challenge to Alekhine, that at Bad Kissingen, Germany, he came second. It was the irrepressible Bogoljuboff who came first, a full point ahead of Capablanca. True, Capablanca beat him in their individual game, but he lost to Spielmann, ever a dangerous adversary for him and one who was to end up with an even score against him when their over-all careers are considered. And—this was unusual with Capablanca—he drew more than fifty per cent of his games (six), while Bogoljuboff drew four.

There were two Berlin tournaments that year. Nimzovitsch won the lesser (though still strong) event and Capablanca had a striking success in the other, a double-round meeting with every player of full grandmaster quality. He came first without losing a game, with $8\frac{1}{2}$ points, ahead of Nimzovitsch 7, Spielmann $6\frac{1}{2}$, Tartakower $5\frac{1}{2}$, Réti and Rubinstein 5 and Marshall $4\frac{1}{2}$.

Here is an entertaining tit-bit from this tournament, with lively play on both sides:

White: Réti. Black: Capablanca. Ruy Lopez, Steinitz Defence Deferred.

1. P-K4,P-K4; 2. Kt-KB3,Kt-QB3; 3. B-Kt5,P-QR3;
4. B-R4,P-Q3; 5. P-B3,P-B4; 6. P-Q4,BPxP;
7. Kt-Kt5,PxP; 8. KtxKP,Kt-B3; 9. B-KKt5,B-K2;
10. QxP,P-QKt4; 11. KtxKt ch,PxKt; 12. Q-Q5,PxKB;
13. B-R6,Q-Q2; 14. o-o,B-Kt2; 15. B-Kt7,o-o-o;
16. BxR,Kt-K4; 17. Q-Q1,B-B6; 18. PxB,Q-R6; White resigns (Diagram 62).

Capablanca was first again at the Budapest Siesta Tournament—ahead of Marshall, Kmoch and Spielmann. And he was first again at Budapest the following year, 1929—above Rubinstein and Tartakower. At Barcelona, a rather weaker tournament in which,

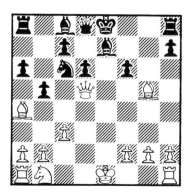

62: Position after White's 12th move.

however, he played a number of beautifully elegant games, he was an overwhelming first, with $13\frac{1}{2}$ out of 14, two points ahead of Tartakower.

But the *piéce de resistance* of the year 1929, as far as tournaments are concerned, was another immensely strong Carlsbad competition with twenty-two competitors. This was won by Nimzowitsch with 15 points, Capablanca sharing second and third prizes with Spielmann with $14\frac{1}{2}$. Once again Capablanca lost to Spielmann, but it was a blunder which cost a piece and the game against Samisch that cost him in turn the first prize.

Rubinstein, who had been a creditable fourth at the Carlsbad tournament with $13\frac{1}{2}$ points, scored his last tournament success this year with a first at Rogaska-Slatina (Rohitsch-Sauerbrunn), with $11\frac{1}{2}$ points, a point ahead of the young Czech, Salo Flohr, who was soon to develop into one of the greatest masters of his time. After this event Rubinstein's results were on a falling curve, owing to mental ill-health. I saw him play in a small event, the Ramsgate Team Practice Tournament, that year, and noticed how strange his behaviour was (it looked like some sort of persecution mania). In the early 1930s he had to abandon competitive chess.

Alekhine won one small event at Bradley Beach, New Jersey, in 1929, where he came an easy first, with $8\frac{1}{2}$ points, L. Steiner coming second with 7. Now at least he chose an opponent for the world championship contest. His choice, which was universally regarded as an attempt to avoid playing Capablanca, was Bogoljuboff—odd, since he had come only eighth at the 1929 Carlsbad event.

But the match was a good one, in which Bogoljuboff showed himself to be a genuine grandmaster. Alekhine had to give of his best; but he was certainly too good for his opponent, whom he beat by $11+ 5- 9=$. The very first game displayed a severity which was the sign of a true and outstanding world champion:
White: Alekhine. Black: Bogoljuboff. Queen's Gambit Declined. Slav Defence.

Aron Nimzovitsch (left) in play against the Hamburg master Brinkmann at the Berlin International Tournament.

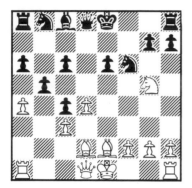

63: Position after Black's 12th move.

1. P-Q4,P-Q4; 2. P-QB4,P-QB3; 3. Kt-KB3,Kt-B3;
4. Kt-B3,PxP; 5. P-QR4,P-K3; 6. P-K4,B-Kt5; 7. P-K5,Kt-Q4;
8. B-Q2,BxKt; 9. PxB,P-QKt4; 10. Kt-Kt5,P-B3;
11. PxP,KtxKBP; 12. B-K2,P-QR3; 13. B-B3,P-R3;
14. B-R5 ch,KtxB; 15. QxKt ch,K-Q2; 16. Kt-B7,Q-K1;
17. Q-Kt6,R-Kt1; 18. B-B4,B-Kt2; 19. B-Kt3,K-K2;
20. B-Q6 ch,K-Q2; 21. 0-0,P-B4; 22. QPxP,B-Q4;
23. PxP,PxP; 24. RxR,BxR; 25. R-R1,Kt-B3;
26. Kt-K5 ch, resigns (Diagram 63).

Poland, with a team headed by Rubinstein and Tartakower, won the FIDE International Team Championship at Hamburg in 1930, with Hungary and Germany in second and third places. Playing for the British Chess Federation in that event was Sultan Khan, the Indian wonder, who had been brought up on the older Indian form of the game but revealed himself as a grandmaster of modern chess when he came to England in 1929. He was second to Tartakower at the Liège tournament. A new United States star appeared in Isaac Kashdan, who came second to Nimzovitsch at Frankfurt-am-Main, and first in a short but select tournament at Stockholm—above Bogoljuboff and Stoltz.

The chief performance of the year, however, was Alekhine's fantastic win at San Remo, where he came first with 14 points out of 15, followed by Nimzovitsch 10½, Rubinstein 10 and Bogoljuboff 9½. This was remarkable, but even more astonishing was his triumph in 1931 at Bled in Yugoslavia. Here, in a double-round tournament in which everybody was of grandmaster strength, he came first with 20½, followed at a most respectful distance, by Bogoljuboff 15, Nimzowitsch 14, Flohr, Kashdan, Stoltz and Vidmar 13½, Tartakower 13, Kostich and Spielmann 12½, Maroczy 12, Colle 10½, Asztalos 9½ and Pirc 8½. Capablanca's tournament performances, fine though these were, paled in comparison; but he showed he was still a formidable force in a match by defeating the young Dutchman, Euwe, by 2+ 0- 8=.

A foretaste of things to come was the win of the Soviet championship in Moscow by a twenty-year-old, Mikhail Botvinnik, with a margin of two points. The Russians had their spearhead; it remained for the cohorts to follow. They were not yet members of the World Chess Federation, so they presented no problem to the rest of the world, as regards team tournaments at any rate. In this respect, the United States' players now showed their great strength. The forward movements of populations as they carry along with them an increased interest in and power to play in chess could not have been bettered by the rise of the U.S.A. to one of the foremost chess countries in the world.

The new Czechoslovak star, Salo Flohr, began to show his great strength. He won first prize in the Premier Tournament of the Hastings Christmas Congress (1931–32) and was to follow this up with repeated successes at the annual Hastings Congresses. In 1932 he came equal first with Prof. Milan Vidmar at Sliac in Czechoslovakia; was second to Alekhine in London and equal second with Euwe below Alekhine again at Berne in 1932. In coming fourth, only half a point behind Euwe and Flohr at the Berne Tournament Sultan Khan too had a fine result. The United States team maintained its position at the head of the International Team Tournament at Folkestone in 1933. But a new name, that of Reuben Fine, appeared in their team. Flohr, in winning first prize at Hastings for the third year in succession (1933–34) and in coming ahead of Alekhine and Andreas Lilienthal, a fine young Hungarian master, began to appear more and more a likely challenger for the world title.

Dr. Lasker made a return to international chess when he took part in a very strong event at Zürich in 1934. Despite advancing years and his long absence from the fray he showed he was still a great player by coming an excellent fifth with a score of 10 points. The world champion, Alekhine, won the tournament with the remarkable score of 13 out of 15, losing only to Euwe, drawing with Flohr and Bogoljuboff and winning his remaining twelve games. Oddly enough, he chose to play another match with Bogoljuboff that year, and beat him easily, as everybody expected, by 8+ 3– 15=.

The chess-world was getting the impression that, while Alekhine was a marvellous player, he was also marvellous at avoiding formidable opposition where his title was concerned. Another circumstance that caused those who knew of it to believe that his star was sinking was that he drank to excess. I often saw him the worse for drink at the International Team Tournament in Warsaw in 1935, and this could not but have a serious effect on his play.

The United States successfully defended their championship at Warsaw, but the most important single appearance at that event was the debut of Paul Keres in the international field. The Estonian, then eighteen, shone with a wonderful brilliance that lighted up the chess-world wherever he went for the next forty-one years.

In this year Alekhine decided to play another match to defend his title, and again there was surprise at his choice of opponent. This time it was Euwe. Why Euwe rather than Capablanca, people wondered, since Capablanca had decisively defeated the Dutchman in a match. Why Euwe rather than Flohr, people wondered, since Flohr's tournament record was much superior. When Euwe won the match and became world champion they wondered even more. Eye-witnesses have said that Alekhine was drinking heavily throughout, and that he even turned up drunk to play. Euwe's win was a narrow one, by 9+ 8– 13=, but it was clear from the games that the result was just. The new world champion had been consistently underestimated and it is highly possible that Alekhine had made the mistake of doing so, when he conceded him the right to play.

Meanwhile the unfortunate ex-world champion, Capablanca, had been left out in the cold, and he made strenuous efforts to achieve such tournament results as would shame and persuade the chess-world into seeing that he was granted another chance at the title. His results in Moscow in 1935 did not help much. This strong event culminated in a tie for first place between Botvinnik and Flohr with 13 points, ahead of Dr Lasker 12½ and Capablanca 12. But the Cuban did achieve a fine result at a double-round tournament in Moscow the following year, where he came first with 13, followed by Botvinnik 12, Flohr 9½, Lilienthal 9, Ragosin 8½, Dr Lasker 8 and Kan, Levenfish, Riumin and Eliskases 7½.

He was also equal first with Bovinnik, with 10 points, at another great tournament, which was held in Nottingham that year. Euwe, Fine and Reshevsky were next with 9½, followed by Alekhine 9, Flohr and Dr Lasker 8½, Vidmar 6, Bogoljuboff and Tartakower 5½, Tylor 4½, Alexander 3½, Sir George Thomas 2 and Winter 2½.

Two other tournaments that year in which Keres shone were

Nauheim, where he was equal first with Alekhine, and Zandvoort, where he was third, below Fine and Euwe.

An Olympiad in Munich (not an international team tournament of FIDE since it allowed only amateurs to participate) was won by Hungary. The real FIDE event in Stockholm in 1937 was won by the United States for the third time with the powerful team of Reshevsky, Fine, Kashdan, Marshall and Horowitz.

Meanwhile Alekhine had been preparing for his return match with Euwe. With remarkable self-discipline he gave up heavy drinking, and by 1937 he was physically fit for the encounter. There were some doubts about his form at chess, however. In Margate, Fine and Keres came equal first with $7\frac{1}{2}$, while he was third with 6. At Kemeri, Flohr, Petrov and Reshevsky were equal first with 12, and he came equal fourth with Keres with $11\frac{1}{2}$. And in a small double-round tournament at Nauheim, Euwe was first, with 4 points ahead of Alekhine and Bogoljuboff $3\frac{1}{2}$, and Sämisch 1.

Nevertheless, once the match, which was held in the Hague, began it was apparent he was going to be the victor. Euwe never had a real chance and Alekhine regained the world championship

The 1927 International Tournament at the British Empire Club. In the foreground, Sir George Thomas plays White against the US champion Frank W. Marshall. In the background, F. D. Yates, Victor Buerger and W. A. Fairhurst.

with the crushing score of 10+ 4– 11=. So he was back in his rightful place, but there were many younger men who were preparing to topple him from his throne: the Soviet Botvinnik, the Czechoslovak Flohr, the two Americans, Fine and Reshevsky, and, most dangerous of all, the Estonian Keres.

This was made clear in a double-round tournament at Semmering-Baden that year. Keres was first with 9 points and then came Fine 8, Capablanca and Reshevsky $7\frac{1}{2}$, Flohr 7, Eliskases and Ragosin 6, and Petrov 5. Keres won a very pleasing game against Flohr in this tournament:

*A modern Hungarian chess set,
with silver and enamel
decorations.*

From the world championship match at Reykjavik, 1972: Bobby Fischer (left), supported by Icelandic bodyguard, endeavours to snatch the crown from Boris Spassky, supported by his seconds Geller and Nej; in the centre chess arbiter Lothar Schmid flanked (left) by Harry Golombek and (right) Arnlaugsson; at the back (above Fischer), Professor Euwe and, with the camera, Chester Fox (USA).

Poster commemorating the final ceremony at Reykjavik, 1972: left to right, Geller, Krogius (Spassky's seconds), Spassky, Fischer, Icelandic bodyguard toasting Fischer's success, Lombardy (Fischer's second), Fred Cramer (Fischer's spokesman) holding basket of telegrams, Professor Euwe (President of FIDE) supported by Golombek (with Möller in reserve), then the President of the Icelandic Chess Federation supported by Fridrik Olafsson (grandmaster). At Fischer's feet is a sack of dollars out of which Chester Fox is carving some money. In the background is the judge's table with Lothar Schmid and Arnlaugsson.

White: Keres. Black: Flohr. Q.P. King's Indian Defence.
1. P-Q4,Kt-KB3; 2. P-QB4,P-KKt3; 3. Kt-KB3,B-Kt2;
4. P-KKt3,P-B3; 5. B-Kt2,P-Q4; 6. PxP,KtxP; 7. o-o,o-o;
8. Kt-B3,KtxKt; 9. PxKt,P-QB4; 10. B-QR3,PxP;
11. KtxP,Q-B2; 12. Q-Kt3,B-B3; 13. KR-Q1,Kt-Q2;
14. P-QB4,Kt-B4; 15. Q-Kt4,Kt-K3; 16. Kt-Kt5,Q-K4;
17. QR-B1,R-Q1; 18. R-Q5,RxR; 19. PxR,P-R3;
20. Kt-R7,Kt-Q5; 21. RxB ch,RxR; 22. KtxR,QxKP;
23. P-KR4,Kt-B4; 24. Q-K4, resigns (Diagram 64).

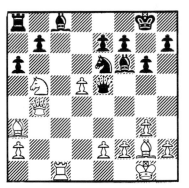

64: Position after Black's 19th move.

Chess pieces carved by Ulyssée Darbouze, depicting King Christophe of Haiti; wood, twentieth century.

chapter 14

The Soviet School triumphs

With Alekhine once more ensconced in his proper niche (although he might have eluded a trial of strength with his rightful rival, Capablanca, and although he was himself on the decline, he was still one of the greatest players in chess history and played as a world champion should), it is time to look at the chess-world at large to see which way the main current was flowing in the late 1930s.

We have seen that the United States was dominating the international team tournaments and doing so by the production of a number of superb players (Kashdan, Dake, H. Steiner, Fine and Reshevsky, all, be it noted, of recent Jewish European stock) and that these events had not as yet included the Soviet Union. We have also noted the rise of Soviet chessmasters to the lofty level of the world's finest masters, and that some of the best players of all outside the Soviet Union—Alekhine and Bogoljuboff for instance—actually came from there.

What we have not indicated so far is the intensive activity that was going on throughout the length and breadth of the USSR in the matter of training and encouraging chessplayers and the popularization of the game. A species of mass-production was used, which was aptly designed to cope with the vast numbers involved. Everyone was classified according to skill. The lowest category was very weak indeed, but players of the first category corresponded to strong amateurs in Britain and America. Above the first category, players were candidates for mastership, and, once they became masters, for grandmastership. They rose in these grades through participation in graded tournaments, a self-feeding process which was of the utmost value in giving them suitable practice.

Naturally, this was not the only reason for the vast expansion in Soviet chess which took place between 1938 and 1963, the period which I have taken as the chronological bounds for this chapter. It should be remembered that the Soviet Union, already the heir to a vast Russian empire, was to become even larger through its acquisitions after World War II. Thus, many of the superb players whom we term Russian have in reality not been Russian at all, but citizens of some territory that might be about as far from Russia as central Africa is from England. To mention a few, there was the Armenian Petrosian, the Estonian Keres, the Latvian Tal, many

Ukrainians (Geller, Stein, Bronstein etc) as well as Tartars, Khazaks, and a variety of other central Asians.

The mixture does not stop there. A great number of the best Soviet players were Jewish and pertained to Jewish, rather than Russian, culture. This brings me naturally to Professor Elo's theory of the vertical movements of population. This lays down that wherever people break through the rigid layers of a class-bound society they produce a stock, by the intermingling of classes, which is prone to give the world geniuses in many ranges of the arts, sciences and games of an intellectual nature. The Soviet Union could not have provided a better illustration for his purposes.

Leaving the Soviet Union for the moment to stew, as it were, in its own borsch, I would like to refer to a small international tournament in which I myself played, at Margate in 1938, as evidence that the world champion was still capable of the most beautiful chess, and also to illustrate the type of combination for which he was famous. Alekhine was first with 7 points, followed by Spielmann 6, Petrov $5\frac{1}{2}$, Book and Milner-Barry 5, Golombek $4\frac{1}{2}$, C. H. O.'D. Alexander 4, E. G. Sergeant $3\frac{1}{2}$, Vera Menchik-Stevenson 3 and Sir George Thomas $1\frac{1}{2}$.

Alekhine lost to Petrov, a highly talented Latvian grandmaster (he alas died in World War II) but he won a famous game—I show it below—against the Finnish master, E. E. Book. Apropos, Spielmann once remarked, 'I can play the combinations Alekhine does, but what I cannot do is produce the positions in which one can use these combinations with anything like his fluency.'

White: Alekhine. Black: E. E. Book. Queen's Gambit Accepted.

1. P-Q4,P-Q4; 2. P-QB4,PxP; 3. Kt-KB3,Kt-KB3;
4. P-K3,P-K3; 5. BxP,P-B4; 6. 0-0,Kt-B3; 7. Q-K2,P-QR3;
8. Kt-B3,P-QKt4; 9. B-Kt3,P-Kt5; 10. P-Q5,Kt-QR4;
11. B-R4 ch,B-Q2; 12. PxP,PxP; 13. R-Q1,PxKt;
14. RxB,KtxR; 15. Kt-K5,R-R2; 16. PxP,K-K2;
17. P-K4,Kt-B3; 18. B-KKt5,Q-B2; 19. B-B4,Q-Kt3;

65: *Position after Black's 14th move.*

20. R-Q1,P-Kt3; 21. B-KKt5,B-Kt2; 22. Kt-Q7,RxKt;
23. RxR ch,K-B1; 24. BxKt,BxB; 25. P-K5, resigns
(Diagram 65).

The combination, or rather the series of combinations having the focal point on White's Q7, present a most pleasing and aesthetic picture. Note too the beautiful contrast of the quiet move (17. P-K4,) in the midst of so much violence.

The year 1938 was notable for the AVRO tournament. This double-round event, so-called after the initials of the Dutch Radio company which sponsored it, was held in the Netherlands with the express intention of designating the challenger for the world championship. The world champion himself competed, and so too did Capablanca. The rest were the select few of the younger players who were likely candidates: Botvinnik, Euwe, Fine, Flohr, Keres and Reshevsky.

The older players, Capablanca and Alekhine, were severely handicapped by the tournament conditions, which entailed travelling from city to city and hence were extremely wearing. Fine, who had deliberately changed his style into that of a more open, attacking game was in stupendous form, but in the end he was overhauled by Keres, who tied with him for first place with 8½ points. They were followed by Botvinnik 7½, Alekhine, Euwe and Reshevsky 7, Capablanca 6 and Flohr 4½. Keres was recognized as the official world-championship candidate, since he had a superior Sonneborn-Berger point count. This is a system of adding together the points obtained by one's opponents, counting their full score when one has beaten them, half their score when one has drawn with them and nothing at all when one has lost to them. The player who acquires the highest score in this way is adjudged the best.

Keres, however, was never to have an opportunity of playing a match with Alekhine, because of the intervention of World War II. Keres once remarked that it was perhaps a good thing that he did not play him at that time, since he was not sufficiently mature for the task of winning the world championship in 1941. His self-deprecation grew out of genuine modesty, but most experts thought that he

Playing chess in 1932, a scene by S. Anderson.

would have beaten Alekhine whose powers were visibly declining.

Sad to relate, the opportunity Keres missed was not to recur again for him as will be shown in the subsequent narrative. It was another and perhaps stronger personality, Mikhail Botvinnik, who was to mount the throne. In respect, it should be observed that while Keres and Fine did indeed share first prize at the AVRO tournament, it was the Soviet grandmaster, Botvinnik, who was the most impressive. Consider the following game, which is characteristic of his mastery in all three spheres of chess, opening, middle-game and ending, and is particularly impressive in the latter stages:

White: Botvinnik. Black: Capablanca. Q.P. Nimzovitsch Defence.

1. P-Q4,Kt-KB3; 2. P-QB4,P-K3; 3. Kt-QB3,B-Kt5;
4. P-K3,P-Q4; 5. P-QR3,BxKt ch; 6. PxB,P-B4;
7. BPxP,KPxP; 8. B-Q3,o-o; 9. Kt-K2,P-QKt3; 10. o-o,B-R3;
11. BxB,KtxB; 12. B-Kt2,Q-Q2; 13. P-QR4,KR-K1;
14. Q-Q3,P-B5; 15. Q-B2,Kt-Kt1; 16. QR-K1,Kt-B3;
17. Kt-Kt3,Kt-QR4; 18. P-B3,Kt-Kt6; 19. P-K4,QxRP;
20. P-K5,Kt-Q2; 21. Q-B2,P-Kt3; 22. P-B4,P-B4;
23. PxP e.p.,KtxP; 24. P-B5,RxR; 25. RxR,R-K1;
26. R-K6,RxR; 27. PxR,K-Kt2; 28. Q-B4,Q-K1;
29. Q-K5,Q-K2; 30. B-QR3,QxB; 31. Kt-R5 ch,PxKt;
32. Q-Kt5 ch,K-B1; 33. QxKt ch,K-Kt1; 34. P-K7,Q-B8 ch;
35. K-B2,Q-B7 ch; 36. K-Kt3,Q-Q6 ch; 37. K-R4,Q-K5 ch;
38. KxP,Q-K7 ch; 39. K-R4,Q-K5 ch; 40. P-Kt4,Q-K8 ch;
41. K-R5, resigns (Diagram 66).

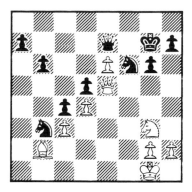

66: Position after Black's 29th move.

Flohr's results had been poor in the last few years preceding World War II. This was due partly to the unsettling nature of the times, which forced him constantly to flee Nazi persecution (he eventually settled in the Soviet Union); it was partly because he simply played too much, and thus converted his style from the flash of genius to the pedestrian. But he had a fine result in a strong tournament which was conducted in Leningrad and Moscow in 1939, winning first prize with a score of 12 points, ahead of Reshevsky 10½ etc. Keres had a setback in this tournament and tied for twelfth place with an eighteen-year-old, Vassily Smyslov, of whom more, much more, will be said later on.

One of the last international tournaments before the war was held in Margate in 1939, and was won by Keres with 7½ points, ahead of Capablanca and Flohr 6½. The Polish master, Najdorf, who was later to emerge as a strong grandmaster with a style of play as colourful as his personality, finished with only 4 points, partly owing to my having beaten him (I had 3½). That Capablanca could still produce model examples of severity against the lesser lights was shown in the following game:

White: Capablanca. Black: G. S. A. Wheatcroft. Sicilian Defence.

1. P-K4,P-QB4; 2. Kt-K2,P-Q3; 3. P-KKt3,Kt-QB3;
4. B-Kt2,P-KKt3; 5. P-QB3,B-Kt2; 6. P-Q4,P-K4;
7. PxBP,PxP; 8. o-o,B-K3; 9. B-K3,QxQ; 10. RxQ,P-QKt3;
11. Kt-R3,R-Q1; 12. Kt-Kt5,B-B5; 13. Kt-B7 ch,K-K2;
14. Kt-Q5 ch,K-K3; 15. R-Q2,KKt-K2; 16. Kt-B7 ch,K-B3;
17. QR-Q1,RxR; 18. RxR,R-Q1; 19. RxR,KtxR;
20. Kt-K8 ch, resigns (Diagram 67).

The 1939 International Team Tournament was held in Buenos Aires. There were some notable absentees, neither the United States nor Hungary participating. In the absence of the Americans, the

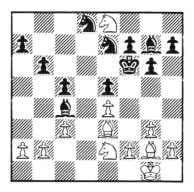

67: Final position.

German team, which now included the Austrian, Eliskases, was unquestionably the best, and duly came first, half a point ahead of Poland. The war in Europe erupted during the competition, and the English team decided to return home, despite having qualified for the top final section. A number of matches between countries which were now enemies were agreed drawn without play. One interesting consequence of the outbreak of hostilities at a time when the best of Europe's players were gathered in Argentina, was an unexpected enrichment of the game in South America. All the German players stayed behind, Eliskases settling in Brazil and the remainder in Argentina. The two finest players to stay were Najdorf and Stahlberg, under whose influence chess-life in the Argentine waxed greatly, and the standard of play began to equal that of Europe.

But the war had a crippling effect on international chess, especially in Europe, and in the matter of international tournaments. At first, however, chess-life went on as normal in the USSR, which had not as yet entered the war. The Soviet championship in Moscow in 1940 ended in a tie between Bondarevsky and Lilienthal with $13\frac{1}{2}$ points each, ahead of Smyslov 13, Keres 12, Boleslavsky and Botvinnik $11\frac{1}{2}$. This was a disappointment for Botvinnik, who had easily won the previous year's championship in Leningrad. It was decided to hold an absolute championship of the Soviet Union in Moscow and Leningrad, with the top six from the Moscow championship tournament taking part. The result was an overwhelming triumph for Botvinnik, who came first with $13\frac{1}{2}$ points (players met each other four times), followed by Keres 11, Smyslov 10, Boleslavsky 9, Lilienthal $8\frac{1}{2}$ and Bondarevsky 8. Botvinnik afterwards referred to it as his greatest tournament success, and for many years he was regarded as without question the leading player of the Soviet Union.

A number of tournaments now took place in Europe, organized by the Germans and with competitors coming largely from occupied Europe. Alekhine, who had clearly thrown in his lot with the German conquerors, played in them, as did also a few masters from neutral countries. In 1941 a tournament for the championship of Europe was held in Munich and ended in victory for the Swede, Stoltz, with 12 points, ahead of Alekhine and Lundin $10\frac{1}{2}$, and Bogoljuboff 9. In a tournament in Cracow, Alekhine tied with Schmidt, with $8\frac{1}{2}$ points, followed by Bogoljuboff $7\frac{1}{2}$, and an interesting, talented young German named Junge, who came fourth with 7 points.

A strong double-round tournament in Salzburg in 1942 was won by Alekhine with $7\frac{1}{2}$, followed by Keres 6, Junge and Schmidt 5, Bogoljuboff $3\frac{1}{2}$ and Stoltz 3. Alekhine also won a European championship that year in Munich with $8\frac{1}{2}$ points, ahead of Keres $7\frac{1}{2}$ and Bogoljuboff 7. He reiterated his supremacy at Cracow, coming first with $7\frac{1}{2}$ to Junge's $6\frac{1}{2}$, while at Prague he was equal first with Junge. Another double-round tournament in Salzburg in 1943 ended in a tie between Alekhine and Keres with $7\frac{1}{2}$.

As military matters went worse for Germany, so their tournaments declined—and Alekhine's fortunes with them. By the end of the war he was playing in minor affairs in Spain and Portugal. When the peace was signed, he tried, despite the shadow of his collaborations with the Nazis, to arrange a match with Botvinnik for the world championship. But he died of a heart attack in Estoril on 23 March, 1946.

Now a problem faced the chess-world. Up to now no one had died while in possession of the title. FIDE therefore decided that the title should go to the winner of a match-tournament. In order to determine which players should compete in this event, a tournament was held at Groningen, in the Netherlands, in 1946. The top three from Groningen were to join Fine, Keres and Reshevsky in a match for the world title. Fine and Keres had been the joint winners of the 1938 AVRO tournament (see page 210) and Reshevsky's results had been of world calibre in the period 1937–1946. Botvinnik was first with $14\frac{1}{2}$, followed by Euwe 14, Smyslov $12\frac{1}{2}$, Najdorf and Szabo $11\frac{1}{2}$, Boleslavsky and Flohr 11, Lundin and Stoltz $10\frac{1}{2}$, and eleven others. This, the first top-level tournament after the war, produced a number of fine games. The first brilliancy prize went to the Swede, Lundin, for the following game against Laszlo Szabo of Hungary:

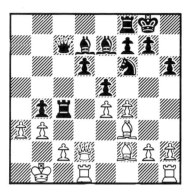

68: Position after Black's 22nd move.

White: L. Szabo. Black: E. Lundin. Sicilian Defence.

1. P-K4,P-QB4; 2. Kt-KB3,Kt-QB3; 3. P-Q4,PxP;
4. KtxP,Kt-KB3; 5. Kt-QB3,P-Q3; 6. B-KKt5,P-K3;
7. Q-Q2,P-QR3; 8. o-o-o,B-Q2; 9. P-B4,P-R3;
10. B-R4,B-K2; 11. B-K2,Q-B2; 12. B-B2,R-QB1;
13. Kt-Kt3,P-QKt4; 14. B-B3,Kt-QR4; 15. KtxKt,QxKt;
16. K-Kt1,P-Kt5; 17. Kt-K2,P-K4; 18. Kt-B1,o-o;
19. Kt-Q3,R-B5; 20. P-QR3,Q-B2; 21. KtxKtP,P-QR4;
22. P-QKt3,PxKt; 23. PxR,R-Kt1; 24. Q-Q3,B-K3;
25. B-K2,Q-K2; 26. BPxP,KtxP; 27. B-K1,P-Q4;
28. P-B3,QPxP; 29. Q-B2,B-KB4; 30. K-B1,Kt-Kt6;
31. BxKt,BxQ; 32. KxB,PxP; 33. B-B3,Q-B1;
34. B-B2,Q-B4 ch; 35. K-Kt2,BxP; 36. PxB,RxP ch;
37. K-B3,R-Kt6 ch; 38. K-Q2,Q-K4, resigns (Diagram 68).

This meant that Botvinnik, Euwe and Smyslov were to join Fine, Reshevsky and Keres in the match-tournament. Many thought it unfortunate that a place was not given to Najdorf, who had obtained fine results in South America, where on the whole he had outdistanced his chief rival, Stahlberg. He emphasized this by picking up first prizes in his next three tournaments. At Prague in 1946 he scored $10\frac{1}{2}$, above Stoltz and Trifunovic 9, Foltys and Gligoric $8\frac{1}{2}$, Golombek $6\frac{1}{2}$, Pachman and Sajtar 6, and seven others. At Barcelona he scored $11\frac{1}{2}$, above Yanofsky $9\frac{1}{2}$, Guimard and Medina 9, etc and at Mar del Plata in 1947, he was first with 14, followed by Stahlberg $13\frac{1}{2}$, Eliskases 12, Pilnik $11\frac{1}{2}$, Euwe and Julio Bolbochan $10\frac{1}{2}$ etc.

By 1947 all the old players of world-championship stature had gone. Lasker had died in 1941, Capablanca in 1942 and Alekhine in 1946. Of the players who could have made headway against them in their heyday, Nimzowitsch had died in 1935 and Spielmann in 1942; Vidmar, Tartakower, Bernstein and Bogoljuboff still lived and played with varying degrees of success and consistency. Tartakower and Bogoljuboff were still powers to be reckoned with. Tartakower won first prize in a rather weak international at Venice and Bogoljuboff was first in an all-German tournament at Luneberg.

But more and more it became apparent that the race was to the swift and young—to players like Keres, who gained a first prize at the strong Pärnu (Estonia) tournament, or to the Hungarian, Laszlo Szabo, who won a rather weaker Hastings at the turn of the year 1947–48. In 1947, too, Botvinnik showed that he was in excellent form by winning first prize in the Tschigorin Memorial Tourna-

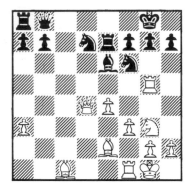

69: Position after Black's 20th move.

ment in Moscow, ahead of Ragosin, Boleslavsky, Smyslov, Kotov and Keres.

The world championship match-tournament was scheduled to start in March, 1948, the first half to be held in the Hague, and the second half in Moscow. Six players were invited: Botvinnik, Keres and Smyslov from the Soviet Union, Fine and Reshevsky from the United States, and Euwe from Holland. But Fine declined the invitation and it was decided to go ahead with only five players. They were to play each other five times.

From the first it was apparent that Euwe was outclassed. The exasperated citizens of the Hague changed their hero's name to *No-it-winnik* (I win nothing), and only Smyslov was kind enough to lose a game to him. Botvinnik, on the other hand, forged ahead. He made a plus-score against everyone, and only against Smyslov did he meet with real resistance. He came first with 14, followed by Smyslov 11, Keres and Reshevsky 10½ and Euwe 4. Against Keres he was particularly severe. Incisiveness could go no further than in the following game:

White: Botvinnik. Black: Keres. Q.P. Nimzowitsch Defence.

1. P-Q4,Kt-KB3; 2. P-QB4,P-K3; 3. Kt-QB3,B-Kt5;
4. P-K3,0-0; 5. P-QR3,BxKt ch; 6. PxB,R-K1;
7. Kt-K2,P-K4; 8. Kt-Kt3,P-Q3; 9. B-K2,QKt-Q2;
10. 0-0,P-B4; 11. P-B3,PxP; 12. PxP,Kt-Kt3; 13. B-Kt2,PxP;
14. P-K4,B-K3; 15. R-B1,R-K2; 16. QxP,Q-B2;
17. P-B5,PxP; 18. RxP,Q-B5; 19. B-B1,Q-Kt1;
20. R-KKt5,QKt-Q2; 21. RxP ch,KxR; 22. Kt-R5 ch,K-Kt3;
23. Q-K3, resigns (Diagram 69).

The chess-world had a new and worthy champion and the full power of the Soviet players was being rapidly revealed.

It was now necessary to devise a fair scheme by which everyone would have an opportunity of piercing the formidable barriers to the world championship. The world, therefore, was divided into various zones, and players from each country would send a representative to take part in an elimination contest. The top players from each Zonal tournament would then play the following year in an Interzonal tournament meeting, and the leading players from this event would qualify for a Candidates' Tournament the next year. Finally, in the year after that, the winner of the Candidates would play for the title against the world champion. A little complicated? Yes, but it worked for many years, with many groans and complaints from those who failed to make each grade, but nevertheless it was quite fair and practical.

After the Zonals in 1947, a massively contested Interzonal took place at Saltsjöbaden in Sweden, not far from Stockholm, in 1948. The Interzonals have always been exceedingly popular, both with spectators and organizers, and this one attracted enormous attention. It was won by Bronstein with 13½, followed by Szabo 12½, Boleslavsky 12, Kotov 11½, Lilienthal 11, Bondarevsky, Flohr, Najdorf and Stahlberg 10½, Trifunovic 10 etc. Eight went forward to join Keres and Smyslov in the Candidates, which was played at Budapest in 1950. This was a double-round affair which ended in a tie between Boleslavsky and Bronstein with 12 points each; the nearest to them was the Soviet grandmaster, Smyslov, with 10. A play-off between Bronstein and Boleslavsky ended in a win for Bronstein by 7½–6½.

Meanwhile a tournament for the women's world championship

had been held in Moscow at the turn of the year 1949–50. The Soviet ladies occupied the first four places, and the eventual champion was L. Rudenko with $11\frac{1}{2}$ points, followed by Rubtsova $10\frac{1}{2}$, Bikova and Bielova 10.

An international team tournament held at Dubrovnik in 1950 resulted in a victory, for the first time, for Yugoslavia, with a team consisting of Gligoric, Pirc, Trifunovic, Rabar, Vidmar jn. and Puc. Argentina were second and West Germany third, with the United States, who had so often won before the war, now in fourth place.

On 16 March 1951, Botvinnik defended his title (for the first time) against Bronstein. Both players were from the USSR and both from Moscow, so the match was played there. It consisted of twenty-four games, and victory and title would go to the man who reached the score of $12\frac{1}{2}$. Should the match be drawn, then the world champion would retain his title. This provision has always seemed to me a little unfair, but it is inherent in the system.

From the first it was apparent that Botvinnik was faced by a most powerful and dangerous adversary. Bronstein was well versed in the openings and was a great innovator in this field. He was also a most imaginative middle-game player. He did, however, have some weaknesses in the ending, and it was this circumstance which saved Botvinnik his title. A most exciting and thrilling match ended in a draw, each player winning five games and drawing fourteen.

Somewhat shaken by this narrow escape, Botvinnik announced his intention of competing more in tournaments, but his first essay in this respect, later in the year, was not successful. He played in the Soviet championship in Moscow, and came fifth with 10 points,

A study in concentration—Botvinnik (USSR) versus Reshevsky (USA) in the 1948 world championship tournament in Moscow.

below Keres 12, Geller and Petrosian 11½, and Smyslov 11; he had the meagre satisfaction of coming half a point ahead of his rival, Bronstein. Equally indifferent were his results in the very strong Maroczy Memorial Tournament at Budapest in 1952. I was playing in this event and observed that the world champion seemed far from sure of himself. Paul Keres, in magnificent form at about this time, was first with 12½ and Geller second with 12. Botvinnik, with 11 points, came equal third to fifth with Smyslov and Stahlberg. One unusual record was achieved by me in this event, when I was awarded a share of a brilliancy prize with Geller for my draw with him, in which I sacrificed two Rooks and a Knight.

The next Interzonal took place partly in Stockholm, partly in Saltsjöbaden in 1952. Five Soviet players qualified en bloc at the top for the Candidates' Tournament: Kotov 16½, Petrosian and Taimanov 13½, Geller 13, and Averbach 12½; three more made up the eight—Gligoric (Yugoslavia) 12½, Stahlberg (Sweden) 12½ and Szabo (Hungary) 12½.

By now the USSR had joined FIDE and, for the first time, they entered for the International Team Tournament, or Olympiad. As expected, their terrifically powerful team came first followed by Argentina and Yugoslavia.

In 1953 the Candidates' Tournament—fifteen players who played a double-round—took place in Neuhausen, not far from Zürich in Switzerland. Bronstein made a gallant bid to repeat his Budapest performance, but he could come only equal second with Keres and Reshevsky, with 16 points. It was Vassily Smyslov who was in wonderful form here, and he came first with 18 points.

Now commenced a period in the history of the world championship in which, despite the valiant efforts of Keres, who came second in both the next Candidates and Interzonal, the title shifted to and fro between Botvinnik and Smyslov. In 1954 a drawn match occurred—seven wins for both sides and ten draws. In 1957 at long last Botvinnik had to concede defeat, but in 1958 he won back his title. Never can players have existed who were so evenly matched as these two, although Smyslov held the title for one year only, he was of the same calibre as his opponent.

A new name and a new genius emerged in 1958 when Mikhail Tal of Riga, Latvia, won the Interzonal Tournament at Portoroz in Yugoslavia. This was a most exciting event: Bobby Fischer made his first international appearance, Petrosian lost his first game for some years, to Larsen, and the lights (I was chief arbiter and can testify to this) gave continuous trouble by failing at vital moments. Tal went on to win the Candidates in Yugoslavia with wonderfully dashing and daring methods in 1959, and in 1960 he won the title by beating Botvinnik with some ease by six wins, two losses and thirteen draws. The following year he was unwise enough to play his return match shortly after an operation. The doctors advised against it, but he replied, 'Who is going to play against Botvinnik, the doctors or I?' That he lost the match, I attribute entirely to ill health.

Botvinnik lost the world championship title to Petrosian in 1963, and now a new system of world-championship qualifications commenced. Instead of a tournament, the Candidates' event became a series of matches. Boris Spassky won this twice in succession, losing the first match against Petrosian, but winning the second to become world champion in his turn in 1969. The remaining story,

Vera Menchik, women's world champion 1927–1944.

how Bobby Fischer became world champion, is told in the next chapter.

Since 1953, the women's world championship has followed a parallel course with the men's, but for a time the Interzonal phase was omitted. Before World War II, Vera Menchik (British) regularly won the world championship. Since 1953, Elizaveta Bikova; 1956, Olga Rubtsova; 1958 and 1960, Bikova and then, from 1962 to the present, Nona Gaprindashvili.

Soviet domination of the Olympiads has been equally all-embracing. Results in the top three places in the 1954 Olympiad were the same as on the previous occasion: USSR, then Argentina and then Yugoslavia. The astonishing point about this Olympiad was that the Argentine abandoned its intention of holding it, and the Netherlands stepped in and did a remarkable job of organization, staging the event in Amsterdam within six weeks.

In 1956 the twelfth Olympiad was held in Moscow. The USSR were first, and the Argentine failed to get into the top places, which were shared by Hungary and Yugoslavia. But they returned in 1958 when the USSR, Yugoslavia and the Argentine occupied the three leading places.

With Bobby Fischer in the team, the United States managed to come second in the Olympiad in Leipzig in 1960. It almost goes without saying that the USSR won and that Yugoslavia came third. In 1962 the United States dropped a couple of places and the winners were the USSR, Yugoslavia and Argentina. In Tel Aviv in 1964, the order was the USSR, Yugoslavia and West Germany. In Havana in 1966 there was a mis-understanding: the USSR were rightfully first and the United States correctly second, but instead of Hungary, third, and Yugoslavia, fourth, the order should have been reversed.

The post-war period saw an immense increase in the power and scope of FIDE, under the inspired and skilful leadership of the Swedish international lawyer, Fölke Rogard. Such events as junior world championships and students' olympiads were introduced. Eventually, too, a scheme of rating players under a system devised by Professor Elo was to come into operation and to prove revolutionary in its effect on grading and classification.

There was a tremendous expansion of chess programmes on radio and television, for example, a weekly half-hour on the BBC Third Programme from 1958 to 1964, and regular series of television shows on both ITV and BBC. Many companies run television programmes in America and there are also regular broadcasts and television programmes in Germany, France, the Netherlands and, above all, in the Soviet Union.

Chess literature has become prolific, especially concerning the openings, where it reflects the vast innovations produced in particular by Soviet players and analysts since World War II. The researches and activities of such grandmasters as Bronstein, Boleslavsky and Geller have been mainly designed to make such defences as the King's Indian and the Sicilian more effective, and there has been great emphasis on dynamism involving in particular an attack on the black squares with the use of an early P-K4.

It used to be said that there was more literature on chess than on all other sports and pastimes combined. This was not exactly the case after the introduction of modern games and their variants. But with the very great increase recently, I believe we may have well returned to the old proportions. The popularization of chess has proceeded most strongly in our time.

chapter *15*

The age of Fischer

By the 1960s Soviet chess had established itself as predominant in the world in every aspect of international importance. Botvinnik, having fully accomplished his task as spearhead of this Soviet advance, retired from the fray to devote himself to research into the theory of computer chess. It seemed he was adequately replaced by the new generation of Soviet grandmasters—in particular by Petrosian, Tal and Spassky. In women's chess the USSR's predominance was even more marked, and the formidable Georgian, Nona Gaprindashvili, was able—like Vera Menchik, her predecessor by some thirty years—to compete on equal terms with most men masters. In team events, too, there was no shaking of the Soviet grasp on the world championship, from the time their team had first participated in the FIDE Olympiad at Helsinki in 1952.

Only in tournament play were there some signs that the world—outside the Soviet Union—had to be taken into account. The Yugoslav grandmaster. Svetozar Gligoric, proved equal to any except the very best Soviet players in the years just after World War II. Later on, first Bent Larsen of Denmark, and then Lajos Portisch of Hungary were to win first prizes ahead of leading Soviet grandmasters.

But even in this sphere, the Soviet still tended to dominate until the advent of one man, Robert James Fischer, commonly known as Bobby Fischer. He wrought a change as significant in the history of chess as the revitalization brought about by the anonymous geniuses who invented castling and the idea of moving a pawn two squares in the opening. The popularization created by these two innovations was equalled by the dynamic effect exerted on chess by the play and personality of Fischer, world champion from 1972 to 1975.

Bobby Fischer was born in Chicago on 9 March, 1943. While quite young, he evinced a passion for the game of chess. Talent, too, he showed, but it was not at first clear whether this was commensurate with his ardent and complete absorption in the game. In fact his former chess tutor, John W. Collins, told me (at the Reykjavik match in 1972) that Bobby was not a particularly impressive eleven-year-old player when he first saw him at the 1955 US Amateur Championship in New Jersey, losing to an elderly and not especially formidable player. What struck him most about that

*The women's world champion,
Nona Gaprindashvili of the
USSR.*

contest was that young Fischer's opponent sat with his hat on throughout the whole game.

However, the boy's enthusiasm for chess was so patent that Collins, who in one way and another was responsible for bringing to international strength most of the modern chessmasters of the United States, took him on as a pupil, tutoring him carefully until he attained grandmaster class. By the age of fourteen he was United States' champion, the youngest player ever to win the title; and in 1958 he qualified from the Interzonal Tournament at Portoroz to play in the Candidates' event the following year in Yugoslavia. I got to know him well during those two years, as I was chief arbiter at both these meetings, and it was apparent that in the sixteen-year-old grandmaster there was at the same time an enormous talent and an equally great determination to achieve his goal: attainment of the stature of world champion, and recognition as the world's strongest player.

Progress towards that goal was complicated by a prima donna-like temperament which at one time threatened to take him out of chess forever. The occasion was another event in the cycle of elimination tournaments for the world championship—the Interzonal at Sousse in Tunisia in 1967. He was in stupendous form that year, and indeed he was leading easily when, as a result of disagreements over playing days with the organizers, he first withdrew and then was excluded.

Bobby Fischer playing in 1971.

For a couple of years it seemed that he might give up chess altogether; fortunately he changed his mind, his interest in chess was restored, and his progress through the various world-championship qualifying tournaments was shatteringly (for his opponents) successful.

In 1970 he was first in the Interzonal at Palma de Mallorca, $3\frac{1}{2}$ points ahead of the rest of the field, and he scored crushing victories in the Candidates' series of matches the following year, winning 6–0 against the Soviet grandmaster, Taimanov, and 6–0 against Bent Larsen in the semi-final. In the final he defeated the former world champion, Tigran Petrosian, by $6\frac{1}{2}$–$2\frac{1}{2}$.

Then in 1972 came his celebrated match at Reykjavik, Iceland, for the title with the world champion, Boris Spassky. It was an event that captured the imagination and aroused enormous enthusiasm—even among non-chess-players. There was the clash between east and west, between the Soviet and the United States, between two different ideologies and between two vastly different temperaments. At one time it was quite possible that the match would not even take place, and this, too, must have contributed to

Perspex pieces in gold and white, made at Huddersfield in England. They won a Design Centre Award.

the drama of the event. After two months' agonizing effort, Bobby Fischer defeated Spassky by 12½–8½ and became the first United States player to be officially recognized as world champion. Long ago, of course, Paul Morphy had been known as the world's strongest player, but that was before the idea of a world-championship title.

The impetus that this event gave to chess throughout the world was enormous and—more important—lasting. At one fell swoop the game had been freed from its captivity in some ivory tower, and was transformed into a popular, newsworthy pursuit. This was reflected in the very mechanics of chess. A friend, coming from Italy in September, 1972, told me that it was impossible to get a chess-board there: they had all been sold to unprecedented numbers of beginners. The situation was similar with books on chess, which suddenly became best-sellers, and chess clubs all over the world reported a doubling or a tripling of membership figures.

One other wholly beneficial effect of Fischer's victory was the change in style of play under his influence. Petrosian had popularized a negative approach to the game, but Fischer was nothing if not positive. His style, deep but direct, was and is aimed at achieving only one goal, that of victory; draws are only marginally better than defeat.

Fischer challenges Spassky (in Reykjavik) for the World Chess Championship in 1972. This is the opening game—Fischer resigned on the 56th move.

Aesthetically, too, his influence was for the good. Classical rather than romantic in his conception of the game, he is the antithesis of a Tal or a Larsen in that he always wants to know exactly at what goal he is aiming. But he will achieve this by the most beautiful

A chess set representing Teesside Industries presented to H. Golombek at the World Junior Championship Tournament at Teesside, in the north of England, in 1973. They were designed by Richard Leake.

and harmonious paths available. The result is that he tends to produce a corpus of most attractive but sound games. As an illustration I give two famous games from the 1972 match, the 6th and the 10th.
White: Fischer. Black: Spassky. Queen's Gambit Declined, Tartakower Variation.

1. P-QB4,P-K3; 2. Kt-KB3,P-Q4; 3. P-Q4,Kt-KB3;
4. Kt-B3,B-K2; 5. B-Kt5,0-0; 6. P-K3,P-KR3;
7. B-R4,P-QKt3; 8. PxP,KtxP; 9. BxB,QxB; 10. KtxKt,PxKt;
11. R-B1,B-K3; 12. Q-R4,P-QB4; 13. Q-R3,R-B1;
14. B-Kt5,P-R3; 15. PxP,PxP; 16. 0-0,R-R2; 17. B-K2,Kt-Q2;
18. Kt-Q4,Q-B1; 19. KtxB,PxKt; 20. P-K4,P-Q5;
21. P-B4,Q-K2; 22. P-K5,R-Kt1; 23. B-B4,K-R1;
24. Q-R3,Kt-B1; 25. P-QKt3,P-QR4; 26. P-B5,PxP;
27. RxP,Kt-R2; 28. R(B1)-B1,Q-Q1; 29. Q-Kt3,R-K2;
30. P-KR4,R(Kt1)-Kt2; 31. P-K6,R(Kt2)-B2;
32. Q-K5,Q-K1; 33. P-R4,Q-Q1; 34. R(B1)-B2,Q-K1;
35. R(B2)-B3,Q-Q1; 36. B-Q3,Q-K1; 37. Q-K4,Kt-B3;
38. RxKt,PxR; 39. RxP,K-Kt1; 40. B-B4,K-R1;
41. Q-B4, resigns.

There was great applause at the end of this game and, a chivalrous gesture on the part of the vanquished player, Boris Spassky joined in.
White: Fischer. Black: Spassky. Ruy Lopez, Morphy Defence.

1. P-K4,P-K4; 2. Kt-KB3,Kt-QB3; 3. B-Kt5,P-QR3;
4. B-R4,Kt-B3; 5. 0-0,B-K2; 6. R-K1,P-QKt4; 7. B-Kt3,P-Q3;
8. P-B3,0-0; 9. P-KR3,Kt-Kt1; 10. P-Q4,QKt-Q2;
11. QKt-Q2,B-Kt2; 12. B-B2,R-K1; 13. P-QKt4,B-KB1;
14. P-QR4,Kt-Kt3; 15. P-R5,QKt-Q2; 16. B-Kt2,Q-Kt1;
17. R-Kt1,P-B4; 18. KtPxP,QPxP; 19. PxKP,QKtxP;
20. KtxKt,QxKt; 21. P-QB4,Q-B5; 22. BxKt,QxB;
23. PxP,KR-Q1; 24. Q-B1,Q-QB6; 25. Kt-B3,QxP;
26. B-Kt3,PxP; 27. Q-KB4,R-Q2; 28. Kt-K5,Q-B2;
29. QR-Q1,R-K2; 30. BxP ch,RxB; 31. QxR ch,QxQ;
32. KtxQ,BxP; 33. RxB,KxKt; 34. R-Q7 ch,K-B3;
35. R-Kt7,R-R8 ch; 36. K-R2,B-Q3 ch; 37. P-Kt3,P-Kt5;
38. K-Kt2,P-R4; 39. R-Kt6,R-Q8; 40. K-B3,K-B2;
41. K-K2,R-Q4; 42. P-B4,P-Kt3; 43. P-Kt4,PxP;
44. PxP, P-Kt4; 45. P-B5,B-K4; 46. R-Kt5,K-B3.
47. R(K4)xP,B-Q5; 48. R-Kt6 ch,K-K4; 49. K-B3,R-Q1;
50. R-Kt8,R-Q2; 51. R(Kt4)-Kt7,R-Q3; 52. R-Kt6,R-Q2;
53. R-Kt6,K-Q4; 54. RxP,B-K4; 55. P-B6,K-Q5;
56. R-Kt1, resigns.

Direct yet deep—the hallmark of a Fischer game.

In the heady days immediately following his triumph in the Reykjavik match, Fischer said he intended affording the former world champion a chance of regaining his title by a return match. But this never came to pass, and as time went on it became clear that such a match would not fit in with the arrangements for a world-championship cycle of events until 1975. Meanwhile, Fischer refrained from taking part in any tournament or match, a not uncommon procedure on the part of newly-fledged champions; he was merely repeating the practice of both Alekhine and Botvinnik.

This has been an age of considerable technical advances in the presentation and carrying out of important chess events. It is more and more usual to demonstrate the most interesting games on large wall-boards; electrically-motivated devices enable the public to

Back to the original concept—a bronze chess set with pieces in the form of modern weapons, by the American sculptor Roy Shifrin.

follow every move, and also to see how the players are faring in time as well as position. Closed-circuit television has also been employed with great effect, notably at the Olympiads in Siegen, West Germany (1970), Skopje, Yugoslavia (1972) and at the match at Reykjavik.

Two brilliant ideas wrought a transformation in the pocket or travelling chess-sets which have become commonly used in the twentieth century. Up to the 1950s pocket sets were either made of wood with the pieces plugged in, or they were leather or fabric wallets, with slots in which celluloid pieces were placed. The first revolution came with the introduction of magnetized metal sets; these are especially useful for sea and air travel. The second idea was conceived by the film producer, Cy Endfield, on location in Africa for the film *Zulu*. He created a metal set (the expensive model was made of silver and gold) with the pieces ingeniously designed so that while retaining their own individual characteristics, they fit into each other to form a small highly portable cylinder.

There was no real change in the shape of the ordinary set which retained the Staunton pattern, with some slight variations, from country to country. However, with the growing rarity of French boxwood, more and more sets tend to be made of plastic, with Hong Kong as the main source of supply.

Artists have continued to produce special pieces, and since World War II, there has been increasing interest in the conception of a set as a work of art. A phase of abstract design, the pieces bearing little or no resemblance to normal chessmen, was followed by a return to more naturalistic ideas. Perhaps one of the most ingenious of these in recent times was made by the young American sculptor, Roy Shifrin. He returned to the original concept of a war game but modernized the weapons. The pieces are bronze, and the infantry pawns fall into line armed with sub-machine guns. The King is a general, the Queen a woman guerrilla; the Bishops are pieces of artillery, the Knights roll in as tanks and the Rooks serve as computerized missile-throwers and radar centres. Together they make an impressive fighting force, ready to do battle until the final checkmate.

chapter *16*

The post-Fischer era, 1972-?

Properly speaking, this chapter should be entitled 'The Period After Fischer's Win of the World Championship', since, although the former world champion has been inactive in chess for some three and a half years (as I write) there is always the possibility that he may return. So the query-mark I have attached to the title above relates only partially to the date and may also apply to the heading, The Post-Fischer Era. I will consider the possibilities and the likelihoods later on in this chapter.

There is no doubt that when Fischer won the world title in the early September of 1972 at Reykjavik, he was fully determined to join in all the chess activities of great importance which were to be held during the period he was world champion. This, by his own perhaps jocular estimate, was for at least the ensuing thirty years. At one moment a reporter had asked him what tactics he intended to employ against Spassky at a certain stage in the match and his reply was, 'I am not worried about what will happen in the next game here, but I am wondering how I will defend my title thirty years from now.'

Such confidence created a euphoria which was widespread, not only in his native America, but throughout the world. Even the chessplayers of the USSR, although disappointed that the world title had not been retained by one of them, recognized the value of a fresh revivifying force and welcomed Fischer's advent. For most of the match in Iceland I represented the World Chess Federation, having been entrusted with the task by the president, Professor Euwe, when he left for home after the earlier part of the match had been played. In that capacity I received letters from all over the world and in particular from the United States and the USSR; surprisingly, quite a number from the Soviet Union backed Fischer.

Clearly, although it was sad to see such a great player as Spassky decline and fall, Fischer's victory was a most wholesome one for the chess-world. The domination of the world championship by the Soviet Union which had begun shortly after Alekhine's death and had been confirmed by every world-championship contest from 1948 onwards—this supremacy was at an end. For the first time for many years people could regard the world championship as genuinely a world title, and no longer a sort of private reserve for the Soviet Union.

*Boris Spassky during the European
Team Championship finals in
Bath, on 12 July 1973.*

Moreover, this was a young champion (only twenty-nine years of age), and a very strong champion; some thought him the strongest in the history of the game, although that had yet to be proved. Above all, he had a definite incisive style that spurned the draw and produced results. Many still remembered the negative policies of Petrosian which had produced a school of players whose supreme objective was the stultifying one of preventing the opponent from doing anything. The chess-world was grateful to Fischer for waking them up from this nightmare of nebulous negatives.

His promises to play too were most welcome. That he had refused so many contracts at Reykjavik in the days following his victory was unusual. Fred Cramer confided to me that about ten million dollars were going down the drain (I use his own words) for want of a signature on Fischer's part. But since most of the offers involved a certain commercialization of the world champion's art, it was regarded as a noble, quixotic gesture on his part.

The first event in which he was due to take part was the Chess Olympiad at Skopje, in the Macedonian republic of Yugoslavia. With the massacre at the Munich Olympiad still fresh in their memory, the authorities took elaborate precautions to prevent a similar occurrence at Skopje. Their preparations were equally elaborate to ensure that Fischer's demands in the way of playing conditions should be adequately met. No less than sixty-three countries sent teams and the world's press came. But no Bobby Fischer. It seems there were difficulties about the fees which were to be paid to the United States team, and in the end a team so weak was sent, that they came ninth. Once again the Soviet team, with three former world champions, Petrosian, Smyslov and Tal (but not Spassky) won the world team championship. But their most impressive player was a young former junior world champion, Anatoly Karpov.

Bobby Fischer did put in an appearance at the next great chess event of the year, a very strong international tournament at San Antonio in Texas. But it was not to play. He merely turned up at the last round in order to watch the proceedings. He had been invited to take part, but refused on the grounds that 'the tournament is too weak and the money's nothing.' In fact the tournament was one of the strongest ever to be held in America, and the first prize of $4,000 was big enough, although admittedly standards changed after the Reykjavik match.

When Fischer arrived, Karpov and Petrosian were leading, with Portisch (the Hungarian grandmaster who was perhaps the most successful of the non-Soviet players except for Fischer himself) half a point away. In the last round Karpov and Petrosian both drew, but Portisch won the following fine game against the Danish grandmaster, Bent Larsen:

White: Portisch. Black: Larsen. Q.P. Benoni Defence Deferred.

1. P-Q4,P-K3; 2. P-QB4,P-QB4; 3. P-Q5,PxP; 4. PxP,P-Q3; 5. Kt-QB3,P-KKt3; 6. Kt-B3,B-Kt2; 7. B-B4,Kt-KB3; 8. Q-R4 ch,B-Q2; 9. Q-Kt3,Q-B2; 10. P-K4,0-0; 11. B-K2,Kt-KR4; 12. B-K3,Kt-R3; 13. Kt-Q2,P-B4; 14. PxP,PxP; 15. BxKKt,P-KB5; 16. 0-0,PxB; 17.PxP,Kt-Kt5; 18. Kt(B3)-K4,P-R4; 19. Kt-Kt5,P-R5; 20. Q-B4,P-R3; 21. Kt-K6,BxKt; 22. PxB,P-Q4; 23. B-B7 ch,K-R1; 24. Q-R4,Q-K4; 25. Kt-B3,QxKP ch; 26. K-R1,Kt-Q6; 27. QR-K1,KtxR; 28. RxKt,Q-Q6; 29. Q-R5,P-R6; 30. P-QKt3,B-B6; 31. P-K7,K-Kt2; 32. PxR=Q ch,RxQ; 33. BxP,BxR; 34. Q-K5 ch,R-B3; 35. Q-K7 ch, resigns (Diagram 70).

So Portisch caught up the two Soviet grandmasters and they tied for first place with 10½ points. Next came the Yugoslav grandmaster, Gligoric, with 10, followed by Keres (USSR) 9½, Hort (Czechoslovakia) and Suttles (Canada) 9, Larsen (Denmark) and Mecking (Brazil) 8½, and eight more.

Fischer was much taken with the game Portisch played and complimented him on playing so vigorously, pointing out that it showed Portisch's rivals the folly of their pusillanimous ways (these were not his exact words).

Even though Fischer himself was still not playing, there was a stir of international activity in chess-life in general, due partially to the impetus he gave the game through winning the championship. Bent Larsen, who had been one of the greatest tournament players of the Fischer epoch, but who now seemed to be on the downgrade, returned to form at a strong Hastings Premier tournament, which was held, as is traditional, over the turn of the year 1972–73. He

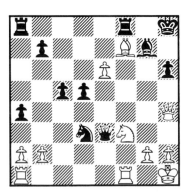

70: Position after Black's 26th move.

came first, half a point ahead of the powerful East German grand-master, Wolfgang Uhlmann, with $11\frac{1}{2}$ out of 15. How strong the event was is shown by the fact that the former world champion, Vassily Smyslov, came ninth, and Ulf Andersson, one of the most promising of the younger school, a Swedish grandmaster in the worthy tradition of Stoltz and Stahlberg, was even lower in equal eleventh and twelfth places.

Another former world champion, Mikhail Tal, seemed to have returned to his former glories in this period. In 1972, he scored two major successes, one a fine first at the international tournament at Sukhumi, on the Black Sea, and the other, the Soviet championship at Baku. He followed this with another remarkable first in an international tournament at Tallinn in Estonia in February, 1973 where he came $1\frac{1}{2}$ points ahead of the strong Soviet grandmaster Polugaievsky. There was speculation that he might be the eventual challenger to Fischer; Tal had been particularly effective against Fischer in the world champion's youth.

But before such a match could take place, the preliminary qualifying tournaments would have to be played. It is true that Fischer had declared himself ready to play a return match with Spassky in 1973, but the declarations came to nothing. Later on in the year, when he visited Manila to observe the first international tournament there (he is reported to have been paid more for his coming for a day or two than the first prize!), he told a press conference that he wanted to end 'all this talk that I am resting and that I am afraid of the Russians.' So he issued a challenge to Spassky: 'Since the Russians are afraid to challenge me, I am going to have to get together an offer myself and challenge him'. He added, 'I do not expect he will accept it, because I'm sure I'll beat him easily. But I want to get a rematch offer on record, because there had been a lot of stuff in the press saying that I want to quit.'

There was another reason for Spassky's non-acceptance. He, like everyone else, was bound to follow the qualifying procedures of FIDE in challenging the world champion. As the defeated champion, he had the right to come in at the penultimate qualifying stage, the Candidates' matches, in 1974. But the automatic right to a return match had been abolished at the end of Botvinnik's regime.

The Interzonals were held in 1973. I use the plural, because it had been decided to have two Interzonal tournaments of equal strength, these to be made up of players who had qualified from Zonal tournaments all over the world. The first was held in June in Leningrad, and the second in July and August in Petropolis, Brazil. Unfortunately, the division into two equal groups seems to have failed in its objective, and the tournament in Leningrad was appreciably stronger than the one in Petropolis. Curiously enough, the division had been made strictly in accordance with Elo ratings (a system devised by Prof. Arpad Elo of Milwaukee that grades players with points in accordance with their tournament results); the answer to why the tournaments were of uneven strength appears to lie in the fact that at Petropolis a number of the competitors belonged to the older group of grandmasters. Their Elo ratings were good, but their stamina was suspect.

The stronger of the two tournaments was held first and it was not without its surprises. True, Karpov and Korchnoi tied for first place with the amazing score of $13\frac{1}{2}$ out of 17. Also typical was that Karpov

Anatoly Karpov at the Alekhine Memorial Tournament, Moscow, in 1971.

did not lose a game and that Korchnoi did lose one to a comparative outsider, but made up for it by winning no less than eleven games, far more than any other competitor. These two, therefore, qualified for the Candidates' series of elimination matches which would take place in the following year to determine who would challenge Fischer for the world title.

But there was a remaining qualifying place. Each Interzonal furnished three players to the Candidates. The remaining two places in the Candidates went to the defeated world champion, Spassky, and to the player whom Fischer had beaten in the finals of the previous Candidates' series—Petrosian.

Before the Leningrad Interzonal started it was anticipated that of Tal, Larsen, Hübner and Gligoric, at least one would qualify. But none of the four came near to doing so. Larsen was fifth with 10 points, as was Hübner; Tal was 10th with $8\frac{1}{2}$, as was Gligoric. The third qualifier was the American, Robert Byrne, with $12\frac{1}{2}$ points, a score which normally would have won such a tournament.

If Karpov and Korchnoi could make such a score in such a tournament then, clearly, one would not have to go further than these two to estimate who would appear in the final of the Candidates.

In the following game against V. Tukmakov, a Soviet grandmaster of no mean calibre, Karpov demonstrates that iron competence which is one of the marks of a true champion:

White: V. Tukmakov. Black: A. Karpov. Ruy Lopez, Morphy Defence.

1. P-K4,P-K4; 2. Kt-KB3,Kt-QB3; 3. B-Kt5,P-QR3;
4. B-R4,Kt-B3; 5. 0-0,B-K2; 6. R-K1,P-QKt4;
7. B-Kt3,P-Q3; 8. P-B3,0-0; 9. P-KR3,Kt-Kt1;
10. P-Q4,QKt-Q2; 11. P-B4,P-B3; 12. B-Kt5,P-KR3;
13. B-R4,Kt-KR4; 14. BxB,QxB; 15. PxKtP,RPxP;
16. Kt-B3,P-Kt5; 17. Kt-Kt1,Kt-B5; 18. QKt-Q2,PxP;
19. KtxP,Kt-K4; 20. Kt(Q2)-B3,Q-B3; 21. KtxKt,PxKt;
22. Kt-B5,BxKt; 23. PxB,QR-Q1; 24. Q-B3,R-Q7;

25. R–K3,RxKtP; 26. QR–K1,R–K1; 27. R–K4,Kt–Q4;
28. Q–Kt3,Kt–B6; 29. RxKtP,Kt–K7 ch; 30. RxKt,RxR;
31. R–Kt7,R–K2; 32. R–Kt8 ch,K–R2; 33. K–B1,R–Q7;
White resigns (Diagram 71).

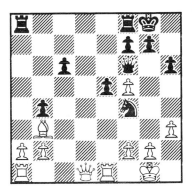

71: *Position after White's 23rd move.*

The Interzonal at Petropolis came later, in July and August 1973. If I have referred to it as weaker than the Leningrad section then I must make it clear that I was using comparative terms, and that it too was a very strong event. Some famous names fell by the way-side, Smyslov, Bronstein, Hort, Keres, Reshevsky and Ljubojevic (a talented Yugoslav who was fast making a name for himself).

There were surprises. Mecking qualified—perhaps not so surprising that he should have a place, since he was a talented player on his home ground. But that he should qualify with a *first* place in such company was indeed remarkable. Three players, Geller, Polugaievsky and Portisch, tied for the second and third qualifying places with $11\frac{1}{2}$. On a play-off some time later the two who qualified were Geller and Portisch.

Mecking, at twenty-one, was the youngest player in the tournament. Here he is beating the oldest player, Reshevsky, who in his time was a famous boy prodigy. He was approximately three times the age of his adversary:

White: E. Mecking. Black: S. Reshevsky. Ruy Lopez, Morphy Defence.

1. P–K4,P–K4; 2. Kt–KB3,Kt–QB3; 3. B–Kt5, P–QR3;
4. B–R4,Kt–B3; 5. 0-0,B–K2; 6. R–K1,P–QKt4;
7. B–Kt3,P–Q3; 8. P–B3,0-0; 9. P–KR3,Kt–Kt1;
10. P–Q4,QKt–Q2; 11. QKt–Q2,B–Kt2; 12. B–B2,R–K1;
13. P–QR4,B–KB1; 14. P–QKt4,P–QR4; 15. KtPxP,RxP;
16. R–Kt1,B–R3; 17. RPxP,RxP; 18. B–Kt3,R–K2;
19. Q–B2,R–Kt1; 20. Kt–Kt5,B–Kt2; 21. P–B4,P–R3;
22. BPxP,PxP; 23. Kt(5)–B3,P–B4; 24. B–R3,Q–B2;
25. Kt–R4,R(2)–K1; 26. Q–R2,Kt–Kt3; 27. PxKP,RxP;
28. BxP ch,QxB; 29. QxQ ch,KxQ; 30. RxKt,Kt–Q2;
31. R–Kt5,B–R3; 32. R–B1 ch, resigns (Diagram 72).

That the Soviet Union was still a dominating influence in European chess was amply demonstrated by the finals of the European Team Championship, which were held in Bath in July. The Soviet team was immensely powerful, containing no less than four former world champions: Spassky, Petrosian, Tal and Smyslov. Eight teams of eight players met each other and the USSR came first with $40\frac{1}{2}$ points, ahead of Yugoslavia 34, Hungary 33, Poland 25, England and West Germany 24, Romania 23 and Switzerland $20\frac{1}{2}$. The Soviet team also included Karpov, and I wrote at the time that his was the form which most impressed me, and that I thought he would probably win the Candidates' series. In view of his successes in 1973 this was a natural assumption. But it was the former world champion, Mikhail Tal, who won the brilliancy prize for the following game:

White: G. S. Botterill. Black: M. Tal. Sicilian Defence.

1. P–K4,P–QB4; 2. Kt–KB3,P–K3; 3. Kt–QB3,P–QR3;
4. P–Q4,PxP; 5. KtxP,Q–B2; 6. B–Q3,Kt–KB3; 7. 0-0,Kt–B3;
8. Kt–Kt3,P–QKt4; 9. B–KKt5,B–K2; 10. Q–K2,B–Kt2;
11. QR–K1,P–Q3; 12. P–QR3,P–Kt5; 13. PxP,KtxKtP;
14. R–R1,0-0; 15. Kt–R5,B–B1; 16. B–QB4,R–Kt1;
17. P–B4,P–Q4; 18. P–K5,B–B4 ch; 19. K–R1,Kt–Q2;
20. B–Q3,KtxB; 21. QxKt,RxP; 22. Kt–Kt3,B–Kt5;

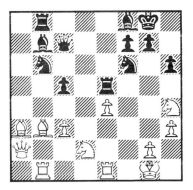

72: *Position after Black's 27th move.*

23. Kt-R2,Kt-B4; 24. Q-Q4,B-R6 25. Q-B3,Q-Kt3;
26. Kt-Q2,RxKt; 27. RxR,B-Kt5; 28. Q-Kt2,P-Q5;
29. Kt-B4,Q-Kt4; 30. QxP, B-Kt2; 31. P-B3,Kt-Kt6;
32. Q-Q3,B-B4; 33. R-Q1,P-R3; 34. B-R4,B-R1;
35. P-R3,P-QR4; 36. K-R2,P-R5; 37. Q-K2,B-B3;
38. Kt-Q6,Q-R4; 39. P-B5,QxP; 40. B-K7,Kt-B8;
41. RxKt,QxR; 42. BxR,B-K6; 43. K-Kt3,B-KKt4;
44. Q-B4,Q-K6 ch; 45. K-Kt4,B-R5; 46. B-K7,BxB;
47. BxP,P-R4 ch; 48. KxP,B-K1; 49. K-Kt4,PxP ch;
50. KxP,P-Kt4; 51. K-Kt4,B-Q2 ch; White resigns.

As if once and for all to settle the question of who was going to come through the Candidates to challenge Bobby Fischer, Karpov, almost at the end of the year, won first prize in an extremely strong tournament in Madrid. This was the strongest tournament ever to have been held on the Spanish mainland, and it was entirely fitting that the youngest player should win it. This was an era when success went to the young, and those countries which possessed a wealth of young talent (the USSR, England and Holland) held the future well and truly in their hands. I have juxtaposed the USSR and England purposely. This year the Soviet player (later grandmaster) Belyavsky won the world junior championship, which was held on Teesside; but he was twice defeated—by Miles and by Stean.

Karpov, as was his wont, went through the tournament unbeaten, and his play had that universal quality which seems to be the stamp of the potential world champion. He also had the other essential, stamina; for this tournament finished in December and within a month he was playing his quarter-final match in the Candidates, against Polugaievsky. It was a strange match, but a most successful one for Karpov, who seemed hardly to do anything at all and yet won three games, lost none and drew five. Polugaievsky told me afterwards that he had never played as badly as he did against Karpov—but perhaps that was precisely because he was playing against Karpov.

In the other quarter-finals Petrosian had a much harder victory over Portisch, only just winning by three wins, two losses and eight draws; Mecking put up a good resistance to Korchnoi but lost by three to one and nine draws, and Spassky had it easiest (as might have been expected) by defeating Robert Byrne by three wins, no losses and three draws.

The semi-final matches were much affected by illness. Petrosian was stricken by pneumonia shortly before he was due to play Korchnoi, and he was not really fit when the match started. Little wonder that he retired when Korchnoi was leading by three wins, one loss and one draw. Both Karpov and Spassky were indisposed at various times during their match, but in the end Karpov emerged a comfortable victor by four wins, one loss and six draws.

Before the final between Korchnoi and Karpov took place, a highly significant FIDE Congress was held in Nice in June 1974, when the rules and conditions for the 1975 world-championship match were laid down. Bobby Fischer had sent in a number of demands through the United States FIDE delegates. Some of these were conceded; in particular, it was agreed that to win the world championship match would require winning ten games. Another of his demands, that draws should not count, had already been agreed at a previous meeting.

But two demands were rejected: that the number of games should be unlimited, and that in the event of the score reaching nine–nine, the match should be regarded as drawn, and the champion would retain his title. Instead of an unlimited number of games it was decided there should be a maximum of thirty-six.

Numerous telegrams had been sent to the Congress by Fischer via his spokesman, Fred Cramer. The last one said that, in the light of FIDE's decisions, he was resigning his FIDE world-championship title. FIDE refused to accept this resignation as final and sent him a telegram asking him to reconsider. No reply ever came.

At the same time that these negotiations (perhaps confrontations is a better description) were going on, the USSR were winning a chess Olympiad at Nice, again with an overwhelming score. They scored 46 to Yugoslavia's $37\frac{1}{2}$; the United States and Bulgaria had $36\frac{1}{2}$, etc. Karpov played on Board One and obtained the prize for the best score on that board with 12 out of 14. His rival, Korchnoi, playing on Board Two, had a second prize with a score of $11\frac{1}{2}$ out of 15.

One of the prettiest games of the Olympiad was the following, for which the winner was awarded the Turover Brilliancy prize of $1,000:

White: M. Stean (England). Black: W. Browne (U.S.A.). Sicilian Defence.

    1. P-K4,P-QB4; 2. Kt-KB3,P-Q3; 3. P-Q4,PxP;
    4. KtxP,Kt-KB3; 5. Kt-QB3,P-QR3; 6. B-KKt5,QKt-Q2;
    7. B-QB4,P-K3; 8. o-o,P-KR3; 9. BxKt,KtxB;
    10. B-Kt3,P-QKt3; 11. P-B4,B-Kt2; 12. Q-Q3,B-K2;
    13. KtxKP,PxKt; 14. BxP,P-QKt4; 15. P-K5,Q-Kt3 ch;
    16. K-R1,PxP; 17. Q-Kt6 ch,K-Q1; 18. Q-B7,Q-B4;
    19. PxP,BxP ch; 20. KxB,R-KB1; 21. QR-Q1 ch,K-B2;
    22. QxP,R-KKt1; 23. PxKt,RxQ ch; 24. PxR,B-Q3;
    25. R-B7 ch,K-B3; 26. B-Q5 ch,K-Kt3; 27. BxR,Q-Kt4 ch;
    28. K-R1,B-K4; 29. P-Kt4,P-QR4; 30. R-Kt7 ch,K-B3;
    31. P-Kt8=Q,QxQ; 32. R-Kt8 ch, resigns (Diagram 73).

Before I come to the match between Karpov and Korchnoi, which was played towards the end of the year in Moscow, I should give a few details about Karpov's early life.

Anatoly Karpov was born at Zlatoust in the southern Urals on 23 May, 1951. He learned chess at the age of four, and by nine he was already a first-category player (roughly the equivalent of a first-class amateur in England and America). His subsequent progress was rapid. When only fifteen he played in a strong international tournament at Trinac in Yugoslavia and easily won first prize ahead of many adult masters. He was an outstanding first, at the junior international tournament at Groningen in the Netherlands (1967–68), an event which was subsequently recognized as the European junior championships.

In 1969 he became the world junior champion by winning a tournament for the title at Stockholm without losing a game. By the following year he had become recognized as the best of the world's younger players. In 1970 he became one of the world's youngest grandmasters by his performance in the international tournament at Caracas, Venezuela, where he was equal fourth with $11\frac{1}{2}$ points. A further advance in 1971 saw him fourth in the thirty-ninth Soviet championship at Leningrad, and equal first with Leonid Stein

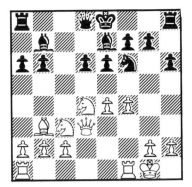

73: *Position after Black's 12th move.*

*The young Russian player
Anatoly Karpov (left) playing
Viktor Korchnoi at Moscow in
1974 for the right to challenge
Bobby Fischer for the world title
in 1975.*

at the very strong international Alekhine Memorial Tournament in
Moscow. Thereafter his career was an almost uninterrupted series
of successes. Equal first with Viktor Korchnoi at Hastings (1971–72),
he had another equal first, as I have said, with Tigran Petrosian and
Lajos Portisch, at the even stronger international tournament of
San Antonio. This, together with what I have written earlier in this
chapter, represents his chess career thus far.

The match between Karpov and Korchnoi commenced on 15
September in the Hall of Columns in Moscow. Ostensibly it was the
final of the Candidates to find a challenger for Fischer. But in reality
it was a contest for the world-championship title, since Fischer was
clearly determined to play on his own conditions and his own conditions alone. The victor was to be the first to win five games, and
Karpov took an early lead. But Korchnoi fought back gallantly and
reduced his lead to one game. If neither had won five games by the
time twenty-four had been played, the rules stated that whoever was
then in the lead was the winner. And this was Karpov with three
wins, two losses and nineteen draws.

Now he was challenger for the world title and FIDE went through the motions of preparing for a match with Fischer. Firstly there was the matter of bids, which had to be made by 1 January, 1975. Mexico City offered a prize fund of 1,000,000 Swiss francs; Milan offered 1,100,000 Swiss francs and the Philippines offered 13,100,000 Swiss francs (about $5,000,000, or £2,200,000).

These bids had to be passed on to the players to see if there was agreement. There was not. If there were a match, said Fischer, he would rather have it in Manila (the Philippines). 'No', said Karpov, 'I prefer Milan'. So the FIDE president, Professor Euwe, decided in favour of the big battalions—the Philippines. Then there was the question of the chief arbiter. Again no agreement, so Euwe chose Paul Klein of Ecuador. But all this was fairly academic, since Fischer did not budge from his two principal claims. Just as Nelson did not know what fear was, Fischer was ignorant of compromise.

Another attempt was made to bring the FIDE and Fischer into complete accord, when Colonel Edmondson (U.S. Chess Federation) asked for the summoning of an extraordinary meeting of the FIDE Congress. There being a sufficient number of countries in agreement, it duly assembled at Bergen-aan-Zee in the Netherlands from 18 to 20 March, 1975. It was an extraordinary congress in every sense of the word, and eventually, after much heated discussion, one of Fischer's demands was conceded: the match was to have a limitless number of games. But Fischer's other demand—that a draw be declared when the situation reached nine to nine—was rejected by a majority of three. Fischer's words on hearing this were, 'It's all over then.' No match took place.

Fischer ignored the request to say by 2 April whether or not he would play, and Karpov became the new world champion on that date. The official ceremony was at the Hall of Columns in Moscow on 24 April and I accepted an invitation to be present in my capacity as president of Zone One of FIDE (most of western Europe). Not all the Zonal Presidents were there, and I noted in particular the absence of the President within whose zone the Philippines lay and also the fact that the United States Zonal President was not there. But it was an impressive and pleasant occasion.

This was the last time I was to see and speak to the great Paul Keres, of whom I had the honour of being a friend for some forty years. He seemed to be making a comeback, even though he was in his sixtieth year, and he had won first prize at a great tournament in Tallinn a month earlier. A month after we met he went to Canada, where he won a tournament at Vancouver. He died of a heart attack at Helsinki on 5 June, 1975 on his way back home. Keres and Rubinstein were the greatest players never to win the world championship. With Keres's death, a whole era of great chess died.

International chess continued as vigorously as ever, despite the retirement of Fischer. There were from time to time rumours of his preparing to play a match with Mecking and once (this seems authentic) he made a trip to Caracas in order to see if such a match could be arranged. But he returned in haste when attacked by journalists. As I write these lines, some three and a half years after his gaining his ultimate objective, the world championship, he still had not played any chess.

What will happen to him? Will he dwindle away like another Paul Morphy and thus add to the pride and the sorrow of chess?

One of the greatest players never to win a world championship, Paul Keres, at the Alekhine Memorial Tournament.

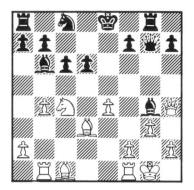

74: Position after Black's 17th move.

Or will he, some day, tiring of inactivity, return to that one talent which 'tis death to hide and play the wonderful chess of which we know that he is capable? He has the right, as the defeated world champion, to play in the Candidates' series in 1977 and then, if he wins it, to challenge Karpov. This is a consummation devoutly to,be wished. What a match it would be! Karpov, whom many thought not mature enough to play and win against Fischer in 1975, would be very experienced and ready in all respects in 1978..

Meanwhile, Karpov has already scored considerable successes as world champion. By winning first prize in an international tournament in Yugoslavia at Ljubljana and Portoroz (June 2–21), he has become the first world champion to win a major tournament for many years. He was first with 11 points out of 15, ahead of Gligoric 10, Furman, Hort and Ribli 9½, Parma and Portisch 8½, Ljubojevic and Velimirovic 8, and eight others. Probably his best game was against the Italian grandmaster, Mariotti:

White: Karpov. Black: Mariotti. Ruy Lopez. Classical Defence.

1. P-K4,P-K4; 2. Kt-KB3,Kt-QB3; 3. B-Kt5,B-B4;
4. o-o,Q-B3; 5. P-B3,KKt-K2; 6. P-QKt4,B-Kt3;
7. Kt-R3,P-Kt4; 8. P-Q4,P-Kt5; 9. KtxP,KtxKt; 10. PxKt,QxP;
11. QxP,QxBP; 12. R-Kt1,R-KKt1; 13. Q-R5,Q-Kt2;
14. P-Kt3,P-B3; 15. B-Q3,P-Q3; 16. Kt-B4,B-Kt5;
17. Q-R4,Kt-B1; 18. P-K5,PxP; 19. B-R6,B-Q1;
20. BxQ,BxQ; 21. BxKP,P-KB4; 22. Kt-R5, resigns
(Diagram 74).

Karpov was in successful action again a month later at Riga where, playing on top-board for Leningrad in a Spartakiad (a team event in which all the republics of the Soviet Union are represented), he obtained the best score with 3½ out of 5, defeating Spassky and Bukhuti Gurgenidze and drawing with Alexander Beljavsky, Petrosian and Tal. A more severe test was to come in a strong international tournament in Milan in August. This was in two parts. The first was a preliminary event among twelve players. The top four qualified for the finals, which consisted of four matches. After winning nicely against Wolfgang Unzicker in the first round he played insecurely, lost a long game to the young Swedish grandmaster, Ulf Andersson, and at one time did not look like qualifying for the finals. He just scraped in with 6½, along with Petrosian and Ljubomir Ljubojevic, half a point behind Portisch's 7. While Portisch defeated Ljubojevic by 2½–1½ in the semi-finals, Karpov could only draw all four games with Petrosian, but he got through on a superior point count in the preliminaries. In the final he beat Portisch by 3½–2½, winning the one game in the second round.

There we leave the world champion, having won two outstanding tournaments. Although he does not have the convincing style of an Alekhine in his heyday, he does at least play like a champion.

Three more important tournaments were held in 1975. One was in September, in Middlesbrough, Cleveland, a memorial to C. H. O'D. Alexander, one of the finest players ever produced by Britain, who died on 15 February, 1974. This was won by the Soviet grandmaster, Geller, with 9½ out of 15, ahead of Smyslov 8½, Bronstein, Hort and Hübner 8, etc. Geller had a triumph too in the Alekhine Memorial Tournament, which was held in Moscow in October. Again he was first—with a higher score this time, 10½ out of 15, ahead of Spassky 10, Cholmov, Korchnoi and Vaganian 9½,

Playing in the Alekhine Memorial Tournament, in Moscow, David Bronstein of the USSR.

Hort and Petrosian 9, Beljavsky and Tal 8½, etc. Finally, a strong Hastings Premier Tournament, held over the turn of the year 1975–76, ended in a triple-tie for first place among Bronstein, Hort and Uhlmann, with 10 out of 15, ahead of Korchnoi 9, etc.

I give a delicate masterpiece won by Bronstein in the first round of this event:

White: J. Kaplan. Black: D. Bronstein. French Defence.

1. P-K4,P-K3; 2. P-Q4,P-Q4; 3. Kt-QB3,Kt-KB3;
4. B-Kt5,PxP; 5. KtxP,B-K2; 6. BxKt,PxB; 7. Kt-KB3,Kt-Q2;
8. Q-Q2,P-QB4; 9. P-Q5,P-B4; 10. PxP,PxKt;
11. PxKt ch,QxP; 12. Q-B3,0-0; 13. Kt-Q2,Q-B4;
14. 0-0-0,QxP; 15. KtxP,Q-B5 ch; 16. Kt-Q2,B-Kt5;
17. R-K1,B-Kt4; 18. B-Q3,QR-K1; 19. R(K1)-B1,Q-K6;
20. P-KR3,B-K7; 21. R-B5,B-R3; 22. BxB,QxQ;
23. PxQ,RxB; 24. R-Q5,RxKt; 25. RxR,R-Q1;
26. R-Q1,P-B5; White resigns (Diagram 75).

A game of which Philidor would have approved. Since I would like to leave the last word with him, the greatest of chess musicians, I quote: 'Pawns are the soul of chess.'

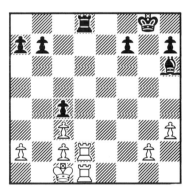

75: Final position.

APPENDIX

QR8	QKt8	QB8	Q8	K8	KB8	KKt8	KR8
QR7	QKt7	QB7	Q7	K7	KB7	KKt7	KR7
QR6	QKt6	QB6	Q6	K6	KB6	KKt6	KR6
QR5	QKt5	QB5	Q5	K5	KB5	KKt5	KR5
QR4	QKt4	QB4	Q4	K4	KB4	KKt4	KR4
QR3	QKt3	QB3	Q3	K3	KB3	KKt3	KR3
QR2	QKt2	QB2	Q2	K2	KB2	KKt2	KR2
QR1	QKt1	QB1	Q1	K1	KB1	KKt1	KR1

76 and 77: Naming the squares by the descriptive notation, first from the White point of view (76), then from the Black (77).

QR1	QKt1	QB1	Q1	K1	KB1	KKt1	KR1
QR2	QKt2	QB2	Q2	K2	KB2	KKt2	KR2
QR3	QKt3	QB3	Q3	K3	KB3	KKt3	KR3
QR4	QKt4	QB4	Q4	K4	KB4	KKt4	KR4
QR5	QKt5	QB5	Q5	K5	KB5	KKt5	KR5
QR6	QKt6	QB6	Q6	K6	KB6	KKt6	KR6
QR7	QKt7	QB7	Q7	K7	KB7	KKt7	KR7
QR8	QKt8	QB8	Q8	K8	KB8	KKt8	KR8

The Descriptive Notation

There are two main methods of recording games, the algebraic and the descriptive notations. The descriptive is far and away the older form in that it is the lineal descendant of the earliest forms of notation of the type 'the King's pawn advances to his third square'. It is used only in English- and Spanish-speaking countries and even there has been losing ground of recent years so that its usage is largely confined to the United Kingdom, to the U.S.A. and to Spain.

The two diagrams left (Diagrams 76 and 77) show the names for each square, the first from the White point of view and the second from the Black.

Before more fully explaining this rather simple notation (in which the one complication is that a square varies in its number in accordance with whether the player has White or Black), I have to give two definitions. A rank is a series of eight squares running horizontally along the board. A file is a series of eight squares running vertically from top to bottom of the board.

Each square has a number from 1 to 8, according to where it is placed on the file; so that the first rank consists entirely of squares numbered 1, the second rank of squares numbered 2, etc. The files are differentiated from each other by the initial letter of the piece which was originally placed on square 1.

With the squares of the board thus numbered all that is necessary to indicate a move is to state which piece moves to which square. Pieces are indicated by their initial letter except in the case of the Knight where one uses the first and last letters so as to distinguish it from the King. This has been simplified a little in the USA and some parts of the UK where the single letter 'N' stands for Knight. A hyphen or long dash, —, shows the actual moving process and a cross 'x' indicates a capture. The process of King-side castling is shown by the symbols 'o-o' and Queen-side castling by 'o-o-o'. Other essential abbreviations are 'ch' for check and 'e.p.' for capturing en passant; there are also 'db ch' which means double check, and 'dis ch' which means discovered check.

The Algebraic Notation

This notation was introduced in Europe in the 18th century by Philip Stamma of Aleppo. It was soon taken up by the German-speaking peoples and spread from there all over the world.

It is even more simple than the descriptive in that each square has only one name, irrespective as to whether the player concerned has the White or Black pieces. Instead of calling the files after the names of the pieces originally placed on the bottom rank the files (from left to right for White) are represented by the letters from a to h. The eight ranks are numbered from 1 to 8, counting from White's first rank. So, in the initial positions the White pieces are on ranks 1 and 2 and the Black pieces on ranks 7 and 8 (see Diagram 78).

Each square is invariably defined by a letter and a number. To the initial letter of the pieces (except the pawn) there is added the square of departure and the square of arrival. In the abbreviated form of algebraic (which is nowadays by far the more commonly employed) the square of departure is omitted. Thus Bf1-c4 means that the Bishop on the square f1 is played to the c4 square. In abbreviated algebraic this would appear as Bc4. With pawns, since they do not require mentioning by name, the procedure is even more brief. Moving the King's pawn to K4 is e2-e4 or in abbreviated form simply e4.

When two similar pieces can go to the same square, the shortened notation is completed in the following way. If, for example, two Knights are on g1 and d2, the move Ktg1-f3 appears in the abbreviated form as Ktgf3. If the Knights are on g1 and g5, the move Ktg1-f3 will be in the shortened form Kt1f3.

78: The initial positions by the algebraic notation.

Bibliography

Alekhine, A. *New York 1924*. New York, 1925.

Alekhine, A. *Das New Yorker Schachturnier 1927*. Berlin/Leipzig, 1927.

Alekhine, A. *My Best Games of Chess 1908–1923*. London, 1927.

Alekhine, A. *Deux cents parties d'échecs (1908–1927)*. Rouen, 1936.

Alekhine, A. *Nottingham 1936*. London, 1937.

Alekhine, A. *My Best Games of Chess 1924–1937*. London, 1939.

Alexander, C. H. O'D. *Alekhine's Best Games of Chess 1938–45*. London, 1949.

Alfonso (X) El Sabio (Alfonso the Wise). *Libros de acedrex, dados e tablas,* ed. A. Steiger. Geneva/Zürich, 1941; *Romanica Helvetica,* 10.

Bachmann, L. *Schachmeister Steinitz,* 4 vols. Ansbach, 1910–21.

Baturinsky, V. *Shakhmatnoe Tvortchestvo Botvinnika,* 3 vols. 1965, 1966, 1968.

Bilguer, P. R. von. *Handbuch des Schachspiels,* ed. Tassilo v. Heydebrand und der Lasa. Berlin, 1843.

Bilguer, P. R. von. *Handbuch des Schachspiels, Nachtrag zu,* by H. Kmoch. Berlin/Leipzig, 1930.

Bland, N. On the Persian Game of Chess. *Journal of the Royal Asiatic Society,* vol. 13, 1852, pp. 1–70.

Bogoljuboff, E. D. *Das Internationale Schachturnier Moskau 1925*. Berlin/Leipzig, 1927.

Botvinnik, M. M. *Championship Chess (Absolute Championship, U.S.S.R. 1941)*. London, 1950.

British Chess Magazine, 1881–present.

Buck, C. A. *Paul Morphy, his later life*. Newport Ky, 1902.

Burton, Sir Richard (trans.). *The Arabian Nights' Entertainments*. 1885.

Burton, Robert. *Anatomy of Melancholy*. London, 1626.

Capablanca, J. R. *My Chess Career*. London, 1920.

Castiglione, Baldassare. *Il libro del Cortegiano* (The Book of the Courtier), translated by Thomas Hoby. London, 1556.

Caxton, William (trans.). *The Right Pleasant and Goodlie Historie of the Foure Sonnes of Aymon*. Westminster 1489, reprinted Early English Text Society, 1886.

Cessolis, Jacobus de. *Liber de moribus hominum et officiis nobilium*. Milan, 1479. Translated by W. Caxton as *The Game and Playe of the Chesse Bruges,* 1474; numerous reprints, latest *British Chess Magazine,* London, 1975.

Cheshire, H. F. *The Hastings Chess Tournament, 1895*. London and New York, 1896.

Chess Monthly, The, ed. L. Hoffer. London, 1879–96.

Chess Player's Chronicle, The, ed. H. Staunton. London, 1841–52, 1853–6, 1859–62.

Cockburn, A. *Idle Passion, Chess, and the Dance of Death*. New York, 1974; London, 1975.

Collijn, L. *Larobok i Schack*. Stockholm, 1921.

Damiano Portugese. *Questo libro e da imparare giocare a scachi*. Roma, 1512; facsimile reprint Nieuwkoop, 1967. Trans. C. Gruget as *Le Plaisant jeu des eschecz*. Paris, 1560. Trans. James Rowbothum, London, 1562, with a dedication to Robert Dudley, Earl of Leicester: 'I knowe that bothe your Lordship with divers other of ye noble-men and gentlemen of this realme can play excellently at this game of ye cheast, and have as deepe knowledge therein as either French men, Italians or Spaniards have.'

Diderot, Denis. *Le neveu de Rameau*. Paris, 1773.

Durgaprasada. *Risala i shatranj*. Delhi, 1890.

L'Echiquier, ed. Lancel. Brussels, 1925–39.

Egenolph (Egenolff), Christian. *Des altern ritterlichen spils des Schachzabels gruntlich bedeutung*. Frankfurt am Main, 1536; reprint Berne, 1923.

Elyot, Sir Thomas. *The Book named the Governour*. 1531.

Féry d'Esclands. *Congrès international des échecs. Compte rendu du congrès de 1867*. Paris, 1868.

Firdausi. *Shāhnāma*. Persia, 1011 AD. French version, *Le livre des rois par Abou'l Kasim Firdausi, publié, traduit et commenté par M. Jules Mohl*. Paris, 1838–78.

Fischer, Robert J. *My 60 Memorable Games*. New York and London, 1969.

Fiske D. W. *The Book of the first American Chess Congress*. New York, 1859.

Forbes, D. *The History of Chess*. London, 1860

Franklin, Benjamin. *Morals of Chess*. 1779; subsequently published in his works, Philadelphia 1812, New York and London, 1825.

Fréret, N. L'origine du jeu des eschecs. *Histoire de l'Académie royale des inscriptions et belles lettres,* 5. Paris, 1729.

Froissart, Jean. *The Chronicles,* 1374; trans. 1523 by Lord Berners.

Ganzo, Julio. *Historia General del Ajedrez*. Madrid, 1966.

Golombek, H. *Capablanca's 100 Best Games of Chess*. London and New York, 1947.

Golombek, H. *World Chess Championship 1948.* London and New York, 1949.

Golombek, H. *Réti's Best Games of Chess.* London, 1954; New York, 1974.

Golombek, H. *World Chess Championship 1954.* London, 1954.

Golombek, H. *World Chess Championship 1957.* London, 1957.

Golombek, H. *Fischer–Spassky 1972.* London, 1973.

Gottschall, H. von. *Adolf Anderssen, der Altmeister deutscher Schachspielkunst.* Leipzig, 1912.

Graham, P. A. *Mr. Blackburne's Games at Chess.* London, 1899.

Greco, G. *Trattato del nobilissimo guioco.* Roma, 1619; Paris, 1669.

Grekov, N. I. *Istoria Shakhmatrtich Sortijazanii.* Moscow, 1933.

Grekov, N. I. *M. I. Tschigorin.* Moscow, 1939.

Gustavus Selenus (Augustus, Duke of Brunswick). *Das Schach- oder Konig-Spiel.* Lipsiae (Leipzig), 1616.

Horsey, Sir Jerome (fl. 1573–1627). *Travels in Russia,* ed. for the Hakluyt Society, 1956, by Sir Edward Augustus Bond.

Horwitz, B. and Kling, J. *Chess Studies.* London, 1851.

Horwitz, B. and Kling, J. *Chess Studies and End-Games.* London, 1884.

Hyde, Thomas. *De Ludis Orientalibus.* 1694.

International Chess Magazine, ed. W. Steinitz. New York, 1885–91.

Jacobi, H. Über zwei ältere Erwahnungen des Schachspiels in der Sanskrit-Litteratur. *Zeitschrift der deutschen morgenländischen Gesellschaft,* 50, 1896, pp. 227–33.

Kagan's Neueste Schachnachrichten. Berlin, 1921–32.

Kmoch, Hans (ed.). *Carlsbad 1929.* Wien, 1929.

Knight, N. *Chess Pieces.* London, 1949.

Knight, N. and Guy, W. *King, Queen and Knight.* London, 1975.

Lange, Max. *Kritik der Eröffnungen.* Berlin, 1855.

Lange, Max. *Paul Morphy, Skizze aus der Schachwelt.* Leipzig, 1859. Trans. and ed. as *Paul Morphy; a Sketch from the Chess World,* by Ernest Falkbeer. London, 1860.

Lasker, E. *Common Sense in Chess.* London, 1896.

Linde, Antonius van der. *Geschichte und Litteratur des Schachspiels.* Berlin, 1874.

Linder, I. M. *Alexander Dmitrievitch Petrov. Piervii Russki Skakhmatni Master.* Moscow, 1952.

Linder, I. M. *Chudoznik Shakhmat Shumov.* Moscow, 1959.

Linder, I. M. *L. Tolstoi i Shakhmati.* Moscow, 1960.

Linder, I. M. *Shakhmatni v SSR 1950–74.* passim.

Lolli, Giambatista (Modenese). *Osservazione Teorico-Pratiche sopra il Guioco degli Scacchi ossia Il Giuoco Degli Scacchi esposito nel suo miglior lume.* Bologna, 1763.

Löwenthal, J. J. *The Chess Congress of 1862.* London, 1864.

Lucena, Luis Ramirez de. *Repeticion de Amores y Arte de Ajedrez.* Salamanca, 1497; facsimile reprint, Madrid, 1953.

Magnus, Olaus, *Historia de gentibus septentrionalibus.* Roma, 1555.

Mason, J. *The Art of Chess.* London, 1895.

Mason, J. and Pollock, W. H. K. *St. Petersburg 1895–6.* Leeds, 1896.

Méry, F. J. P. A. Les matinées du Louvre—Paradoxes et rêveries. *Une revanche de Waterloo,* pp. 34–8. Paris, 1856.

Mieses, J. and Lewitt, M. *Le tournoi d'Échecs de Saint-Sebastien.* Paris, 1911.

Minchin, J. J. *Games Played in the London International Chess Tournament 1883.* London, 1884.

Murray, H. J. R. *A History of Chess.* Oxford at the Clarendon Press, 1913.

Murray, H. J. R. *A Short History of Chess,* rev. B. Goulding-Brown and H. Golombek. Oxford at the Clarendon Press, 1963.

Noldeke, Prof. Karnamak, Geschichte des Artachsir-i-Papakun aus dem Pehlewi übersetzt. *Bezzenberger's Beiträge,* IV. Göttingen, 1878.

Nimzovitsch, Aron. *My System.* London, 1929.

Nimzovitsch, Aron. *Die Praxis meines Systems.* Berlin, 1929.

Orbeli, I i K. *Trever Shatrang. Kniga o shakhmatakh.* Leningrad, 1936.

Philidor, François-André Danican. *L'Analyze des échecs.* London, 1749.

Philidor, François-André Danican. *Analyse du jeu des échecs.* London, 1777.

Philidor, François-André Danican. *Studies of Chess containing Caissa, A Poem by Sir William Jones; A Systematic Introduction to the game and the whole Analysis of Chess by Mr. A. D. Philidor.* London, 1810. (The Introduction to the Game is anonymous, but it reads like William Lewis and is certainly not Sarratt whom he attacks.)

Ponziani, Domenico Lorenzo. *Il guioco incomparabile degli*

scacchi. Modena, 1764 and 1782.

La Régence, monthly magazine, ed. Kieseritzky. Paris, 1849–51.

Reinfeld, F. *The Book of the Cambridge Springs International Tournament,* 1904.

Réti, Richard. *Die Neuen Ideen in Schachspiel.* Vienna, 1922.

Réti, Richard. *Modern Ideas in Chess.* London, 1923.

Réti, Richard. *Masters of the Chess Board.* London, 1953.

Rio, Ercole del. *Sopra il guioco degli Scacchi, Osservazioni pratiche d'anonimo Autore Modenese.* Modena, 1750.

Rousseau, Jean Jacques. *Les Confessions.* Paris, 1781 and 1788.

Salvio, A. *Trattato dell'inventione et arte liberale del guioco di scacchi.* Napoli, 1604.

Savenkov, I. T. *K voprosu ob evolyutsii shakhmatnoi igri.* Moscow, 1905.

Sergeant, P. W. *A Century of British Chess.* London, 1936.

Sergeant, P.W. *Charousek's Games of Chess.* London, 1919.

Sergeant, P.W. *Morphy's Games of Chess.* London, 1921.

Sergeant, P. W. and Watts, W. H. *Pillsbury's Chess Career.* London, 1922.

Shakhmatny Listok, Moscow, 1922–31.

Shakhmatny Bulletin, Moscow, 1955–75.

Shakhmaty v SSR, Moscow, 1931–75.

Sidney, Sir Philip. *Defence of Poesie.* 1595.

'*64*' (magazine), Moscow, 1924–35.

'*64*' (journal), Moscow, 1935–41.

Stamma, Philip. *Essai sur le Jeu des Echecs.* Paris, 1737.

Stamma, Philip. *The Noble Game of Chess.* London, 1745.

Stamma, Philip, ed. L. Bledow und O. von Oppen. *Stamma's hundert Endspiele.* Berlin, 1856.

Staunton, H. *The Chess Player's Handbook.* London, 1847.

Staunton, H. *The Chess Handbook by an Amateur.* Philadelphia, 1859.

Staunton, H. *The Chess Tournament, 1851.* London, 1852.

Staunton, H. *The Chess-player's Companion.* London, 1849.

Staunton, H. *Chess Praxis.* London, 1860.

Steinitz, W. *The Modern Chess Instructor.* Vol. 1, New York, 1889; vol. 2, New York, 1895.

Steinitz, W. *The Book of the Sixth American Chess Congress 1889.* New York, 1891.

Tarrasch, Siegbert. *Dreihundert Schachpartien.* Leipzig, 1895.

Tarrasch, Siegbert. *Die Moderne Schachpartie.* Nurnberg, 1912.

Tarrasch, Siegbert. *The Game of Chess.* London, 1935.

Tartakower, Savielly. *Die hypermoderne Schachspiele.* Wien, 1925.

Trivet, N. (ed.). *Annales.* London, 1845.

Vida, M. G. *De arte poetica . . . de ludo scacchorum (Scacchia Ludus).* Roma, 1527.

Vidmar, M. *Das zweite internationale Schachturnier in Karlsbad.* Potsdam, 1912.

Vogt, Carl Frederich (alias W. Lewis). *Letters on Chess.* London, 1848.

Voltaire, François-Marie Arouet. *Dictionnaire Philosophique.* 1764.

Walker, G. *Chess Studies.* London, 1844.

Walker, G. *A selection of games at chess, actually played by Philidor and his contemporaries.* London, 1835.

Walker, G. *Chess and Chess Players.* London, 1850.

Walker, W. G. *Games at Chess.* London, 1836.

Watts, W. H. *The Grand International Masters' Chess Tournament at St. Petersburg 1914.* London, 1914.

Wiener Schachzeitung, 1898–1916, then 1923–1938 ed. Marco *et al.*

Zijlstra, D. *Rondom het Al-Adli handschrift. Complete schaak-analyse,* 2 vols. Amsterdam, 1936.

FURTHER READING

The Bibliography I have given opposite is a fairly wide and representative selection of the books and works I consulted when writing this history. I have omitted mention of a vast number of tournament books, chess magazines and journals, biographies and diverse studies of the game of chess in all its aspects. But I have picked out those works which I regard as important both positively (in the sense that they contributed much to the history of chess) and negatively in that they spread myths about the course and history of chess. This latter pursuit, as I realised quite early on in my career, was indulged in by, roughly speaking, about 80% of the writers on the subject.

For further reading it is possible to confine oneself very largely to writers in the English language, though it has to be admitted that a knowledge of French, German, Spanish, Russian, Italian and Latin is exceedingly useful.

Undoubtedly Murray's *History of Chess* is the great work on the subject. Murray united great learning with a passionate industry that betrays an equally fervent interest in the game. He is particularly good on the earlier history of the time when chess was called by other names. His *Short History* is also useful (and more readable). I contributed a chapter on what were then (1963) the latest developments and am now engaged in preparing a second edition of the work which will not only bring it up to date but also modernize previous chapters.

I must make one exception to the exclusion of foreign languages here, for the German writers of the 19th and 20th centuries have made great contributions to the study both of ancient and of modern chess history. Van der Linde's *Geschichte und Litteratur des Schachspiels* is a fine work on the older history; and the writings of Tarrasch, Tartakower and Réti are essential reading for the study and understanding of modern chess. Fortunately, good translations exist of Réti, and the other important writers on the game in this aspect, Steinitz and Lasker, wrote in English for the better part of their lives.

For the literary aspects of chess Knight's *Chess Pieces* and Salzman's *Chess Reader* are both useful and entertaining and they also provide many indications as to possible sources of chess history.

ACKNOWLEDGEMENTS

My grateful thanks are due to the Oxford University Press for their permission to quote the following passages from H. J. R. Murray's *A History of Chess* (Oxford, as the Clarendon Press, 1913); Chapter 2, first paragraph; Chapter 3, third paragraph; Chapter 6, Murray's paraphrase of the "Innocent Morality".

I also acknowledge permission for the following quotations: from the *Romance of the Rose* (in Chapter 7), translated by F. S. Ellis, and published by J. M. Dent & Sons Ltd. in the Temple Classics Series; from Richard Réti's *Modern Ideas in Chess,* published by Dover Publications; from H. G. Wells's *Certain Personal Matters,* by permission of The Estate of H. G. Wells; and from the *British Chess Magazine.*

PICTURE CREDITS

Permission to reproduce photographs has kindly been given by the following (the picture numbers in italics refer to colour illustrations).

INDEX   Games given in the text

A

Alekhine–Bogoljuboff Match (1929), 199

Alekhine–Book (Margate 1938), 209

Alekhine–Wolf (Pistyan 1922), 192

Anderssen–Dufresne (Berlin 1853), 147

Anderssen-Kieseritzky (London 1851), 133

Anderssen–Morphy Match (1858), 144

Anderssen–L. Paulsen (part game, Vienna 1873), 155

Anderssen–Staunton (London 1851), 132

Anderssen–Steinitz (Vienna 1873), 154

B

Bardeleben–Steinitz (Hastings 1895), 168

Bauer–Lasker (Amsterdam 1890), 161

Bernstein–Capablanca (San Sebastian 1911), 187

Bernstein–Capablanca (St. Petersburg 1914), 190

Blackburne–Zukertort (London 1883), 158

Bogoljuboff–Alekhine Match (1929), 199

Bogoljuboff–Réti (New York 1924), 195

Book–Alekhine (Margate 1938), 209

Botterill–Tal (Bath 1973), 223

Botvinnik–Capablanca (AVRO 1938), 211

Botvinnik–Keres (Hague–Moscow 1948), 214

Bourdonnais–McDonnell (London 1834), 126

Bronstein–Kaplan (Hastings 1976), 239

Browne–Stean (Nice Olympiad 1974), 235

Brunswick, Duke of and Count Isouard–Morphy (Paris 1858), 142

C

Capablanca–Berstein (San Sebastian 1911), 187

Capablanca–Berstein (St. Petersburg 1914), 190

Capablanca–Botvinnik (AVRO 1938), 211

Capablanca–Réti (Berlin 1928), 196

Capablanca–Spielmann (New York 1927), 197

Capablanca–Wheatcroft (Margate 1935), 211

Castellvi–Vinoles (Catalonia 15th century), 98

Charousek–Tschigorin (Budapest 1896), 170

D

Dufresne–Anderssen (Berlin 1853), 167

F

Fischer–Spassky (6th match game, Reykjavik 1972), 225

Fischer–Spassky (10th match game, Reykjavik 1972), 225

Flohr–Keres (Semmering–Baden 1937), 202

H

Harrwitz–Morphy (Paris 1858), 141

Hromadka–Rubinstein (Mährisch–Ostrau 1923), 195

J

Johner, P.–Nimzowitsch (Dresden 1926), 197

K

Kaplan–Bronstein (Hastings 1976), 239

Karpov–Mariotti (Ljubljana–Portoroz 1975), 238

Karpov–Tukmakov (Leningrad Interzonal 1973), 196

Keres–Botvinnik (Hague–Moscow 1948), 214

Keres–Flohr (Semmering–Baden 1937), 202

Kieseritzky–Anderssen (London 1851), 133

L

Larsen–Portisch (San Antonio 1972), 230

Lasker–Bauer (Amsterdam 1890), 161

Lasker–Pillsbury (St. Petersburg 1895–6), 169

Lasker–Pillsbury (Cambridge Springs 1904), 177

Lasker–Schlechter (part game Berlin 1910), 181

Lasker–Steinitz (London 1899), 171

Lasker–Tarrasch (Dusseldorf 1908), 179

Lasker–Tarrasch (St. Petersburg 1914), 191

Leonardo da Cutri–Ruy Lopez (Madrid 1575), 108

Lewitzky–Marshall (Breslau 1912), 188

Lundin–Szabo (Groningen 1946), 213

M

MacDonnell, Rev.–Steinitz (Dublin 1865), 151

McDonnell–De la Bourdonnais (London 1834), 126

Marriotti–Karpov (Ljubljana–Portoroz 1975), 238

Marshall–Lewitzky (Breslau 1912), 188

Mecking–Reshevsky (Petropolis Interzonal 1973), 233

Mongredien–Steinitz (London 1862), 150

Morphy–Anderssen (Paris 1858), 144
Morphy–Brunswick, Duke of–Count
    Isouard (Paris 1858), 142
Morphy–Harrwitz (Paris 1858), 141
Morphy–Harrwitz (Paris 1858), 142
Morphy–L. Paulsen (New York 1857),
    135
Morphy–L. Paulsen (New York 1857),
    136
Morphy–E. Rousseau (New Orleans
    1849), 138

N

Neumann–Steinitz (Dundee 1867), 153
Nimzowitsch–P. Johner (Dresden
    1926), 197

P

Paulsen, L.–Morphy (New York
    1857), 135
Paulsen, L.–Morphy (New York
    1857), 136
Paulsen, L.–Anderssen (part game
    Vienna 1873), 155
Pillsbury–Lasker (St. Petersburg
    1895–6), 169
Pillsbury–Lasker (Cambridge Springs
    1904), 177
Portisch–Larsen (San Antonio 1972),
    230

R

Reshevsky–Mecking (Petropolis
    Interzonal 1973), 233
Réti–Bogoljuboff (New York 1924),
    195
Réti–Capablanca (Berlin 1928), 196
Rousseau, E.–Morphy (New Orleans
    1849), 138
Rubinstein–Hromadka (Mährisch–
    Ostrau 1923), 195

Ruy Lopez–Leonardo da Cutri
    (Madrid 1575), 108

S

Saint Amant–Staunton (Paris 1843),
    130
Schlechter–Lasker (part game, Berlin
    1910), 181
Spassky–Fischer (6th match game,
    Reykjavik 1972), 225
Spassky–Fischer (10th match game,
    Reykjavik 1972), 225
Spielmann–Capablanca (New York
    1927), 197
Staunton–Anderssen (London 1851),
    132
Staunton–Saint Amant (Paris 1843),
    130
Stean–Browne (Nice Olympiad 1974),
    235
Steinitz–Anderssen (Vienna 1873), 154
Steinitz–von Bardeleben (Hastings
    1895), 168
Steinitz–Lasker (London 1899), 171
Steinitz–Rev. MacDonnell (Dublin
    1865), 151
Steinitz–Mongredien (London 1862),
    150
Steinitz–Tschigorin (Havana 1889),
    160
Steinitz–Tschigorin (Havana 1892),
    162
Szabo–Lundin (Groningen 1946), 213

T

Tal–Botterill (Bath 1973), 233
Tarrasch–Lasker (Dusseldorf 1908),
    179
Tarrasch–Lasker (St. Petersburg 1914),
    191
Tschigorin–Steinitz (Havana 1889), 160
Tschigorin–Steinitz (Havana 1892), 162

Tschigorin–Charousek (Budapest
    1896), 170
Tukmakov–Karpov (Leningrad
    Interzonal), 232

V

Vinoles–Castellvi (Catalonia 15th
    century), 98

W

Wheatcroft–Capablanca (Margate
    1938), 211
Wolf–Alekhine (Pistyan 1922), 192

Z

Zukertort–Blackburne (London 1883),
    158

INDEX General

A

Abbazia 1912, 187
Abdalghaffar-al-Ansari, 44
Abu'n Na'am, 43
Abu Shararu, 44, 46
Adli, Al-, 43, 44
Adviser, the, 14
Ala'addin as-Tabrizi, 49
Albin, Adolf, 167, 169, 188
Albin Counter-Gambit, 188
Alekhine, Alexander, 180, 184, 188,
    189, 190, 191, 192, 193, 194, 195,
    196, 197, 198, 199, 200, 201, 202,
    208, 209, 210, 211, 212, 213, 225,
    228, 229
Alekhine–Bogoljuboff match, 1929, 199
Alekhine–Bogoljuboff match, 1934, 201
Alekhine–Capablanca match, 1927,
    197–198
Alekhine–Euwe match, 1935, 201
Alekhine–Euwe match, 1937, 202
Alekhine Memorial Tournament,
    Moscow 1971, 236
Alekhine Memorial Tournament,
    Moscow 1975, 238
Alexander, C. H. O'D., 201, 209, 238
Alexander Memorial Tournament,
    Middlesbrough 1975, 238
Alexander II, Pope, 52
Alfil, 50
Alfin (Alphyn, Aufin), 64, 67, 87
Alfonso VI, King of Leon and
    Castile, 59, 60
Alfonso el Sabio (Alfonso the Wise),
    61
Algebraic notation, 39, 117, 241
Allgaier, Johann, 123
Allison, W. S., 136
American System, 147
Amsterdam 1890, 161
Analyze du Jeu des Echecs (Philidor), 120,
    121
Anatomy of Melancholy, 10, 85
Anderssen, Adolf, 129, 131, 132, 139,
    141, 142, 143, 147, 148, 152, 154, 155

Andersson, Ulf, 231, 238
Arabian Nights' Entertainments, 34, 40
Art of Chess, The (James Mason), 157
Artaxerxes (Artakhshir), 27
Ascham, Robert, 83
Asp (Knight), 27
Ash-shatranj, 50
Ashtapadas, 12
Astrological (Elephant) chess, 12
Astronomical chess, 63
Asztalos, Lajos, 200
Atkins, H. E., 172
L'Atlantide, 90
Attahasa, 14
Augustus, Duke of Brunswick, 142
Automaton, 122
Averbach, Yuri, 216
AVRO International Tournament,
    1938, 210

B

Bacon, Francis, 113
Backgammon (nard), 11, 12, 31, 34
Baden 1914, 189
Baden–Baden 1870, 152, 154
Baden–Baden 1925, 196
Bad Kissingen 1928, 198
Bagueret, 116
Baidaq (Foot-soldier, pawn), 39
Balhait (Shahraim), 32
Bāna, 12
Barcelona 1929, 198, 199
Barcelona 1946, 213
Bardeleben, Kurt von, 159, 167
Barmen 1905, 177
Barnes, Thomas, 148
Beljavsky, Alexander, 234, 238, 239
Bénoit, Pierre, 96
Bergen-aan-Zee, FIDE Congress, 1975,
    237
Berger, A., 159, 168, 171
Berlin 1881, 157
Berlin 1897, 171

Berlin 1918, 191
Berlin 1920, 192
Berlin 1928 (two tournaments), 198
Berne 1932, 200
Bernstein, Ossip, 172, 177, 178, 184,
    187, 190, 213
Bernstein, S., 194
Bibliothèque Nationale, 57
Bigelow, Horace, 194
Bikova, Elizaveta, 215, 217
Bilguer, Paul, Rudolph von, 129
Bird, H. E., 132, 141, 154, 158, 162, 166
Birmingham 1858, 140
Bishop, 80, 83
Bishop and Knight mate, 121
Bishop's Opening, 100, 101
Bishop sacrifice, double, 161
Bisignano, Prince of, 111
Bissy de, 115
Bjelova, 215
Blackburne, J. H., 148, 151, 153, 155,
    156, 157, 158, 159, 160, 162, 165, 166,
    167, 169, 190, 196
Bland, Nathaniel, 32
Bled 1931, 200
Blindfold Play, 120, 135, 172
Blumenfeld, Benjamin, 178
Boerken, Rodovane, 56
Bogoljuboff, E. D., 189, 192, 193, 194,
    195, 196, 197, 198, 199, 200, 201, 202,
    208, 212, 213
Boi, Paolo, 93, 108, 111
Boke of the Duchesse (Chaucer), 78
Bolbochan, Julio, 213
Boleslavsky, Isaac, 212, 213, 214, 218
Bondarevsky, Igor, 212, 214
Böök, Eero, 209
The Book named the Governor, 93
The Book of the Courtier, 94
Botvinnik, Mikhail, 200, 201, 202, 210,
    211, 212, 213, 214, 215, 216, 219, 225
    v. Bronstein, World Championship
        match, 1951, 215
    v. Petrosian, World Championship

match, 1963, 216
v. Smyslov, World Championship match, 1954, 216
v. Smyslov, World Championship match, 1957, 196
v. Smyslov, World Championship match, 1958, 216
v. Tal, World Championship match, 1960, 216
v. Tal, World Championship match, 1961, 216
Boy prodigies, 118
Bourdonnais, Louis Charles Mahé de la, 125, 126, 128, 129
Bradley Beach 1929, 199
Brassey Institute, 168
Breslau 1889, 161
Breslau 1912, 188
Breslau 1925, 196
Breyer, Gyula, 192, 194
Brilliancy Prize (for a draw), 216
British Chess Association, 147
British Chess Magazine, 12, 48, 76
Brodie, 132
Bronstein, David, 209, 214, 215, 216, 218, 233, 238, 239
Brunswick, Duke of, 142
Buck, C. A., 144
Buckle, W. T., 131
Budapest
  1896, 170
  1912, 188
  1913, 189
  1921, 192
  (Siesta), 1928, 198
  1929, 198
  Candidates' Tournament, 1950, 214
  Candidates' Tournament Play-off (Bronstein–Boleslavsky), 214
Buenos Aires 1927, 197
Buoncompagno, Giacomo, Duke of Sora, 107
Burn, Amos, 159, 160, 161, 171, 177, 181, 184
Burton, Sir Richard, 40
Burton, Robert, 10, 85
Byrne, Robert, 232
Byzantium, 28, 55

C
Café de la Régence, 114, 115, 129, 141
Calabrese, Il Calabrois, 112
Calthrop, S. R., 136
Camels, 26
Cambridge Springs 1904, 169, 172, 177
Cambridge Springs variation, 177
Candidates Tournament, Neuhausen 1953, 216
Candidates Tournament, Yugoslavia 1958, 216
Canterbury 1930, 108
Capablanca, José Raoul, 147, 184, 188, 190, 191, 192, 193, 195, 196, 197, 198, 199, 200, 201, 208, 210, 211, 213
Capablanca–Euwe, match, 1930, 200
Capablanca v. Lasker, World

Championship match, 1921, 192
Caputo, Tomaso, 108
Caracas 1970, 235
Carlsbad 1923, 194
Carlsbad 1929, 199
Carrera, Pietro, 116
Castellvi, Francisco de, 97
Castiglione, Baldassare, 94
Castling, 63
Castling, free, 118
Catherine de Medici, 93
Caxton, William, 64, 86
Centre Counter Defence, 100, 143
Ceron, Aldonso, 107
Cessolis, Jacobus de, 63
Chandaraki, 25
Chariots (Rooks), 15, 16
Charlemagne, 56, 57
Charousek, Rudolf, 169, 170, 171
Charles the Bold, Duke of Burgundy, 85
Chatrang, 27
Chatrang-namak, 20, 27
Chaturanga, 12, 14, 15, 19
Chaturanga, four-handed, 19
Chaucer, Geoffrey, 78
Checkmate, 19, 27
Chessmen, English, 122
Chessmen, French, 122
Chess Monthly (ed. L. Hoffer), 158
Chess Pieces (ed. Knight), 26
Chess Player's Chronicle (ed. Staunton), 130
Chess Player's Handbook (ed. Staunton), 131
Chess Studies, George Walker, 123
Chinese Chess Federation, 25
Chinese riverside game, 10
Chinese River Game, 23, 24
Chronicle, 90
Closed-circuit television, 220
Cochrane, John, 123, 130
Cockburn, Alexander, 138
Cohn, W., 171
Cole, H. H., 47
Colle, Edgar, 200
Collins, John W., 219, 220
Cologne 1898, 170, 171
Comes, 69
Common Sense in Chess (Lasker) 182
Comnena, Anna, 28
Comnena, Emperor Alexis, 28
Confessions, J. J. Rousseau, 116
Cook, Nathaniel, 133
Corzo, J., 187
Courier Game, 95, 96
Coxford, Priory of, 55
Cracow 1941, 212
Cramer, Fred, 229, 235
Crocodiles, 62
Cunningham, Alexander, 120
Curvus, 69

D
Dake, Arthur W., 208
Dalverzin-Tepe, 12
Damiano, 101

Damiano Gambit, 99, 106
Deacon, Frederic H., 148, 151
Dean, 148
Defence of Poesy, 94
Derivation of chess, 13
Deschapelles, Alexandre, Lunis Honoré le Breton, 125
Deutsche Schachzeitung, 167
Dewarsarm, 20
Dickins, A. S. M., 12
Dictionnaire d'Anecdotes, 85
Diderot, Denis, 115, 120,
Dilaram, 39, 40
Divan, The, 129, 133
Dobell, H. E., 167
Dom treasury, 57
Don Juan of Austria, 108
Dreihundert Schachpartien (Tarrasch), 165
Dresden 1892, 165, 197
Dresden 1926, 197
Dublin 1865, 151
Dubois, Serafino, 148, 150
Duchamp, Marcel, 84
Dufresne, Jean, 143, 147
Dundee 1867, 153
Duras, Oldrich, 177, 180, 184, 187, 188
Durgaprasada, 40
Dus-Chotimirsky, fedor, 178
Dutch Defence, 136

E
Edmondson, Colonel, 237
Edward I, King of England, 84
Edward III, King of England, 90
Egenolff, Christian, 83
Eginhard, 57
Einsiedeln poem, 68
Elephant, 13, 15, 37, 80
Eliduc, 87
Eliskases, Erich, 201, 202, 212, 213
Elizabeth I, Queen of England, 93
Elo, Prof. Arpad, 209, 211, 231
Elyot Sir Thomas, 93
Endfield, Cy, 226
Englisch, Berthold, 158
Enlarged Chess, 62
En passant, capturing, 82
Epstein, 151
Ercole del Rio, 117, 118
Ermengaud I, Count of Urgel, 50
Ermessind, Countess, 51
Essai sur le jeu des Echecs (Stamma), 117
European Team Championship Finals, Bath 1973, 233
Euwe, Prof. Max, 194, 197, 198, 200, 201, 202, 210, 213, 214, 228, 237
Evans Gambit 143, 162
Evergreen Game, 147
Evilmerodach, 65
Evolution of the game of Chess, 21
Exerxes, 66

F
Falkbeer, Ernst Karl, 141
Fana, Begum, 40

Faras (Horse, Knight), 39
Farzin, 27
Fenollar, Abbot, 97
Ferrand, Count of Flanders, 85
FIDE (Fédération Internationale des Echecs), 196, 217
Fidhcheall, 77, 78
Field, The, 155
Figure game, 22
Fil (Elephant), 39, 50
Filidori, 119
Fine, Reuben, 200, 201, 202, 208, 210, 211, 213, 214
Firdausi, 10, 26
Firz (fers) = Minister or Queen, 38, 57, 68, 78, 79
Fischer, Robert James (Bobby), 141, 217, 219 *et seq.*, 229, 230, 235, 237
    v. Larsen, match, 1971, 221
    v. Taimanov, match, 1971, 221
    v. Petrosian, match, 1971, 221
    v. Spassky, match, 1972, 222
Fiske, Prof. Willard, 12, 13, 136, 144
Fitzgerald, Edward, 25
Flamberg, Alexander, 178, 189
Flohr, Salo, 199, 200, 201, 202, 210, 211, 213, 214
Foltys, Jan, 213
Foot-soldiers (pawns), 15, 16
Forbes, Duncan, 19, 68
Forgacs, Leo, 177
Foubert, 115
Four-handed chess, 62
Foure Sonnes of Aymon, 86
Frankfurt-am-Main 1887, 159
Frankfurt-am-Main 1930, 200
Franklin, Benjamin, 115, 124, 134
Fraser, James Cunningham, 129
Frederick the Great of Prussia, 97, 115
Frederick William I of Prussia, 96
French Defence, 143
Fréret, 79
Froissart, 90
Fuller, 136
Furman, Semyon, 238

G
Gagarin, 84
Gambit, 107
Gambit Tournament, 172
Game of Chess, The (Tarrasch), 166
Ganzo, Julio, 19
Gaprindashvili, Nona, 217, 219
Gasper Lord, 94
Gav, 26
Geller, Ejfim, 209, 216, 218, 233, 238
Gerard, Bishop (later Pope Nicholas II), 52
German Chess Federation, 159, 178
Geschichte und Litteratur des Schachspiels, 22, 57
Giraffes, 62
Giuoco Di Scacchi (Lolli), 118
Giuoco Piano, 99

Gligoric, Svetozar, 211, 215, 216, 219, 230, 238
Go (wei-chi), 10, 11, 22
Goddonove, Boris Federowich (Boris Godounov), 56
Golden Palace, 22
Goldsmith, Oliver, 103
Golombek, Harry, 209, 213
Good, Dr. Jack, 13
Goring Gambit, 148
Gøteborg 1920, 192
Gotha, 58
Gottingen Manuscript, 98
Graham (*Mr. Blackburne's Games at Chess*), 156
Greco, Gioachino, 111, 112
Greco Counter-Gambit, 112
Grétry, André, 119
Grimm, Jakob, 115
Groningen Junior International Tournament, 235
Groningen 1946, 213
Grünfeld, Ernst, 192, 193, 194
Grünfeld Defence, 192
Gryphon, 62
Guimard, Carlos, 213
Gunsberg, Isador, 159, 160, 162, 167, 190
Gurgenidze, Bukhiti, 238
Gustavus Selenus, 142
Gutmayer, Franz, 194
Gwydbwyll, 78

H
Hafs, Abu, 34
Hague, The, 1921, 192
Hamburg 1885, 159
Hamburg 1910, 180
Handbuch (Bilguer), 129, 131, 170
Hannak, 148
Hanover 1902, 172
Haravijaya (Victory of Siva), 14
Harrington, Lord, 117
Harrwitz, D., 129, 130, 131, 141
Harshacharita, 12
Harun al-Rashid, 34
Hastings
    1895, 167, 168
    Victory Tournament, 1919, 192
    1922, 193
    1931–32, 200
    1933–34, 201
    1947–48, 213
    1971–72, 236
    1972–73, 230, 231
    1975–76, 239
Hastings Chess Club, 167
Havana 1913, 188
Havana Chess Club, 165
Havasi, Kornel, 198
Hayat Begum, 40
Henry III, King of England, 52
Henry VIII, King of England, 93
Historia General del Ajedrez, 19
Historia de Gentibus Septentrionalibus, 58
History of Civilisation (Buckle), 131

Hoby, Thomas, 94
Hoffer, Lepold, 158
Horowitz, Israel, 202
Horsemen (Knights), 37
Horses (Knights), 15, 16
Horsey, Sir Jerome, 56
Hort, Vlastimil, 230, 233, 238, 239
Horwitz, Bernard, 129, 130, 132
Howard, Frederick, Earl of Carlisle, 130
Howard, Henry, Earl of Surrey, 83
Hübner, Robert, 232, 238
Huon of Bordeaux, 88
Hyde, Thomas, 34
Hypermoderne Schachpartie (Tartakower), 193, 194

I
Ibn-Ammar, 60
Ibn-al-Sabbana, 59, 60
Iljin-Genevsky, Alexander, 196
Illustrated London News, 139
Il giuoco incomparabili degli scacchi (Ponziani), 118
Immortal Game, 133
Indian, North-West, 13
Innocent Morality, 66
International Chess Magazine (ed. Steinitz), 160
Internationale Schachkongress zu St. Petersburg, 1909 (Lasker), 182
International Team Tournament
    London 1927, 198
    Hamburg 1930, 200
    Folkestone 1933, 200
    Warsaw 1935, 201
    Stockholm 1937, 202
    Buenos Aires 1939, 212
    Dubrovnik 1950, 215
    Helsinki 1952, 216, 219
Isouard, Count de Vauvenargue, 142
Ivan Grozny (Ivan the Terrible), 56

J
Jabir al-Kufi, 44, 47
Jacobi, Samuel, 14, 15
Jacobs, Herbert, 48
Jacques, 133
Jaenisch, Carl Priedrich, 131, 134
Jaffe, Oscar, 194
Jahan Begum, 40
James I, King of England, 113
Janowski, David, 165, 167, 169, 170, 171, 172, 177, 178, 181, 187, 190, 194, 195
Jehan, Shah, 40
Joan of Arc, 80
Johannes Gallensis (John of Wales), 66
John, King of England, 84
Junge Klaus, 212
Jurevitch, Vladimir, 172

K
Kan, Ilya, 201
Karlsbad 1907 (see also Carlsbad), 178

Kārnāmak, 27
Karpov, Anatoly, 230, 231, 234, 235
  et seq., 237, 238
Karpov v. Polugaievsky, match, 1974,
  234
Karpov v. Korchnoi, match, 1974,
  234, 236
Kaschau (Kassa), 1918, 191
Kashdan, Isaac, 200, 202, 208
Kāvyalankāva, 15
Kecskemet 1927, 197
Kemeri 1937, 202
Kempelen, von, Wolfgang, 122
Kennedy Capt., 132
Kennedy, E., 132
Kennicott, 136
Keres, Paul, 201, 202, 208, 210, 211,
  212, 213, 214, 216, 230, 233, 237
Kermur M. de, Sire de Legal (usually
  known as Legal), 115, 120
Kieseritzky, Lionel, 132, 138, 141
Kiev, Dukedom of, 55
Kiev, 1903, 172
King, the, 14, 15, 34, 38, 56, 79
King's Gambit, 121, 189
King's Gambit, Allgaier variation, 118
King's Indian Defence, 171, 218
Kling, Joseph, 129
Kmoch, Hans, 198
Knight, Norman, 26
Knight against pawn, 121
Knott, 136
Knut (Canute), 69, 76
Kolish Ignatz, 147, 153, 154, 157
Kon (horse), 58
Korchnoi, Viktor, 231, 235, 236, 239
Korchnoi v. Mecking, match, 1974,
  234
Korol (King), 56
Kostich, Boris, 192, 200
Kotov, Alexander, 214, 216

L

Ladya (boat=Rook), 58
Lajlaj, al-, 45, 46
Lange, Max, 129, 144
Larsen, Bent, 216, 219, 222, 230, 232
Lasa, Baron Tassilo von Heydebrand,
  129
Lasker, Edward, 193, 195, 232
Lasker, Emanuel, 161, 166, 167, 168,
  169, 171, 177, 178, 179, 180, 181,
  182, 184, 191, 192, 195, 196, 201,
  213
Latrunculi, 78
Legal, 115, 120
Leipzig 1877, 155
Leipzig 1894, 165
Leningrad Interzonal, 1973, 231
Leningrad–Moscow 1939, 211
Leonardo da Cutri, 106, 108
Leonhardt, Saladin, 177, 178, 184, 187
Letters on Chess, 98
Levenfish, Grigori, 201
Lewis Chessmen, 75
Lewis, William, 98, 123

*Liber de moribus hominum et officiis
  nobilium*, 63
Libre del jochs partitis, 98
Lichtenheim, 136
Liège, 1930, 200
Lilienthal, Andreas, 200, 212, 214
Linde, Antonius van der, 22, 57
Lions, 62
Lipke, Paul, 165
L'Isle and Dudley, Lord de, 94
Libre des eschecs moralisé en Francois, Le,
  64
Ljubljana and Portoroz, 1975, 238
Ljubojevic, 233, 238
Lodge, 32
Lodz 1906, 178
Lolli, Gian Batista, 118
Lombard School, 63
London
  1851, 131, 139, 140
  1897, 171
  1899, 170, 171
  1892, 166
  1887, 160
  1862, 147
  1866, 151
  1872, 154
  1883, 152, 158
  1886, 159
  1899, 171
  1922, 193
  1932, 200
London Club, 131
Lopez, Ruy de Segura, 93, 106
Louis XIII, King of France, 119
Löwe, Edward, 132
Löwenthal, J. J., 135, 137, 139, 140,
  141, 148
Lucas van Leyden, 96
Lucena, Luis Ramirez de, 43, 82, 97,
  98
Lucena position, 101
Ludus Scacchorum, 63–64
Lundin Erik, 212, 213
Lüneberg 1947, 213

M

MacDonnell, Rev. G. A., 148, 151,
  153
Mackenzie, George Henry, 158, 159
McDonnell, Alexander, 126
McGinley, P. T., 76
Madrid 1574, 131
Madrid 1973, 234
Maelzel, 122
Mahdi, Caliph Al-, 34
Mahmud Al Ghazni, 26
Mährisch-Ostrau 1923, 195
Main chator, 21
Maiselis, I. J., 84
Malayan chess, 21
Ma'mun Al, 44
Manchester 1890, 165
Mannheim 1914, 191
Mansubat, 43
Mar del Plata 1947, 213

Marache, Napoleon, 136
Marco, Georg, 165, 168, 169
Margate 1937, 202
Margate 1938, 209
Margate 1939, 217
Marie de France, 87
Marienbad, 1925, 196
Maroczy, Geza, 169, 170, 171, 172,
  177, 178, 180, 184, 187, 193, 194,
  195, 198, 200
Maroczy Memorial Tournament,
  Budapest 1952, 216
Marshall, Frank, 171, 177, 178, 179,
  184, 187, 188, 190, 191, 195, 197,
  198, 202
Mason, James, 157, 158
Mattison, Herman, 196
Maurian, Charles Amédée, 138
Mayet, Carl, 132
Mayot, 115
Mecking, Enrique, 230, 273
Medina, Antonio, 213
Meek, Alexander, 136
Menchik-Stevenson, Vera, 209, 217,
  219
Mennel, 83
Mephisto, 159
Méry, F. J. P. A., 126
Metellus, 68
Mieses, Jacques, 177
Milan 1975, 190, 238
Miles, Tony, 234
Minister, the, 14, 15
Modena school, 117, 118
Modern Chess Instructor (Steinitz),
  160, 162
Modern Ideas in Chess (Réti), 149, 180,
  182
Moderne Schachpartie (Tarrasch), 165
Mongredien, A. W., 148, 151
Monte Carlo 1901, 172
Monte Carlo 1902, 172
Monte Carlo 1904, 172
Montgomery, H. P., 136
Moors, the, 59 *et seq.*
Morals of Chess (Benjamin Franklin),
  124
Morphy, Alonzo, 137
Morphy, Ernest, 137
Morphy, Helena, 144
Morphy, Paul, 124, 134 *et seq.*, 155,
  222
Morphy, Paul: His Later Life (C. A.
  Buck), 144
Mortimer, James, 158
Moscow 1925, 196
Moscow 1935, 201
Moscow 1936, 201
Mouret, Jean-Francois, 123
Mu'aqrab, 47
Mu'awiva, Caliph Yazid I ben, 39
Mucklow, James, 132
Mujannah, 47
Munich 1900, 171
Munich Olympiad 1936, 202
Munich 1941, 212
Muraddid, 47

Murray, H. J. R., 12, 13, 15, 28, 47, 50, 55, 56, 62, 67, 68, 81, 82, 98, 99, 130
Mush-tik, 12
Mushtain Al, 33
Mutamid, Al-, 59
Mutawakkil, Caliph, 43
Mutazz, Ibn Al-, 33
My Chess Career (Capablanca), 187
Muzio Gambit, 111

N
Nagy, Geze, 198
Najdorf, Miguel, 211, 212, 213, 214
Napoleon Bonaparte, 84, 115, 123
Nation, The, 12
Nauheim, 1936, 202
Nauheim, 1977, 202
Neckum, Alexander, 76
Neue Ideen im Schachspiel (Réti), 194
Neumann, Gustav, 153, 154
Neveu de Rameau, Le (Diderot), 115
New Orleans Chess Club, 139
New York
  1857, 134, 139
  1889, 160
  1894, 167
  1910, 187
  1913, 188
  1922, 193
  1924, 195
  1927, 197
Newham, Samuel, 132
Nicephorus, 28
Nimzowitsch, Aron, 155, 178, 184, 189, 190, 192, 196, 197, 198, 199, 200, 213
Noa, Josef, 158
Noble Game of Chess, the (Stamma), 117
Notation, Algebraic, 39, 117, 241
Notation, Descriptive, 240
Nottingham 1886, 159
Nottingham 1936, 201
Nuremburg 1883, 159
Nuremburg 1896, 169
Nuremburg 1906, 177
Nushirwan, 27

O
Olaus Magnus, 58
Oleg the Wise, 55
Olympiad (International Team Tournament)
  Amsterdam, 1954, 217
  Moscow, 1956, 217
  Munich, 1958, 217
  Leipzig, 1960, 217
  Warna, 1962, 217
  Tel Aviv, 1964, 217
  Havana, 1966, 217
  Siegen, 1970, 226
  Skopje, 1972, 226, 229
  Nice, 1974, 235
Olympiad (Students'), 217

Omar, Caliph, 30
Omar Khayam, 25
Orbeli, 47
Origin of chess, 11
Origine du jeu des échecs, 79
Ostend, 1905, 177
Ostend, 1906, 177
Ostend, 1907, 178
Owen, Reverend John, 140, 141, 148, 151

P
Pachman, Ludek, 213
Palma de Mallorca Interzonal, 1970, 221
Paris, 1867, 153
Paris 1878, 155
Paris 1900, 171
Paris Olympiad 1924, 195
Parma, Bruno, 238
Parnu 1947, 213
Paulsen, Louis, 134, 136, 147, 148, 154, 155
Pawns, 63, 80, 104
Pawns, two versus one, 121
Pawns, isolated versus united, 121
Peckham, Archbishop, 55
Perigal, George, 129
Perrin, Frederick, 136
Persia, 20, 28
Petroff, Alexander, 100, 134
Petropolis Interzonal, 1973, 231, 233
Petrosian, Tigran, 208, 216, 219, 222, 230, 236, 238, 239
  v. Portisch, match, 1974, 234
  v. Spassky, World Championship match, 1966, 216
  v. Spassky, World Championship match, 1969, 216
Petrov, V., 202, 209
Petrus Damiani, Cardinal, 52
Philidor, Francois André Danican, 114, 115, 118–122, 239
Philidor's Legacy, 115
Philip II of Spain, 93
Philip IV of Spain, 112
Philosopher, the, 13
Philosophy of History, 115
Pieshka (foot-soldier, pawn), 58
Pil (Elephant), 27
Pillsbury, Harry Nelson, 166, 167, 168, 169, 170, 171, 172, 177
Pilnik, Herman, 213
Pirc, Vasja, 200, 215
Pistyan 1912, 188
Pistyan 1922, 192
Pius IV, Pope, 106
Pleiades, the, 129
Pocket sets, 226
Polerio, Giulio Cesare, 108, 111
Polugaievsky, Lev, 231, 233
Ponziani, Domenico, 118
Ponziani Opening, 118
Popert, W. W., 129, 130
Porges, Moritz, 169
Portisch, Lajos, 219, 230, 233, 236, 238

Portoroz Interzonal 1958, 216
Praeceptor Germaniae, 165
Prague 1908, 180
Prague 1946, 213
Prokofiev, Serge, 84
Puc, Stojan, 215

Q
Quaedam moralitas de scaccario (Innocent morality), 66
Queen, 37, 68, 79, 83, 87
Queen against advanced passed pawn, 121
Queen and pawn versus Queen, 121
Queen versus Rook, 121
Queen versus Rook and pawn, 121
Queen's Gambit Accepted, 102, 117
Questo libro e da imparare giocare (Damiano), 101

R
Rabar, Braslav, 215
Rabrab, 43, 47
Radio and television, chess on, 218
Ragosin, Viacheslav, 201, 202
Rāja, the, 14, 15, 16
Ramsgate Team Practice Tournament, 1929, 199
Raphael, Benjamin, 136
Rating systems, 217
Ratnākara, 14
Razi, ar-, 43
Renaissance, 81
Renaud de Montauban, 86
Repeticion de Amores y Arte de Ajedrez (Lucena), 98
Reshevsky, Sammy, 194, 201, 202, 208, 210, 211, 213, 214, 233
Réti, Richard, 149, 151, 160, 180, 188, 191, 192, 193, 194, 195, 196, 197
Revanche de Waterloo, une (F. J. P. A. Méry), 126
Ribli, Zoltan, 238
Richard Coeur de Lion, 85, 86
Riumin, Nikolai, 201
Robert de Hunstaneston, 55
Robespierre, Maximilien, 115
Robey, James, 168
Rockingham, 122
Rogard, Folke, 217
Rogaska Slatina (Rohitsch–Sauerbrunn) 1929, 199
Roman de la Rose, 87
Rook and Bishop against Rook, 121
Rook and pawn against Bishop, 121
Rook and pawn against Rook, 121
Rosenthal, Samuel, 154, 158
Rothschild, Baron, of Vienna, 154
Rotlevi, G., 184
Rousseau, Eugène, 138, 153
Rousseau, Jean Jacques, 116, 117
Rowbothum, James, 122
Royal Asiatic Society, 32
Rubaiyet, 25

Rubinstein, Akiba, 172, 178, 180, 182, 184, 188, 190, 193, 195, 196, 199, 200
Rubtsova, Olga, 215, 217
Rudenko, L., 215
Rudge, Miss Mary, 171
Rudrata, 15
Rueb, Dr. Alexander, 196
Rukh (Rook), 27, 28, 80
Ruodlieb, 67, 68
Ruy Lopez (opening), 99, 101, 118, 136, 143

S

Saint Amant, Pierre Charles Fournie de, 126, 129, 140
St. Petersburg
    1895–6, 169
    1909, 180
    (Qualifying) 1914, 189
    1914 (grandmaster tournament), 189, 190
    Chess-Club, 169
Sajtar, Jaroslav, 213
Saltsjobaden Interzonal, 1948, 214
Salvio, Alessandro, 111, 120
Salvio Gambit, 111
Salwe, Georg, 172, 178, 184
Salzburg 1942, 212
Salzburg 1943, 212
Sämisch, Fritz, 194, 202
San Antonio 1972, 230
San Remo 1930, 200
San Sebastian 1911, 184
Sassa (Sissa), 32
Savenkov, E. V., 21, 55, 58
Sayyal, 44
Scacchia Ludus, 102
Scacci alla rabiosa, 83
Schach oder könig spiel, Das (Gustavus Selenus), 142
Schachzabel, 83
Schallopp, Emil, 159, 169
Scheveningen 1906, 177
Scheveningen 1913, 188
Schiffers, Emanuel, 169
Schlechter, Karl, 168, 169, 170, 171, 172, 177, 178, 180, 181, 184, 188, 191
Schmidt, Paul, 212
Scotch Game, 118
Schwarzwald chess-clocks, 154
Sebastian, King of Portugal, 108
Sellman, Alexander, 158
Semi-Tarrasch, 136
Semmering-Baden 1937, 202
Semmering Panhans Tournament, 1926, 197
Sergeant, E. G., 209
Seu de Urgel, 50
Shah (King), 27
Shāh-nāmah, 26, 27
Shakmate, 56
Sharrkan, 40
Shatranj, 30 *et seq.*

Shifrin, Ray, 226
Showalter, Jackson Whipps, 169, 171
Siang-chi, 22
Sicilian Defence, 135, 136, 218
Sidney, Sir Philip, 94
Silbermann, Dr., 80
Simpson's Divan, 160
Skipworth, Rev. A. B., 158
Sliac 1932, 200
Slon, 58
Smyslov, Vassily, 211, 212, 213, 216, 230, 231, 233, 238
Sonneborn–Berger point count, 210
Sopra il giuoco degli Scacchi (Ercole del Rio), 117, 118
Sousse Interzonal, 1967, 220
Soviet Championship, Moscow 1940, 212
Soviet Championship, Moscow 1951, 215
Soviet Championship, Baku 1972, 231
Spassky, Boris, 219, 225, 228, 231, 238
Spielmann, Rudolf, 183, 184, 189, 193, 197, 198, 200, 209
Stahlberg, Gideon, 212, 213, 214, 216, 231
Stalemate, 19, 63, 95
Stamma, Philip, 117
Stanley, Charles Henry, 136
Staunton, Howard, 129, 130, 132, 139, 142
Staunton Chessmen, 133
Stean, Michael, 234
Stein, Leonid, 209, 235
Steiner, Endré (Andreas), 198
Steiner, Herman, 208
Steiner, Lajos, 197, 199
Steinitz, Wilhelm, 118, 144, 148, 149 *et seq.,* 157, 158, 159, 160, 162, 166, 167, 168, 169, 170, 171
Steinitz Gambit, 153
Stockholm 1930, 200
Stockholm Interzonal, 1952, 216
Stoltz, Gosta, 200, 212, 213, 231
Ströbeck, 95
Sturlasson, Snorre, 69
Subandhu, 11
Suhle, Berthold, 49
Sukaikir, B., 49
Sukhumi 1972, 231
Sulaiman, Sultan, 50
Suli, as-, 34, 43
Sully, Odo, Bishop of Paris, 52
Sultan Khan, Mir, 200
Szabo, Laszlo, 213, 214, 216
Szen, Joseph, 132

T

Taimanov, Mark, 216
Tal, Mikhail, 180, 208, 216, 219, 222, 230, 231, 232, 238, 239
Talib, Caliph Ali ben Abu, 30
Talkhand, 26
Tallinn 1973, 231
Tallinn 1974, 237

Tarrasch, Dr. Siegbert, 159, 161, 162, 165, 167, 168, 169, 170, 171, 172, 177, 178, 179, 184, 187, 190, 191, 193, 194
Tartakower, Savielly (Xavier), 184, 188, 189, 192, 193, 194, 195, 197, 198, 199, 200, 213
Teichmann, Richard, 165, 168, 169, 184, 187
Temesvar, 188
Teplitz-Schönau 1922, 193
Thomas, Lady, 171
Thomas, Sir George, 48, 126, 168, 193, 201, 209
Thomas a-Becket, 84
Thompson, James, 136
Thorgil's Saga, 70
Time limit, 148
Tinsley, Samuel, 168
Trever, 47
Triberg 1921, 192
Trifunovic, Peter, 213, 214, 215
Trivet, Nicholas, 85
Trollope, Anthony, 122
Tschigorin, Mikhail Ivanovitch, 157, 158, 160, 162, 165, 167, 168, 169, 170, 171, 172, 178, 194
Tschigorin Memorial Tournament, Moscow 1947, 213
Turover Brilliancy Prize, 235
Two Knights' Defence, 129, 162
Tylor, T. H., 201

U

Uhlmann, Wolfgang, 231, 239
Ulf, Jarl, 69
Ummayad, Hisham, 74
Unicorns, 62
Unsuri, 26
Unzicker, Wolfgang, 238

V

Vaganian, Rafael, 238
Vajda, Dr. Arpad, 198
Vasavadatta, 11
Venice, 1948, 213
Vere, Cecil de, 151, 153
Vergani, Beniamino, 168
Versus de scachis, 68
Vicent, 98
Vida, Marcus, Hieronymus, 162
Vidmar, Prof. Milan, 180, 184, 188, 193, 197, 200, 213
Vidmar, Milan jun., 215
Vienna, 188
    1872, 152
    1873, 152, 154
    1882, 157
    1898, 170, 171
    1903, 172
    1908, 180
    Jubilee 1913, 188
    Trebitsch 1913, 188
    1922, 193

Vierge, 79
Vignay, Jehan de, 64
Vignoles, Narciso, 97
Vikings, 20, 58, 63, 69, 75, 76
Vogt, C. F., 98
Voltaire, 115, 117
Vortex opening, 47

W
Walbrodt, Carl August, 165, 169, 170
Walker, George, 107, 129
Wang-Po, 13
Wedgwood, 122
Wei-chi (Go), 10
Weiss, Max, 159, 160
Wells, H. G., 114
Werlinsky, Boris, 196
White Rock Pavilion, Hastings, 168
Wiener Schachzeitung, 165

William the Conqueror, 85
Williams, Elijah, 132
Wilno, 1912, 188
Winawer, Simon, 153, 155, 157, 158, 159, 169, 170
Winawer variation, 154
Winchester Poem, 76
Winter, William, 201
Wolf, Heinrich, 193
World Championship
    (individual), 152
    (Junior), 217, 234
    (Women's), 217
    Tournament, Hague–Moscow 1948, 214
    Tournament (Women's), Moscow 1949–50, 215
World Chess Federation (FIDE), 190
Wu-Ti, Emperor, 13
Wyvil, Marmaduke, 132

X
Xerxes, 32

Y
Yanofsky, Daniel, 213
Yates, F. D., 181, 193, 195
Yaw a kit ul Mawakit, 33

Z
Zandvoort 1936, 202
Zatrikion, 28, 29
Zebu, 13
Zeitschrift des Deutschen Morgenländischen Gesellschaft, 14
Zonares, John, 28, 29
Zukertort, Johannes, 144, 153, 154, 155, 157, 158, 159
Zürich 1934, 201

5

Still More Doubt.

7

Checkmate.